DANCE IS A CONTACT SPORT

BY

Joseph H. Mazo

A DA CAPO PAPERBACK

Library of Congress Cataloging in Publication Data

Mazo, Joseph H
    Dance is a contact sport.

    (A Da Capo paperback)
    Reprint of the ed. published by Saturday Review Press,
New York.
    Includes index.
    1. New York City Ballet. 2. Ballet. I. Title.
[GV1786.N4M38 1976]   792.8'09747'1   76-6557
ISBN 0-306-80044-6

ISBN: 0-306-80044-6

First Paperback Printing

This Da Capo Paperback edition of *Dance Is a Contact Sport* is an
unabridged republication of the first edition published in New York in 1974.
It is reprinted with the permission of E. P. Dutton & Co., Inc.

Published by Da Capo Press, Inc.
A Subsidiary of Plenum Publishing Corporation
227 West 17th Street
New York, N.Y. 10011

This is for my parents,
Anne and Louis Mazo,
Who always knew that I could write a book.
With love.

Contents

Picture insert follows page 160.

Prologue

I have a habit of falling in love with women I've never met, especially ballerinas. Others also enchant me from a distance—actresses, musicians, tan-armed tennis players, rich-breasted receptionists, unbearably fragile madonna-faced young Puerto Rican girls on the uptown IRT—but most of all, I am susceptible to ballerinas.

The title "ballerina" should not be tossed to every female dancer. It belongs only to those entrusted with leading roles in classical ballet. On stage, ballerinas are magically desirable. Vulnerable but strong, fragile yet enduring, they flutter as quickly as eyelashes, then float as softly as sleep. The women who sail with them in the white-skirted convoy, and the men who escort them, also are laden with magic. The girls of the corps de ballet flash by as fickle as jibs in a changing wind, almost as beautiful, but less unobtainable, than their queen. The cavaliers escort their women with proud deference, waiting the time to show their own power.

When I was much younger, my infatuation often led me to a disreputable-looking building on New York's West 55th Street, where, for a small fee, I could gratify my longing. The City Center Theater, once the Mecca Temple of the Shriners, by then had become the mecca of American dance and the home of The New York City Ballet. There was a girl there, stretchable as taffy and el-

egant as fine china, with a name you could roll over your tongue
like a great wine: Allegra Kent. Others danced with her, anonymous odalisques and renowned queens regnant, and I loved them
all.

The men on the stage deserved such women: they were virile
and vibrant, courtly and commanding. I especially remember a
small, dark young Dionysus who leaped across the stage as if shot
from a cannon. His name was Edward Villella. I liked him because
he had lots of elevation. ("Elevation" was my first dance word. I
picked it up listening to conversations in the City Center lobby,
which is so small you can't help overhearing other people's talk,
and used it a great deal until I learned a few more words to alternate with it when I wanted to show people I knew about ballet.)

Allegra and Eddie and their colleagues dazzled my eyes, but I
was even more impressed by a man I never saw, the one who
taught these elegant athletes to swim in their pool of music. His
name was George Balanchine, and the people in the City Center
lobby said he was a genius. Even I could tell that.

A bit later, as an actor and director-in-training, I ached my way
through enough dance classes to learn that what Eddie and Allegra
and the rest were doing required intense dedication, as well as talent and skill. I played enough roles to understand that their performances were dramatic events, and staged enough plays to realize
how rich were the patterns, how mighty the encounters through
which they moved. I heard and played enough music to know that
Balanchine was making it visible for me. And always, I fell in love
with women I never had the chance to meet.

Although I relished other forms of dance, and other styles of
ballet, I returned constantly, more enamored than ever, to my
dream harem on West 55th Street, to the speed and exhilaration
and drama of The New York City Ballet. Long before I became a
theater critic, the company moved from its ungraceful quarters to a
mausoleum-white palace in the new Lincoln Center arts complex.
In the New York State Theater, NYCB had not only a spacious
foyer and grand promenade (it was harder to overhear conversations, now), but a house designed specifically for its style of dancing. Fortunately, the queens, their trains and their consorts, and

Balanchine's reverence for music and his revolutionary thoughts about space and shapes, made the journey safely. The company had changed—the women I worshiped in the mid-sixties were not the same ones I had adored in the late fifties, but the new delights were as precious and bright as their predecessors. True, the company had become part of the accepted scheme of things, the ballets were sometimes less daring, the audience less adventuresome, the theater less full, but it remained NYCB. The structure and style remained intact.

By the time I came to write about dance, the New York City Ballet long had been conceded one of the great performing ensembles of the world. It had begun to acquire detractors. There has always been a group of spectators who find Balanchine's ballets "cold." There were traditionalists who found his use of twelve-tone music, and his invention of steps to suit it, iconoclastic, and romantics who thought his more contemporary idiom too severe. Now, these were joined by an avant garde who proclaimed that Balanchine had nothing new to say. Critics remarked that his great days were behind him. Jerome Robbins produced *Dances at a Gathering*, and some insisted the future of the company was with him. Others said the future of dance was not with ballet at all, or that the future of ballet was not with NYCB. Some of the commentators were dancers.

I had begun to meet them; not ballerinas, of course, but still, real dancers. They looked smaller off stage, but less fragile. Not all were beautiful. Many had small, thin voices and seemed ill at ease if not talking about dance. Others were intelligent companions, who astonished me only occasionally by chatting while one leg rested on the desk or the table. Their presence was less overpowering in a private room than on the public stage. They were human after all. Human enough to tell me terrible things about NYCB: Balanchine technique is not classically pure, Balanchine style and speed breed injuries, Balanchine wants only "Balanchine dancers."

The man, his work and his company still fascinated me, and despite their obvious humanity, dancers continued to delight. I began to learn more about what they did on stage, and how and why they did it. I learned a little about what they did off stage, and came to understand that they, even more than the rest of us, are bound by their profession. It sets them a bit apart, as a habit segregates a religious from society.

When an opportunity to watch a class or rehearsal came, I enjoyed it, not merely because I feel at home in theaters but because one of my great pleasures is to watch anyone doing anything, providing he does it well—and dancers must. An incompetent actor will bruise nothing but his ego; a slovenly dancer can destroy a tendon. I will watch artists, plumbers or switchboard operators, if they are good at their craft, feeling my way into the rhythm of the work. After a time, I think of questions. I'm not alone in this hobby: A favorite urban pastime is to peer through a window in a fence while men turn a sandy pit into a building. If you watch long enough, you begin to wonder about the techniques involved and the people who employ them. Why do they do this work? How did they learn it? Where do they go when they leave the pit and the girders for the night? It's like seeing the cars coming from the opposite direction on the highway and considering the histories and probable destinations of the passengers. I decided I wanted to learn more about the architecture and construction of ballet, and about its builders.

I had met some of the NYCB dancers and liked them. I had enjoyed a brief interview with Balanchine and tasted his wit and his presence. I wanted to know these people and then, through a book, to let others know them. Virginia Donaldson, press representative for the company, always had been even more gracious than her duty required, and I put my suggestion to her: Could I spend one full season with the company as a kind of house guest, watching class and rehearsal, talking with the dancers, studying the life of the colony? Virginia carried the idea to Barbara Horgan, Mr. Balanchine's personal assistant. In the autumn of 1972, Barbara escorted me backstage, to speak with Mr. B.

He sat on a wooden bench in the corridor leading from the stage to the dressing rooms and elevators, a compact man with gray hair, looking down at his neatly folded hands, then up, intently but with great courtesy, at me. Sitting beside him, I told him what I wanted, and why. I explained that I thought the public should know more about the grueling work of dancers, about the making of a ballet, about the conduct of a great performing company and about the reasons that even a great company finds it impossible to operate at a profit. He listened, giving me the kind of attention most people offer only to their most cherished dreams: Balanchine is one of those rare men who can devote his entire being to the matter at hand. "You know," he said, "this is not four-hour-a-day job. You must come when I come, go home when I go home; then perhaps you learn." (Balanchine's style of speech is not so much "accented" English as rhythmic phrasing. Every sentence shapes itself into a musical pattern appropriate to the content. It scans.) I assured him that was how I had hoped to work. "All right," he said. "Is a good idea. We do it."

Six months later, in April, 1973, I went to live with The New York City Ballet. It was a lucky choice of season. Balanchine and Jerome Robbins each offered a new work. Neither ranked with its choreographer's masterpieces nor earned great acclaim, but neither was a disaster. Both showed the craftsmanship and invention of the dance-maker's art. However, the chief interests of the season were not choreographic. Melissa Hayden, one of the company's long-established stars, was in the process of retiring; City Center was deeply in debt; competition from other companies was high and audience attendance low; the company feared the following season might be curtailed because of a strike by musicians. And the fall, 1973, season was indeed delayed, not by picketing musicians but by striking dancers. The changing attitudes of performers, which allowed such a previously unheard of event to occur, were becoming evident while I was in residence. To everything there is a season; mine was a season of change.

Throughout my stay, I had the freedom to come and go as I pleased, backstage and in the front of the house. I attended orchestra rehearsals, dance rehearsals, company class, students' class, performances, technical sessions and discussions. I pestered executives, administrators, stage hands, conductors, wardrobe artists and musicians. I was allowed access to the company's director, Lincoln Kirstein, and to its three ballet masters, John Taras, Jerome Robbins and George Balanchine. Hospitality was extended by Mme.

Barbara Karinska, the great costumer, by Norman Singer, executive director of City Center of Music and Drama, Inc., and by
the members of the New York City Ballet Guild. I could come and
go as I chose, and mostly, I chose to go with the dancers.

Their hospitality was even more generous, if that is possible,
than that extended by the managements of the company and the
theater. In a surprisingly short time, they made me feel as if I
belonged with them. The first morning I attended company class, a
tall, slender young woman in blue practice clothes came over to
me, smiled a welcome and said, "Hi. I'm Teena McConnell." So it
began. After I had been with the company for a few weeks, I made
a note in one of my ever-present steno pads: "Today I really feel a
member of the family—Violette kissed me good morning." When I
started to leave a rehearsal early for a rare night off, Bruce Wells
pointed me back to my chair. "Oh, no," he said, "we're in this
together. If we stay, you stay." And one morning late in the season, after I had conducted an interview instead of attending company class as usual, about six dancers stopped to say, "You weren't
in class this morning. We missed you. Mr. B. missed you. He
asked, 'Where is man with pencil?' " I felt honored, and at home.

A stranger among more than eighty people is bound to become
better acquainted with some than with others. A few of the dancers
I knew only to greet; others to chat with; some answered questions,
some went further and proposed them; many simply accepted me
in their conversations and their lives; and some, more than I could
have hoped, offered friendship. A journalist can quote only those
people with whom he has talked, which is why some members of
the company are mentioned in this book more often than others.
Furthermore, some remarks fit more easily into a scheme of writing
than others, and a great deal of warm and lively talk and freely offered information had to be omitted if this book were not to become as long as a dowager's heirloom pearls.

I owe more than I can repay to the entire staff of the New York
State Theater, and to the full company, orchestra, staff and crew
of The New York City Ballet. Everyone associated with NYCB
did all he could to make my work easier, and my visit a joy. Still,
special acknowledgment must be made of those who, ex officio,

served as my hosts. The company's stage managers, Ronald Bates, Kevin Tyler and Roland Vazquez, made sure I had comfortable vantage points backstage. Edward J. Ryan, general manager, and Thomas F. Kelley, manager of the New York State Theater, allowed me the freedom of the audience side. Barbara Horgan introduced me to the paths through the theater and the ways of the company. Virginia Donaldson not only gave me office space but guarded my health, shooing me out to lunch and warning me against smoking too many cigarettes. Lincoln Kirstein and George Balanchine, whose house it is, gave me the most gracious of all welcomes, allowing me to use their home as if it were mine. And to the dancers—I love you all.

Writing is lonely work. There is no more intimidating sight than several hundred sheets of blank paper that need to be filled—and nobody in the world can help you do it. But not all the work of a book is in the writing. There are times of planning and preparation, of rejoicing in anticipation or relaxing before the next round. Then, you can have help, if you are lucky enough to find it. I did. Let me allow the mention of a few to serve as thanks to the many. Marcia Powell and Bob Gales helped turn an idea into a publisher's contract, and Marcia closed the circle by typing the manuscript. My editor, Tom Davis, "talked me through it," as the dancers say, with guidance as gentle as his taste is sure. Peter and Lorraine Wynne helped make the work of trimming a bit of gourmet cooking, rather than a bout of butchery. Fellow critics and dance buffs, some of whom have been watching ballet and writing about it far longer than I, gave me encouragement, not only by telling me how anxious they were to read the book, but by assuring me that as soon as it was done, I could get back into the habit of sleeping more than five hours a night. As examples, let me mention Patricia and Clive Barnes, Dorita and Leighton Kerner and Dick and Kitty Cunningham.

People who may think they had no part in the work were perhaps the most important of all: Those who helped me celebrate the beginning of my project, then listened to the same ballet stories forty times; those who were neglected for weeks on end, or put up with me during all the trauma, trepidation, snarling, swearing, relaxing and rejoicing of a first book, and who somehow have managed to forgive me everything and remain my friends at the end of it—thank you.

And at the last, since in a sense they started the whole business, I give thanks to Allegra Kent and Edward Villella—and to the ballerinas, the dancers, and all the women, known or merely glimpsed, whom I have loved.

DANCE
IS A
CONTACT
SPORT

1

Class

Degas and Hollywood, you lied to me: They don't look like that. I wanted my dancers to be delicate, fresh-faced darlings, neatly pressed and pleated, prettily made up. I imagined them curling bird-light hands around the barre, tilting their chins with an air of innocent superiority, stretching seductively as kittens as they negligently tied shoe ribbons. They don't look like that at all.

Dancers sweat. After class, the main rehearsal hall of the New York City Ballet smells like Secaucus, New Jersey, before they closed the pig farms. The stage-sized room, on the top floor of The New York State Theater, is windowless. From their square, louvered cages in the ceiling, fluorescent lights tear at the eyes. Faces, hands and chests perspire until they shine like the mirror that fills the front wall. The mirror reflects the fronts of dancers, and the plaid-shirted back of George Balanchine, who doesn't sweat.

Balanchine stands still as a heron waiting for a fish, balanced and secure, his compact body leaning slightly forward from the waist. His eyes switch back and forth, watching. Tightly-stretched skin across his temples leads to a crest of gray-white hair. The hawk's nose arches aggressively; the triangular mouth is tight. In old, gray, flopping slacks and Western shirt, tom-tomming the rhythms on his belly, he drills his flock. He is the greatest classical choreographer alive, the man who transformed the art, teacher of this class, leader of this company, master of this vessel, after God.

When you think about American ballet—athletic, cool and quick—you are thinking about George Balanchine. When you think about dancers—long-legged, slender girls who move as quickly as delight—you are thinking about him. He invented them. Balanchine knows the three elements any great dance-maker must: space, time and sex. He is master of music and of movement. He knows speed and stillness. He knows beautiful women—sometimes in the Biblical sense—and cats and books and haute cuisine. He knows his dancers. Autocrat, aristocrat, architect who builds in living bodies, master of this vessel, but always after God. "I do not create," he likes to say, his soft, nasal voice elongating the vowels. "Only God" (he points a forefinger in His direction) "creates. I only put the pieces together."

The pieces with which he works are leaping across the gray-tiled floor of the rehearsal room, but you look at him. Whatever else is happening, whoever else is present, you look at Balanchine. In well-worn clothes, he is elegant. In the midst of imbalance, he is certain. Whatever he is doing, he does it utterly. It is because of him the dancers on the practice floor are panting and perspiring.

Look into the mirror as they pull and stretch. Listen to the shoes and the knees creaking behind you. Look at the dancers' faces. One twists his tongue between his lips, a little boy with a really tough arithmetic problem; a dark young man stares as grimly as a middleweight contender having his gloves dusted after a knock-down; a sexy little blond with a stylish line tenses her throat muscles until they stand out like mountain ridges on a relief map; a tall, plain-faced young woman bends to smooth the tension from her thighs; a pert brunette, whose brown eyes are too bright and set, blinks back perspiration.

Look into the mirror. It's there, like the wicked queen's, to destroy illusion. It's there to show the dancers exactly what they are doing, and why it isn't right. It isn't enough to be trapped in a windowless rehearsal room, or in your own fallible body, or in the belief that humans can do anything as impossible as classical ballet—you have to be trapped in the mirror, too, and in the myth the audience has dreamed for you: be beautiful, be serene, be shimmering in white with a tiara in your hair.

They don't wear tiaras to class, except on matinee days when there's no time afterwards to make up. They don't wear white, either. Flower-faced Allegra Kent has black leg warmers swelling around her ankles like fungi. Michael Steele sports a blue-and-gold polo shirt reading, "Sun Valley Day Camp." Peter Martins, muscular and blond, wears a scoop-necked orange shirt, black tights and a broad belt, an outfit that makes him look more like Captain Marvel than Apollo.

Leg warmers do exactly what their name implies. They are bulky and sweaty and usually look like the scarf your spastic Aunt Evangeline knitted for Christmas. Some dancers use heavy men's socks, cut out at the toe to fit over ballet slippers. Others prefer long woolies that cover the thighs, and a third group chooses to pull bulky knit tights over the usual thin ones. None of them stay clean for very long, and gray-tinged pink is not the most romantic of colors. (Did Claire Bloom sweat in "Limelight?" Did her leg warmers turn gray?)

Several dancers are wearing the bulging rubber pants—tan or dark blue—known as "instant warm-ups" or "Woolworth saunas." These are among the least decorative fashions ever invented; the wearer seems to have become permanently entangled in an air mattress. But a dancer too rushed to warm up properly, or one who must lose weight in a hurry, can't worry about aesthetics.

NYCB is a team without practice uniforms. In class there are sweat shirts and tee shirts, tank tops and no tops, tie dye and faded dye. Deni Lamont hates tights and wears only a leotard, giving his leg muscles a chance to show off during his bullfrog leaps. Frank Ohman takes class in a ski suit of Santa Claus red that gives him an advantage denied most dancers—pockets. Tiny, porcelain-pretty Elise Flagg is all in pink, a little girl showing off her new pajamas. Elise, with her big eyes and determined mouth, looks as if she comes tucked in a case and must be carefully packed away each evening to prevent her from breaking. She's so sweet you could sip her through a straw.

On the other side of the hall, Gloria Govrin chats in the tiny voice that was installed in her throat by mistake. Gloria is big; much too big to have that shy voice. After all, Gloria can perform a double saut de basque. (It doesn't matter if you don't know what a double saut de basque is. Unless you're a dancer and muscled like Tarzan, you can't do even one.) A famous, but probably apocryphal, Gloria story recalls that some years back she was gaining too much weight, and sideliners suggested that Balanchine fire her. "But I like Gloria," Mr. B. reportedly said. "She's the kind of girl you can SEE on the stage."

On the floor, the dancers bend and stretch. Voluptuous Gloria and diminutive Elise. Peter Martins, the Danish golden god, and Robert Maiorano, the Brooklyn middleweight. Gloriann Hicks, body of Salome, long brown hair wrapped around her throat like a choker. Melissa Hayden, fifty-year-old torso erect and rigid as a suit of armor, determined jaw challenging you under the scarf that serves her as helmet. Kay Mazzo, long-necked, fine-boned, sparkling-eyed. Helgi Tomasson, reserved and cool, with the neat body of the ideal shortstop. Jean-Pierre Bonnefous, chest like the boiler of a locomotive, face of a shy, affable innkeeper, disposition of a St. Bernard puppy. Polly Shelton, slight, dark and sharp-faced. Penelope Dudleston, constructed like a siege tower, flying a pennant of blond hair. Pretty and plain. Sleek and slovenly. Halloween-thin arms and thick-set torsos. They're not supposed to look like that. They should be more alike. They should look like dancers. At the least, they should look like "Balanchine dancers."

There's a lot of talk about "Balanchine dancers." Dance fans say Balanchine likes his girls tall, with long legs and long necks. Mr. B., they point out, enjoys looking at beautiful women, and has his own ideal of balletic beauty. Balanchine, you are told, can choose any dancers he wants for his company and everyone knows he wants "Balanchine dancers." Except that Elise is not a Balanchine dancer, nor is Gloria, nor is Milly Hayden, for twenty-two years a principal dancer and piece of company bedrock. Neither do the men seem to run to any single somatype. Where are the "Balanchine dancers?"

On stage.

Dancers in class and dancers on stage are not the same. Physical differences, so clear when you look at a group of girls in the rehearsal hall, sitting ten feet from them and thinking as much of girls as of dancers, become insignificant when you are in the seven-

teenth row of the theater watching the same set of women perform
as an ensemble. Choreography, costumes and planned groupings of
similar-sized dancers minimize differences in physique; facial features provide less distraction at a distance; a relatively uniform
style of make-up adds to the impression of similarity, and the fact
that one neck is a bit shorter than the next does not mean that both
are not, when you come to think about it, long necks. That is part
of the secret of a corps de ballet. The spectator, directed by the
choreographer and by tradition, looks for uniformity, not individuality, just as a guest at a dinner party has been trained to look for
individuality in the midst of uniformity. Who wants to spend the
evening with a group of people who look alike—even if they do?
Who wants to spend the ballet with a corps that looks like a collection of individuals—even if it does?

Look in the classroom mirror again. So many of the women are
racehorse sleek, long-legged, long-necked, small-headed, lean-
bodied. So many of the men have thin waists and high chests and
pursed, slightly sardonic mouths. Linking the differences is a same-
ness. It's the sort of thing that lets you select, in a crowd, the
business-school graduate, the aspiring actress, the professional pro-
letarian. Filling the mirror and the classroom floor are dancers.
Balanchine dancers. The New York City Ballet.

NYCB is considered one of the great ballet companies of the
world. The usual tally includes two in the Soviet Union, Lenin-
grad's Kirov and Moscow's Bolshoi; one in Great Britain, The
Royal Ballet; one in Copenhagen, The Royal Danish Ballet; and
two, American Ballet Theater and NYCB, in the United States.
Some scorekeepers include the Stuttgart company; the Paris Opera
Ballet still has some adherents, and there are a couple of other con-
tenders. Still no more than ten companies on the planet can be considered world class—and there are a lot of companies. There is one
in Peking and one in Salt Lake City; there are several in the British
Isles; a whole flock in the U.S.S.R.; and two in Huntsville, Ala-
bama. All perform ballet, that peculiar art form based on social
dances of long ago and on the Italian pageantry that Catherine de'
Medici brought to France when she arrived to marry the duc d'Or-
leans, later Henry II.

There are other kinds of theatrical dancing and great companies that perform them, but only ballet has engraved as commandments the five classical positions of the feet, the pointed toes and turned-out legs, the specifically defined placements of the arms, and the long code of set steps that has been developing since before the reign of Louis XIV. The first modern ballet was *Le Ballet Comique de la Reine*, produced in 1581; the first ballet school was the Dancing Academy founded by Louis XIV eighty years later. American classical ballet, as we know it, got its start in 1933: Lincoln Kirstein (twenty-seven, Boston, prep school, Harvard, patron of the arts) invited George Balanchine (thirty, St. Petersburg, Imperial Ballet School, Conservatory of Music, dancer, choreographer) to visit America. Kirstein wanted to create a ballet school equal to the great ones of Europe and to build an American ballet company. He had the vision, the gall and the money. Balanchine had the vision, the gall and the choreographic genius. The School of American Ballet gave its first class on January 1, 1934. In March, using students of the school, Balanchine began to make his first American work, *Serenade*. A touring troupe, American Ballet, came into being the next year. The vision and the gall, the money and the genius mated repeatedly, producing a series of major works and several incarnations of the company. In 1948, the current avatar, Ballet Society, was invited to join the New York City Center of Music and Drama as The New York City Ballet.

Meanwhile, Balanchine had choreographed for opera, Hollywood and Broadway. Kirstein had founded and edited a dance magazine—a brilliant one—done time in the army, written several books and helped artists along in their careers. Nobody, including Lincoln, seems to know exactly how much money he has invested in NYCB over the years, but the figure tossed around the company is $3 million. Norman Singer, executive director of City Center, and Mary Porter, Kirstein's secretary, will tell you that "Lincoln's put so much into this he's not a rich man any more." It depends on what you mean by rich. He takes no salary for his work as director of the company, and never has. He paid the dancers' salaries when a musician's strike put them out of work for four weeks in 1970. "It was $50,000," he says. "I could afford that. Today it

would be $250,000 and I couldn't afford that." Still, he's not likely
to starve. The Kirstein money comes from Filene's, the celebrated
Boston department store, and it is lovely to think that Balanchine's
great ballets were paid for by ladies hunting through piles of
"slightly irregular" underwear in Filene's bargain basement. It
takes a lot of underwear to build a world-class ballet company.

It also takes work. Most professional dancers take class every
day. Some take more than one. Those who don't usually regret it.
Remember, ballet is impossible. It has more varied postures than
the *Kamasutra*. It repeals the laws of gravity and inertia. It can't be
done. If God had wanted us to stand with our toes pointing in opposite directions, he would have bought a load of ball bearings and
installed them, instead of using hip joints. Nobody was meant to
sing opera, either, or to run the mile in under four minutes, or to
take a tapered club and try to wallop the blazes out of a small white
sphere coming toward him at ninety-eight miles an hour. These are
unnatural acts, but a few damn fools insist on trying, and some of
them succeed. They do it by combining talent, desire, guts, dumb
luck and hard work.

The word "class," as used by dancers, is misleading. They are
not out on the floor of the main hall to learn new steps. Sup-
posedly, after eight or nine years of training, they know them all.
The pros take class to refine their technique, to clarify it and to
bring it closer and closer to the impossibility of perfection. More
important, they work to put the steps together. "All right, now
you know the steps," Balanchine will say to a girl who recently has
left the company's school and joined the troupe. "Now you must
learn how to dance." Every morning, members of NYCB gather in
the main hall for that purpose.

In rehearsal, and certainly in performance, there is no time to
think about perfection. A man who stops to consider the purity of
his fifth position is going to find himself six beats behind everybody else and running like hell to catch up. A girl with exactly
ninety minutes in which to learn a ballet is not going to worry too
much about whether or not her toe hits her calf in just the proper
place during the piqué turns: She just wants to know when to do
the turns. A dancer who has been through two hours of rehearsal,

and has three still to go, is not about to dance full out—she'd never make it through the two ballets she is due to perform that night. Instead, during rehearsal she "marks it," walks through the steps, twirls her finger to indicate pirouettes, leans a few degrees to the side to show an arabesque. This is necessary for survival, but it is hell on technique. You get sloppy, your body memory is corrupted, you lose your strength. The antidote is class.

Musicians practice, distance runners do their miles, nuns meditate and dancers take class. There, they can build strength, purify technique and acquire the stamina to survive. Beyond that, they can learn more about their bodies, increase their concentration and become better acquainted with the floor beneath and the air around them. At least, that is what class should be. Too often, dancers forget to breathe. Many rely so much on the mirror they forget to feel their bodies, until it becomes the reflection, not the dancer, that is moving. Dancers, like the rest of us, are imperfect. The things they fail to learn are perhaps the most important, but in class they can discover at least how to do the improbable, if not the impossible. Balanchine, who never talks merely with words, swings an imaginary baseball bat and tennis racket to compare class with an athlete's practice. "It's all the same—baseball, tennis, ballet—you need technique, rhythm, style, strength. Especially in ballet you need strength. In sports, you must have technique, but it is even more important in ballet because if you don't have it, you fall down." His tone is perfectly matter-of-fact.

In performance, a dancer works for the audience. In class, he works for himself and for the teacher. One ballet master will emphasize purity of technique, another security of placement. Balanchine wants speed. Mr. B. teaches company class nearly every morning because it is his company; its purpose is to dance his ballets and to dance them his way. The one characteristic of "Balanchine dancers" that even Balanchine, who hates the phrase, admits they share, is speed. There are companies that dance more precisely, companies that dance more serenely, companies that dance with greater dramatic power, but nobody dances faster.

Balanchine is a musician, and his music must be played at concert tempo. Most choreographers slow the music to suit the dancers; he speeds the dancers to suit the music. Teaching, he slaps out the beat on his slightly convex stomach, quick and sharp. "Now, faster. . . . Again, this time faster." It's not enough to jump high, you have to land on your toes and take off again, land and bend your knees and grasshopper a diagonal across the room. Faster.

Even at the barre, the thick wooden rod secured to floor and wall on which dancers support themselves with one hand while working in place, the feet flash out and back like darting fish. After the barre comes the center work, steps and combinations of steps in the middle of the room. Taking a Balanchine class is like doing sixty minutes of wind sprints. His teaching is less severely classical than that of other masters, it puts less stress on the niceties, but it is more athletically demanding. Peter Martins, an NYCB principal who was trained at The Royal Danish Ballet, insists that despite the speed, "Balanchine's style is easy. You don't have to close your feet in a perfect fifth position every time, or bring your heels all the way down, or square your hips perfectly—and those are the things that are really hard, the things that take years and years. That's why the company looks terrible in class, but why it looks so great on the stage."

"Easy" is a relative term. When NYCB visited the Soviet Union in the autumn of 1972, the company was given the honor of a class taught by a famous Russian ballet master. They had a bit of trouble with it. "It was so slow," John Clifford says, "s-o-o-o slow and stretched out. They hold each pose forever." Of course, when Balanchine gave a class, the Russian dancers had their chance to be astonished. "He'd come up to me and whisper, 'Are you up to doing one of your tricks?' " Clifford recalls, "and when I said 'Sure,' he invented a fast combination that the Russians couldn't believe."

The very precise technique Martins learned in Denmark asks the muscles to do different things than the technique he now practices with NYCB. Making certain your heel and opposite toe touch exactly every time you finish a step in closed fifth position—and that is fairly often—demands more concentration and more stringent discipline of the muscles than does the speed beloved by Mr.

B. But the pure classicism is suited to ballets made in the European tradition. Balanchine works in New York, a city enamored of power and speed, and his freer, faster style needs other things.

"In other companies, in other classes, you have plenty of time for a preparation before each step," Bobby Maiorano explains. "You set yourself, center your weight, then move. Here, you can't do that." Here, you must simply move. You must be centered, your weight placed, your body aligned, your concentration set, but you can't take the time to feel it all out. You do it in the moment it takes Balanchine to say, "And—!" Then, you move.

Moving begins officially at 11 A.M. Tuesdays through Fridays, and an hour and a half before matinees on Saturdays and Sundays. Monday is the day of rest. Most of the dancers like to warm up before class begins; a few real workhorses put in a full hour, particularly when recovering from an injury or trying to work into shape. During the season, the New York State Theater is well stocked with dancers by 10:30 in the morning, and it stays that way until twelve hours later. Toward the end of the season, the overtime sheets on the bulletin boards begin to fill up. Some days, the performers may put in only three or four hours, "which is plenty hard enough," but emergency rehearsals and other hard times make up for the short sessions.

By 11 A.M., anywhere from 25 to 75 percent of the eighty-four-member company is in the main rehearsal hall, finishing pre-class chats and warm-ups. Bobby Maiorano says, "Mr. B. gives a very hard class, a very fast barre. If you aren't warmed up beforehand, it gets to you." Some dancers have several personal warm-ups, and choose among them depending on the weather, the state of their bodies and the scheduled teacher. "Oh, it's John," says Susan Pilarre one morning, grimacing in mock dispair as the ballet master comes in, "and I did my pre-Balanchine warm-up, not my pre-Taras warm-up." John Taras, ballet master of the company along with Balanchine and Jerome Robbins (who never teaches), gives the company class when Mr. B. is out of the city or occupied elsewhere. His classes are less showy than Balanchine's, more devoted to stretching and purity of form. "Show the leg please, show it . . . neatly please, neatly. . . ." Balanchine concerns himself with

speed and style, Taras concentrates on precision. The first morning
he teaches this season, his entrance wins a round of applause. "We
like John," Melissa Hayden confides. "He's kinder to the body than
Mr. B." He also begins precisely at eleven, which Balanchine never
does.

At eleven on Balanchine mornings, the dancers still are exercis-
ing, doing splits and stretches, hanging from the barre or pulling
themselves over the floor, practicing steps or sewing shoes. (At any
given time, some dancer somewhere is sewing shoes; it is their national pastime.) Most of the conversation concerns today's rehearsal
schedule or last night's performance, the most recent injury or the
latest find in chiropractors. Around the perimeter of the room,
tucked against the wall in the space underneath the hip-high barre,
are airline bags, traveling bags, leather-trimmed Louis Vuiton
bags, plastic supermarket bags, woven bags, canvas bags, shoulder
bags and shopping bags, filled with spare shoes, sewing gear,
lambs' wool and tissues (for wrapping toes), tights, underwear, hair
pins, bobby pins, safety pins, scarves, sweaters, make-up, pocket-
books, purses, *The Idiot*, *The New York Times*, gothic novels, *Dance*
magazine, candy bars, chewing gum, cigarettes and cans of Coke.
(Dancers drink Coca-Cola for breakfast—the diet-conscious drink
Tab. They also drink it for lunch, dinner and in-betweens. Despite
the presence of a few abstainers, the theater is pretty much a car-
bonated skid row.)

By 11:03, somebody decides to start class. Usually the volunteer is either Suki Schorer, a former principal dancer who now
heads the company's lecture-demonstration program for school
children and still takes company class, or Carol Sumner, a soloist
who teaches the younger students at NYCB's official training
ground, The School of American Ballet. She begins with pliés, the
slow, straight-back deep knee bends that form the preparation for
balletic jumps. To understand what is happening, stand up, touch
your heels together and turn your legs from the hips so the toes of
your left foot point in exactly the opposite direction from the toes
of your right, making an angle of 180 degrees. Keep your torso and
head perfectly straight, hips squared, weight centered. Now, bend
your knees outward in a direct line over the center of your feet rais-

ing your heels only slightly off the floor, and that only when you no longer can keep them down. Then press your heels down and rise immediately, but slowly and smoothly, ending as you began. You have just executed a full (grand) plié in the first position (without the arm movements, of course), and if you have done it properly, your legs hurt like hell.

Carol Sumner, in blond hair and blue leotard, stands in her place and does the exercise while leading the class. She and the other dancers are lined up, each with one hand on the barre that circumnavigates the room. The overflow uses iron-footed portable barres set in the middle of the floor; one or two rely for support on the piano on which Gordon Boelzner (or Jerry Zimmerman or Dianne Chilgren) is playing a little plié music. "Other side," says Carol, and everyone turns around, puts his other hand on the barre, and does the same thing again. Faces are firm with concentration, hands explore hips and thighs to be sure they are in the correct position, torsos glide up and down as if on hydraulic lifts. The barre keeps the dancers neatly aligned, like toy soldiers in a shop window, but some of them plié more quickly and some throw in a backward stretch now and again, so the line moves in human fashion after all. They continue with bends, reaches and stretches until Balanchine materializes.

Mr. B. is not really fond of pliés and stretches, but he knows they need to be done, just as he knows that one or two dancers will rush into class late and require a few minutes for warming up. He gives them their time and then, between 11:08 and 11:11, he appears in the room as if someone had rubbed a lamp. He walks around the floor, exactly the way a person who can materialize should walk, watching, making a correction or two, waiting until the exercise is finished. Then he claps his hands to stop the piano and takes charge. "As normal," he says, "battement tendu."

Every Balanchine class begins with battement tendu. The dancers stand in fifth position—the feet, one directly in front of the other toe-to-heel, nestling together to form a box, the first joint of each big toe projecting beyond the opposite heel—then extend one leg so it stretches as fully as possible from thigh to pointed toe, sliding the toe forward so that it touches the floor directly in the center of the body. Slide it back, go to the side. Slide it back, go behind you. Do it quickly. Gordon Boelzner is playing battement tendu music, setting the pace. Balanchine claps his hands. "Now again, faster."

After battement tendu comes battement tendu jeté, then frappé, fondu, rond de jambe. Always sharp, always fast. The sweat starts to shine. Nipples begin to protrude under the leotards. Hair shakes loose from tightly-piled ricks and tickles necks and faces. "This is not to make you feel good," Balanchine tells them. "This is not to loosen you up in the morning. It's not like massage, where you don't have to do anything but someone works on you and something happens to your body. The teacher can't massage, he can only suggest what you should do. After this, after class, everyone must exercise alone."

He walks around the room in his soft-soled shoes, joking, correcting, kicking an errant foot into line. When Balanchine looks at a dancer, he seems to slip inside the other's body like a hand wriggling itself into a glove; he feels an error in form as much as he sees it. He corrects with his body, too. Working with Marnee Morris at the barre, he stamps down with his heel to show the wrong technique, then lets his foot float to the ground in the proper style.

The class divides, some dancers stepping away from the barre to give the others room for grands battements, in which legs sweep as high as they can without distroying the line of the hip. Young dancers start out working for a high extension, but eventually it becomes clear that a clean, straight beat is better than a head-high sloppy one. Some people are built to swing their toes up to the level of their ears, some are not. There's nothing you can do about it. Work, loosen the hip joint, stretch the thigh muscles—sooner or later, you reach your stopping place. Then, aim for precision. The working leg is to form a 90-degree angle with your body—not 87 degrees, and not 92. Your chest must not jiggle. Your hips are not to sway. There's an eccentric pattern to a class doing grands battements at the barre. Some legs are held slightly below waist level, some shoot eye-high. Victor Castelli swings his as if he had hinges for hips; Allegra Kent, doing a variation of her own, slips her right foot behind her left ear. Peter Martins' leg stays even with his waist, but rides up and back as smoothly as a carousel horse.

Bart Cook, a slim red-haired dancer whose open face is marked

by a rash, does the grands battements on half-toe as Mr. B. ex-
horts, "Stay——and stay——and stay." Throughout the long,
slow cadence Bart holds a deep plié with one leg while extending
the other in front of him, low but spear-straight. His entire body
begins to tremble, his mouth opens in a small, tight, shaking O.

The class moves from the barre to the center of the huge room.
Some of the men slip their forearms under the moveable barres,
lifting the heavy iron legs off the floor, and carry them over to the
wall. Balanchine, several dancers and the pianist roll the instrument into the front right corner of the hall. Girls sit on the
floor edge near their dance bags, changing from ballet slippers into
toe shoes. The softer footgear is pulled off, tissues, lambs' wool or
both come out of dance bags and the girls begin the ritual of pro-
tecting their feet, tucking the lambs' wool between their toes and
folding the tissues around them as neatly as if wrapping sandwiches. Ballet slippers can be used for most of the barre, but once in
the center, the girls go up on pointe and need shoes designed to
support them. Toe shoes are constructed with a little box in the
front that creates a small flat surface, like the hind end of a row-
boat, on which the dancer stands. An application of Fabulon, a
kitchen-floor product, adds a hard surface to the shoes, and increases their protective qualities. Fabulon sells very well in neigh-
borhoods inhabited by dancers.

The women tend to be terribly self-conscious about their feet.
Those beautiful, strong legs end in a collection of bruises, bumps
and bunions. Ballet shoes fit tightly, sometimes tightly enough to
limit circulation, and the feet inside constantly are asked to do
things for which they were not designed. Calcium deposits form,
tendons pull, muscles tear. They don't show that in the movies, either.

The luggage is pushed back into place, dancers dabble their feet
in the resin box, and the class lines up facing the wall-wide mirror.
Center work begins with steps from the classical canon—glides,
turns, arabesques and jumps—which then are developed by the
teacher into choreographic patterns. Although the barre is virtually
the same every day (each teacher has his own routine), the steps in
the center vary. Balanchine orders his center work systematically,

using related steps one after the other and then building combinations from them. He shows each step, sketching it in lightly with his feet. The dancers do it full out. Balanchine wants energy, he wants excitement, he wants size and style and sizzle. "Don't be stingy, don't save it for later," he urges. "There is no later. Only now. What are you saving for? It's like telling very young people, 'Put $5 a week in the bank and when you are eighty-seven, you'll have $5,000.' And everybody thinks, 'Oh, what I'll do then,' not thinking that maybe then $5,000 will be worth 50 cents. Look at me: I'm there already—old, I mean—and I don't have a penny in the bank. I buy my wine and I drink it."

The rehearsal pianist, working from a pile of sheet music, plays anything that suits the rhythm of the step—the swelling theme from the Chorale of Beethoven's *Ninth* or "Teddy Bear's Picnic." Gordon Boelzner works without music. Gordon has been at this since 1960; he knows what the dancers need and what Balanchine wants. While watching Mr. B. mark out the step, he picks up the rhythm, then plays whatever seems appropriate to it—"Bali H'ai," "Roll Out the Barrel," "Humoresque" ("My FAvorite PASTime AFTer DARK is GOOSing STATues in the park, if SHERman's horse can STAND it WHY can't you?"). The dancers enjoy Gordon.

Balanchine demonstrates jumps, leaning slightly to the side, arms open and head cocked. He looks as easily elegant as Fred Astaire, a comparison that would please him. "Be like Fred Astaire," he tells the dancers, "Do like Fred Astaire." When the late movie on the tube stars Astaire, you know where the dancers will be after work. Mr. B. soft-shoes through the steps and calls his nasal, elongated "And—." Gordon hits "Five-foot two, eyes of blue. . . ." The dancers try to do like Fred Astaire.

"You are falling; you should descend." Balanchine stands in front of Maiorano. "Separate the jumps. Stay longer on the ground." Bobby, his bulky knit rehearsal clothes getting heavier with perspiration, pauses to set himself, points his brown eyes straight ahead, takes a demi-plié, leaps, lands and realigns his athlete's body before taking off again. "That's RIGHT." Balanchine's "That's RIGHT" is an ecstatic cry of mutual success. It pulls every eye to the scene of triumph. The world can't be all bad as long as Mr. B. can crow, "That's RIGHT."

He works on timing and separating the jumps because he wants soft landings. Early in the season, when middles still are wrapped in fat, you hear a solid thud each time a dancer touches down. Later on, the thuds grow softer. They are supposed to disappear entirely. Toward the end of June, Balanchine will point at one of the men, lean in at him and say, very quietly, "What a waste! You waste a day, a week, a year. Do you know why I say you waste? What did I teach you about landing? Softly. Softly." The dancer, setting shoulders, hips and abdomen in their proper places, will take his plié and jump, and once in the air, will seem to hold himself above the floor with some inner-generated anti-gravity ray. He will land softly.

Balanchine wants his dancers to land on their toes, touching their heels only very slightly to the ground. It allows them to land more softly and take off again more quickly. It also, according to the people who do it, "strains the tendons if you aren't warmed up. And over the years, it strains them anyway. But it's faster, it looks better, it has more style."

As the season goes on, routines at the barre become shorter, the steps in the center more difficult, the combinations increasingly complex. From leaps, Balanchine may develop a series of cabrioles for the men. They pile into a group at the back of the room and step forward in pairs and trios to travel a long diagonal, jumping to land with one leg deeply bent in plié, the other angled behind them, then they kick the supporting leg back to touch the hanging one. Peter Martins and Jean-Pierre Bonnefous, the local strong men, are throwing in doubles. Almost everyone else looks ready to throw in the towel. Thighs twitch as if they'd been subjected to electric shock, necks tense, raising muscle ridges which form watercourses for perspiration, mouths are pulled taut. Balanchine watches each dancer go past, swinging his body to help them along, like a bowler using body English. "That's RIGHT."

Watching, you begin to see how ungainly many balletic jumps really are. The room seems filled with grasshoppers, bullfrogs and kangaroos. Sometimes, during Balanchine's classroom combinations, the men shoot up in high, arching trajectories. Knees snap straight, unfolding as the dancers land, only to take the strain again as the men rebound like mortar shells. By sitting very still, you can begin to feel your muscles sending out a miniature echo of each move. You can begin to understand how difficult it is to do these steps, and how much more difficult to turn the steps into dance, to make the awkward look graceful and the impossible seem perfectly normal.

When Mr. B. gives an adagio class, based on slow stretches and arabesques, the tension is different—the elastic is pulled instead of snapped. Now, the emphasis is not on speed but on line, on achieving a precise relationship between legs and torso, shoulders and head, body and arms. Instead of cracking his finger-snaps like ships and calling, "Faster. Again, faster. Now, only for those who want to do it, faster," Balanchine leaves a long, deliberate beat between each snap and croons, "Now stay——and stay——and stay."

As the class moves to center, Mr. B. beckons the two newest members of the company to places in the front. "Don't hide. If you hide, how can I see you? Come forward, come forward." He smiles like Gretel's witch. Stephanie Saland and Wilhelmina Frankfurt move from their comfortable obscurity into places in the front row. "That's RIGHT. You're out of the school now, it's time for you to start learning."

At seventeen, Wilhelmina, so very thin, so quietly intense, with serious brown eyes and a nervous upper lip that pulls up to show protruding front teeth, is doing exactly what she wants to do. She is dancing for Balanchine. Other kids her age still are wavering between Swarthmore and Antioch, or between City University and NYU, wondering whether to major in math or speech therapy, brazenly snuggling up to the world and secretly hoping it won't get fresh. Willie is a dancer. Her big decisions won't come until those other girls are involved with their first jobs, their first babies, their first divorces. Right now, all Willie can see is the hand in front of her face.

"Look at your hand," Balanchine tells her. To look at it, she has to turn her head and tilt it slightly, lengthening the line of the throat and accenting the opposing plane of her shoulders. It is the carriage of the shoulders, neck and head that gives ballet dancers their peculiar appearance of sensuous fragility. This is an aristocratic art, and aristocrats, by tradition, don't work. No matter what the lady is doing, no matter how great the strain, her head must be proud and serene, literally above it all. The shoulders always are sloping and soft, the neck forever relaxed. No matter how high you jump or how quickly you spin, your shoulders, neck and head should complete the design of your body, never betraying your effort, never even hinting that dancing is work.

The top of the body completes the line that begins at the toe. Putting one foot in front of you seems to be a relatively simple operation, but putting one foot exactly in front of you is not so easy. The developed foot must come directly to the center of the body. "Right in front of your nose," Balanchine tells the class. "Right THERE," and he kicks at a foot a few inches off center. This is battement tendu, the same step that began the class, but now it is performed without the barre. Now, all the dancer's weight must be centered, the line must run cleanly from the top of the head, down through the midriff, through the left leg and into the left foot, leaving the right leg free to move. A properly weighted dancer with a sense of his relationship to the floor seems to grow from it like a tree, drawing strength from beneath him. Legs sweep forward from the hips, feet stretch taut, toes in pink satin shoes feel for a position on the floor. Everyone is trying to put his foot right in front of his nose. They look like a gang of city youngsters playing "Step on a line and break your spine."

Now, Mr. B. leads them into arabesques, poses that contrast a straight line—running from the grounded toe up the supporting leg and torso and directly past the ear—with a curve that sweeps down from the head and around the chest, down the abdomen and along the working leg which is stretched out behind. "Look where you're going," Balanchine says, "your nose wants something." If your nose wants something, you have to stretch your neck to get it, you must extend your upper body around the imaginary curve, you have to reach. They hold position, on one leg, reaching, led by their noses, until the trembling takes their thighs.

Now, the women do their arabesques on pointe. Whenever Balanchine gives a class that emphasizes pointe work, he has the men do the same exercises, on half-toe. "You can do this, too," he tells them, "so that some day, when you are teachers, you will know how to teach the girls." As the women rise onto their toes and lean into the arch of the arabesque, Balanchine claps his hands. "It's not balance," he says, "it's timing." Going up onto the toe at the proper moment, taking a plié before the rising, establishing a rhythm for the exercise—these are the keys. Without timing, the steps cannot be done in the proper style; without phrasing, they have no meaning. Each step must develop as a flowing sequence, the way a flower opens. The phrase begins with the first hint of a bend at the knee, develops down toward the ground, reverses itself and reaches up, then out, finds a climax as it is held in stillness, and finally, in a decrescendo, comes to rest. Without timing and phrasing, class could be no more than a series of peculiar gymnastic exercises. With them, it is the beginning of ballet.

As the season goes on, bodies lose their haze of fat and come into sharp focus. All the dancers in class are doing the same step, but it looks slightly different on each. Melissa Hayden's arabesques are strong and weighted in the ground; her chest arches in a determined, no-nonsense curve, like the figurehead of a man-of-war. Colleen Neary is clipper-ship tall, long-legged, high-headed, cool and built for speed. Patricia McBride arches deeply, joyously, seeming to move forward even when completely still. Kay Mazzo reaches out to you with her body, but the aristocratic tilt of her head warns against over-familiarity. Kay pulls up her shoulders and shakes the delicate head from side to side, angry with herself. The arabesque wasn't quite right. She goes to the bulletin board to check the rehearsal schedule as a second group of dancers takes its turn to work.

There is not enough room on the floor to accommodate the entire company during class. The dancers divide into three groups, two sets of women and one of men. The males are outnumbered in the company, fifty to thirty-four. Two groups exercise, talk, sew shoes or simply watch while the one on the floor gets its workout. Heads are serene, shoulders squared, feet directly in front of noses,

arms curving to embrace the air. There are still things to be accomplished: Balanchine works on hands. He wants them firm, but
appearing soft, free at the wrists but solid. "Hands must grow, like
leaves," he tells them. "Not like that—it looks like dead chicken."
Most of the dancers take tension in their hands, and it shows. Even
on stage, the corps girls sometimes seem to have claws instead of
fingers. They are working in a hard, driving world and the tension
has to go somewhere. It claims their hands, their necks and their
eyes.

Balanchine takes his dancers' hands and molds them into shape,
the forefingers extended. He holds them by the wrists and has
them flex their hands, trying to feel softness in the joints. "Hands
must grow. Just grow." He looks around the room. "All right.
Very good. We keep working like this and some day we will have
it."

Maybe. Perhaps some day when there is less tension in the
company and in class. Some NYCB dancers refuse to take Balanchine's class, or else take it as seldom as possible. They say the
speed at which he works helps to create the tension he tries to
avoid. "He wants fluidity," they insist, "but he doesn't know how
to teach it. Some other teachers show you how to dance, how to
use your muscles, but he doesn't. He sacrifices technique to speed,
and to his 'look.' " Several of the troupe's leading dancers—Edward
Villella, Gelsey Kirkland, Allegra Kent—take company class only
when Balanchine does not teach, if then. They prefer to study elsewhere.

Balanchine believes his dancers should take his class, because it
is designed to prepare them to perform his ballets. The dancers say
the kind of class you should take "depends on your body." Those
who warm up slowly, or who want to work for precision of technique, would rather take class with Stanley Williams at The School
of American Ballet, with John Taras, with Maggie Black or other
celebrated teachers. Some request their mentors to make a cassette
recording of sequences of steps and the counts for each, so they can
practice at home.

Many dancers will study with nobody but Mr. B. They want
him to approve of them, to notice them, to see what they can do
and give them roles in his new ballets. They also want to learn

from him. John Clifford insists that, "Mr. B. knows more about ballet than anyone in the world." He certainly knows more than anyone in the world about American ballet—he invented it.

Before starting to give combinations, Balanchine is teaching pirouettes, walking the room, slapping dancers on the shoulders as they spin. The slaps are to correct the dancers' balance: they are pushing too much with one shoulder, throwing themselves off center. "It's hard to figure out if you're overbalancing one shoulder," explains Kay Mazzo. Dancers should come equipped with stabilizers. From pirouettes, Balanchine moves on to tours en l'aire— turns in the air. Victor Castelli, the young man with the mile-high extension, is having difficulty. He falls backwards on landing. Balanchine stands in front of him, his body making the moves as his voice describes them. Victor mirrors him, holding his stomach tight, leaning slightly forward. "Not such a big preparation"—Balanchine pushes the dancer's arms in closer to his body— "And——." Victor does his plié, pushes off, spins once, and lands—and stays in place. "That's RIGHT. Well, you have time; you practice and you will do it."

The hour-long class is coming to a close. The dancers gather in the back of the room. Mr. B. sets them a combination of spins and jumps. "And——." The piano starts. They move onto the floor in their groups of two and three, pushing down into plié, then up into the spins; heads snap sharply, legs cut through the air to find the ground. Press down, rise onto half-toe, spin, reach with the leg. Again. Faster. "Good," says Balanchine. "If we go on like that, one day we'll get what we want. Not today. Because today it won't happen. Not tomorrow. Tomorrow it won't happen. Next day it won't happen. Maybe next month. Maybe next year." He pauses, thinks a moment, looks around the room. "Maybe never."

As he leaves, the dancers start packing their bags, putting on sweaters and eyeglasses, getting ready for rehearsal. One, standing at the barre wiping perspiration from his face, looks at himself in the mirror. "I look like death. By the end of the week, we all do. We're drained. There must be a reason we put outselves through this." He reaches for his heavy bag. "The reason is, if you want something as badly as we want to dance, you'll do anything to get it. Anything at all."

2

Preparations

The company usually gets five or six weeks of rehearsal before the spring season, but in 1973, City Center is one-and-a-half-million dollars in debt. Only three weeks fit into the budget. The ballets won't be quite as well drilled this season. It will take a bit longer for the performers to melt the pads of fat acquired during a seven-week layoff, a little more time before they can be casual about paying bills. Not until April 10 is there a reason for the dancers—the kids, as all but the most senior refer to themselves—to telephone their special number at the New York State Theater for a recorded announcement of the day's schedule. "Eleven to 12, Main, Class, Mr. Balanchine; 12 to 2, Main, *New Raymonda*, Balanchine; 2 to 4, Main, *Goldberg Variations*, Leland; 2 to 3, Practice Room, *Symphony in C*, Dunleavy . . ." and so on until the chipper, "Thank you."

Copies of the schedule are posted in the rehearsal rooms. During the season, they also will be push-pinned to the on-stage bulletin board. The rehearsal schedule is to dancers what the program card is to high school students. It is studied and groaned over in the dancers' lounge, which looks like the cafe of a small-town bus station. Three tables with stained white plastic tops are surrounded by lunchroom chairs. Against one wall stand a long-suffering brown sofa and a spitoon-style ash tray. A candy machine accosts you from a corner, offering Oh Henry; Snicker's Munch; Burry's Lemon Creme ("artificially flavored") cookies; Burry's Biggies (peanut butter and cheese cookies); Chunky, Kit Kat chocolate wafers and peppermints. Health food.

In the cozier basement lounge, machines dispense fruit and microwave-cooked sandwiches, but the basement lounge, like the dressing rooms and the stage, is occupied during rehearsal period by the New York City Opera. The dancers don't take over until the day their season begins. Until then, they stay on the fifth floor, snacking from the candy machine, showering and changing clothes in locker rooms, and between rehearsals, reading, sleeping, chatting and sewing shoes in the lounge, sometimes known as The Submarine. "It's got porthole-shaped lights, speakers in the roof, a sprinkler system and a tendency to instill claustrophobia."

A long corridor, punctuated now and then by brown doors and huge orange packing crates and filled with chattering dancers, all apparently under twenty, leads to the main rehearsal hall. Facing the lounge is a pair of double doors that opens onto the smaller studio, the practice room. Both rooms are constantly in use. During the first week of rehearsal, twelve ballets are on the schedule; by the third week, there will be twenty. Balanchine is making a new ballet, Jerome Robbins is rehearsing three, the pieces to be performed early in the season need drilling, dancers must be trained to replace those who have left the company or have relinquished roles.

On the first day of rehearsal, the men of the corps de ballet (remember, it means "body of the ballet," and a fat lot of good the head and heart would be without it) line up in the middle of the main hall. In their grubby practice clothes they look like a reform school class posing for senior pictures. Rosemary Dunleavy, assistant to the ballet masters, prepares to lead them through *Stars and Stripes*, a Balanchine crowd-pleaser that will send the audience home happy on opening night. As usual, Rosie wears black leotard and tights and thick eyeglasses. A pale blue sweater has its arms tied around her waist. Rosie also owns a brown sweater, but it doesn't premiere until later in the season.

Small, sharp-nosed Rosemary seems to have been designed as

an executive secretary, brisk but polite with the big clients. Instead, she became a dancer, then a ballet mistress. She keeps the corps steps of Balanchine's ballets in the file cabinet of her head, to be referred to as needed.

Balanchine, Robbins and Taras, the resident choreographers and ballet masters, have neither the time nor the inclination to lead every rehearsal of their works. Balanchine is in his office playing music, or at the school, or consulting with Lincoln. Robbins is making three ballets. Taras—well, nobody is quite sure where Taras is: probably off again, staging *Apollo* or one of his own ballets for still another company. Which leaves Rosie to teach the old dances to new dancers and to keep the repertory in trim.

She has the men move around, trying to maneuver them so the shortest are on the ends of the line, the tallest in the center. There's a lot of back-to-back measuring and finger-pointing, and a few interim games of leap frog, before the lineup is satisfactory. Finally, Dianne Chilgren is allowed to start pounding Sousa out of the concert grand, and people start to move.

Rosie stands on one of the gray folding chairs and leans back so she is sitting on the barre. "Stay closer together," she calls. "Here you have to step out because the other line is coming forward." They strut, bending their knees like hinges, lifting their feet high. "One, two, nice and sharp, five, six," Rosemary counts cadence. It doesn't look nice and sharp. It looks sloppy. Some of the men dance full-out, jumping high and bouncing along, others walk through it, and a third group, new to this ballet, counts out loud and tries to learn the plays. Every few seconds the ballet mistress claps her hands and everything stops. She corrects a mistake, coming off her perch to demonstrate the step. Rosie roosts again, says, "And—," Dianne plays march time and dancers step and strut. Rosie claps her hands, the men mop up perspiration, corrections are made and everything starts again.

Stars and Stripes is a brash, showy ballet that uses the stage as a drill field on which to parade military strides and salutes dressed up in classical uniforms. Obviously, it should be performed with military precision. The lines of dancers should be absolutely straight. The men should plié, take off, do mid-air turns and land

again in unison. It should look so much like a West Point gradua-
tion parade that you wait for one of the cadets to faint from heat
prostration. It doesn't. It can't. There are eighteen rehearsal days
until opening, and more than twenty works need honing. Most rehearsals are for the corps, and the same corps people show up in
most of the ballets. They can practice only one work at a time. The
American Guild of Musical Artists, the dancers' union, allows five
hours of work a day during rehearsal periods. After that, overtime
sets in. Human stamina allows dancers to work rather less than
that before exhaustion sets in. A standard ballet such as *Stars* may
get only six or eight hours of rehearsal before it is performed.

Some of these men have not danced *Stars* in months; some have
never danced it with their current partners, some have never
danced it at all. Despite that, the audience will expect the lines to
be clean, the steps pure, the timing perfect. The audience will just
have to be disappointed. As much as the spectators, and Rosie, and
the dancers would like the ballet to be done with drill-team precision, they will have to settle for hurried professionalism.

At the same time as the main hall is filled with *Stars*, Robert
Maiorano and Lynda Yourth are in the practice room groping toward one another like wrestlers. Lynda bends her square, farmer's-
daughter body back into a crab, comes out of it on the count of
four and reaches her leg around Bobby's head and shoulders. They
stretch. They contract. They crawl like kids playing dog, except
that kids don't have to count beats as they play. The dancers are
facing in opposite directions, creeping away from one another,
fingers splayed, heads up, thighs pulling. Bobby is having difficulty timing his creeps: "I was fantastic at crawling when I was a
kid, but. . . ." They move back to the center of the room and start
again, an amoeba practicing fission.

Bob and Lynda are rehearsing the pas de deux from *Episodes*, a
ballet Balanchine made to the spare music of Anton von Webern,
music filled with unexpected pauses, plinks and thuds. As the
dancers grapple, their harsh moves begin to clarify the logic of the
music, delineating its geometry and the emotional hypotheses behind it. Making *Stars and Stripes* in the blare of Sousa, Balanchine
found salutes and spins, marching ranks and aggressive legs, and

encased them in pure classical technique. In this section of *Episodes*, he had the dancers turn their toes in rather than out, twist and stretch, entwine one another like ivy strangling a tree. In a courtship rite stripped of romantic trappings, they search, assault and hold on. They do everything that classical ballet says they must not do and, somehow, beneath the eerie neoclassical architecture of the dance, you see the classical pylons that support it, as they do Webern's music. (The music will sound quite different when played by the orchestra in performance than it does in rehearsal with only the piano. That is one of the reasons the dancers work to counts—so as not to be confused by the change in musical texture.)

Lynda has danced *Episodes* before, with another partner. Bobby is trying to learn. Jurg Lanzrein guides the rehearsal. Jurg, an energetic young Swiss, is the company choreologist, a man trained to write down the steps of dances in special symbols, and to read them back the way a secretary reads back dictation. Holding his charts, he supervises the crawling. He examines his notes, rests them on the piano, and kneels down to give Maiorano a short course in dogsmanship, counting each move of hand or foot.

Not all of the study comes from notes. Lynda remembers the way she danced the ballet with Nicholas Magallanes. "That's what Nicky did," is the theme song of this rehearsal. Nicky has been with NYCB forever. He's given up most of his roles now, but when he joins the company, later in the season, he will watch rehearsals and say, "I created that part . . . that was made on me . . . Mr. B. did this ballet on me. . . ." The record book holds some impressive statistics about Nicky. He's also a fine teacher, and has a peculiar talent for finding the easiest way to do each step. It's one of the reasons he's been able to keep dancing for more than twenty years. Therefore, Lynda sometimes ignores Jurg's careful notes to rely on, "That's what Nicky did." But Nicky's body is not Bobby's body, and a dance alters with the dancers who perform it.

They keep at it, Jurg with his notes, Lynda with her kinesthetic memory, Bobby with his determination. They wrestle. Maiorano lifts his partner on his back, pulls her through stretches that end in grunts of relief, and learns to crawl on the proper counts and end up in the right place.

Two days later in the practice room, Balanchine makes some changes in another passage of *Episodes*. This time, as a couple steps forward, the choreographer claps his hands to stop them. He closes his eyes, feeling the new idea kicking in his body, then allows it to grow until it takes control of him. He demonstrates the step with assured, clearly defined motions; the dancers imitate him; it is done. As the couple steps out, the man bends and kneels and his arm, which is intertwined with his partner's, comes over, forward and down in a soft pumping motion. They repeat the sequence at each step of the short promenade. A beautiful ritual unfolding has been added to the dance, and it is a good bet that ninety-eight percent of the audience won't notice.

Episodes has been around since 1959. It is a major effort, and an adventurous one. Even now, many members of the audience find the music "too modern," and think the grasping, the women flipped upside-down, the angled knees and elbows which describe that music are "not real ballet." In the spring of 1973, fourteen years after he made the ballet, sixty-nine years after he was born, Balanchine still is too revolutionary for much of his public. And, fourteen years after he made the ballet, he still is working on it. He has wanted to change it since before the company moved from City Center to Lincoln Center back in 1963. There wasn't time. He made some changes last summer, when the company was in Munich. He'll make some more this season. He will go on altering *Episodes*, some sections this year and some next, until he is satisfied.

Balanchine reworks his ballets for a simple reason: "I change things because I don't like them. I have to work fast—very fast, on union time—throw things together. It's different in other kinds of work: A writer can set it down, and if he doesn't like it, he can rewrite, he can do over again until he likes it. I have to put something on stage; I have to be ready on a certain night. So later on, when there is time, I change." If he does not like the way a section looks, eventually he will remake it. If a dancer cannot do a specific step comfortably, after a time Balanchine will alter it for him. The changes come gradually. The important thing is that the dance should seem as right to him as it can at this particular time, and fulfill the music.

Ballets also change without help from the choreographer. They are passed from performer to performer as whispers pass around a circle in the old party game: The first player tells his neighbor, "The cat has fleas," and it comes back to his other ear as, "She's got fat knees." Rehearsals are pretty much like that. On the first Saturday of the rehearsal period, Jerome Robbins is working in the main hall, while in the practice room, Rosemary trains the corps girls in *Scotch Symphony*, drilling the opening night cast and then the understudies. As the mass of girls crumbles into a series of small clusters, Suzanne Erlon, who has been doing this ballet for years, gasps, "That way? I never did it that way before." Obviously, she's been doing this ballet incorrectly for years. Nobody makes much of it; whoever taught Suzanne the ballet got it wrong. It happens all the time. It's easily corrected.

As the pattern of the corps changes again, one of the understudies asks nobody in particular, "Are we on pointe for this?" and gets an emphatic, universal, "No!" The rule is: when in doubt, stay off pointe. Your feet will last a lot longer.

The mass reassembles and the evolution begins again. Step, stop, correct, repeat. Try it with the second team. Step, stop, check the count, start again. Try not to bump into one another. Try to hear the piano at the same time as you listen to Rosie's counting. Newcomers watch the older dancers, the older ones watch one another. Everybody watches Rosemary. Somebody has to know how this thing goes. At the end of an hour, it has started to make sense. At the end of an hour, it stops. You can almost hear the schoolbell ring as the girls grab their dance bags and move on to their next session.

Scotch Symphony leaves the room; *Agon* comes in. The trick here is the counting. There is no corps, in the classical sense, in *Agon*. It is a ballet for twelve dancers Mr. B. made to a beautifully complex score by Stravinsky which seems to shift time signatures every five bars. There's no nice, even oom-pah-pah here, as there is in *Stars*, no sweeping melody as there is in Mendelssohn's *Scotch Symphony*. Even with a relatively simple score, such as *Stars*, dancers don't move "to the music." You can do that in a ballroom or discothèque, where the steps are more or less repetitive and the music more or less simply structured, but not in ballet. There are too many changes of direction to deal with, too many pauses and shifts of accent, too many sets of phrases. In theatrical dancing, you work by counts. To do *Scotch Symphony*, a dancer has to be able to count to eight. *Agon* takes him up to twenty and for *Episodes*, with its counts of twenty-seven, he needs a degree in math. Each set of counts defines a sequence of movements, and in a ballet in which the music changes time signature frequently, the counts change with it.

The dancers count in unison as they move: "One, two, three . . . one, two, three . . . one, two, three, four, five . . . one, two, three, four, five, six, seven, eight. . . ." It's like trying to run the four-minute mile while doing your calculus homework. Karin von Aroldingen is learning Gloria Govrin's role. They take a short section and drill it again and again. "We turn on one, we turn on two, on three we step. . . ." Suddenly, Karin breaks the pattern. "Oh, I forgot." Her soft eyes are upset; she sets her determined jaw even more firmly. She and Gloria share a nervous grin, then Karin massages the heavy muscles of her thighs, tosses back her blond hair and starts again, following Gloria through the athletics of arithmetic. "We turn on one, we turn on two, on three we step . . ."

Bruce Wells, a tall soloist with a reputation as a fine classical stylist and an intelligent dancer, says quite casually that it took him—it takes anybody—a year to learn *Agon*, because "Everyone has his own count." The ballet was made in 1957 and has passed through a lot of dancers. You count it the way you can, the way it works for you, and just try to stay even with your opposite number. "We get away with murder in this one," Bruce remarks. "It's so complicated the audience doesn't know if it's a little bit wrong—and it usually is." Melissa Hayden adds that the only way to do the thing is to keep your mind on your counting and not listen to the orchestra, "because the orchestra makes mistakes, too, or goes too fast to keep it together. Then everyone, especially the new people, gets nervous and watches everyone else and we all get confused. Just keep your mind on your counts, and after a few performances, you start to breathe with it and it makes sense.

"I know it, because I was in the cast when Mr. Balanchine made it. He taught it to us, he counted it for us, and he taught it *right*. These kids learn it from one another, or from someone who doesn't really know, and that's where the confusion starts. When Mr. B. did it, we had much less trouble. One day Stravinsky came to see rehearsal and asked, 'How fast could I do it?' so we did it a *little* faster."

The next day, Balanchine does conduct the *Agon* rehearsal. John Clifford hopes everyone in the cast knows it, "because if they forget, Mr. B. just changes it. He says all his changes make it better—and they never make it worse—but it gets confusing. You start doing what you did last year and suddenly see your partner doing something else." Clifford, a choreographer himself, thinks more of Balanchine than the DAR does of its ancestors, and expresses his regard, as he expresses everything else, with exuberance.

The rehearsal picks up pretty much where it left off a day ago. A bunch of people in the middle of a large room make curious feline movements while counting to twenty. When the sequence doesn't time out, there is a bit of nervous laughter, and everyone stops counting and stretching and joins a huddle trying to figure out what went wrong. They look like a bunch of engineers trying to decide why the bridge fell down. Balanchine gets up from his chair, moves into the group and begins rearranging people, pointing with his finger or pushing on their shoulders: "You are here, and you are here, and you come down so. That's RIGHT."

They go on, with Mr. B. counting it out for them. Sitting in his chair, he slaps out the rhythm on his thighs, then on the chair metal. He is almost inside the music—or it is inside him. He alters a counting sequence, making it three groups of fours instead of four groups of threes. "Is simpler this way."

Throughout the session, John Clifford substitutes for any dancer, male or female, who is absent, his short, strong body delighting in the steps, his curly hair bouncing up and down. He knows all the parts. John, who began his career as a show dancer, has the knack of watching somebody perform a series of steps and then, almost immediately, doing it himself. Some dancers have to watch a sequence over and over, to step through it again and again, until their muscles remember. Others respond to movement almost without being conscious they are doing it. There are actors who can learn a big part in three hours, and others who still get the words wrong on closing night. With actors, it's largely a matter of how quickly the sounds sink into their ears—with dancers, it depends on kinetic memory, on how quickly the movement sinks into their bodies.

A dancer learns steps as a child learns to tie a shoelace or ride a bicycle—by repetition, practicing until the muscles know the pattern better than the mind does. Since dancers already know the classical canon of steps, they concentrate on linking the steps of a given passage into a sequence, and performing it to corresponding counts. The memory of counts and the memory of steps reinforce one another, the pathways of nerve impulses become well-traveled, and the sequence of the passage turns into habit. Once the habit has been ingrained, it remains in the muscles for a long time. Music can recall it, helping the body move from one step to the next, then from one passage to the next. Fortunately, there is a logic to choreography: it may not always be apparent to the spectator, but the dancer, who knows the terms, can reconstruct the kinesthetic syllogism. There is a reason that movement B should follow movement A, and a dancer's muscles have been trained to understand that.

When Balanchine rehearses *Agon*—or any ballet—he gives the performers a chance to work their muscles into the habit of the moves. Despite his problem of creating on union time, despite the schoolbell schedule of rehearsals, he works as much as possible at his dancers' pace. He seems to have as much time as a redwood.

In the outside world, it is Sunday. It may also be raining, or windy, or going through a freak April blizzard. There's no way to tell, because there are no windows in the rehearsal rooms or in The Submarine. The weather forecast for every day is "bright and fluorescent."

Virginia Donaldson's office, on the third floor of the theater, has a window. (It isn't raining.) Virginia is the press representative for the New York City Ballet, a charming, rather harassed woman who sometimes seems to have the job of telling journalists things nobody has bothered to tell her. The fact that it is Sunday doesn't mean she isn't working. The original schedule for the season called for the premieres of two ballets. Now, there may be three new ballets. Or four. It all depends on what Jerry Robbins is going to do, and Jerry hasn't told anyone what he is going to do, probably because he doesn't know yet. If there are going to be more than two premieres, it would be nice to find out, because the newspapers would like to know, tickets for critics should be available, and a bit of advertising might be useful. Right now, the best Virginia can do is get a full press list, and warn the box office that if there should be more premieres, they will be on Thursdays.

By the time the dancers leave the theater Sunday night, they have rehearsed six of the fifteen ballets to be presented during the first week of the season (each act of *Jewels* properly is considered a separate work), two productions that will be added to the repertory during the second week, and four ballets-in-the-making. They've earned a rest.

Monday is the day off, the day to have a massage, visit a chiropractor, take a few extra classes, do the laundry. Hang around a ballet company long enough and you'll come to believe that its chief end-product is dirty laundry. During the season, Mondays provide the only time dancers, especially corps dancers, have to themselves. During rehearsals things are a bit easier and a good deal of the talk in The Submarine is concerned with the movies. There's not much of a rush to Broadway, the opera, or classical or rock concerts. Tickets to those things are expensive. Besides, those entertainments tend to happen while dancers are working. Movies, though, always are available, and by the end of rehearsal period, it seems as if every dancer in the corps has seen every film in New York and is ready to start again.

The second Tuesday of rehearsals looks pretty much like the first one. Rosemary is working on *Scotch Symphony*, taking the men through the passages the women learned last week. The two performers who lead the men's corps, the demi-soloists, are relinquishing their roles and being replaced by men from further back in the line. They, in turn, are being succeeded by dancers new to the ballet.

The routine is established by now: Those who know it teach those who don't. Rosemary calls out the steps as the boys go through them, the section is repeated with the piano, mistakes are corrected, and the next passage is taken the same way. It's rote learning, doing the steps until the muscles remember them in sequence. Physically, it isn't as demanding as class, where everybody dances with full energy, but the repetition is tiring. Then, just as the steps are becoming routine, Rosie says, "All right, now, let's do it at tempo." To do it "at tempo" is to dance at performance speed. Now everybody has to work full steam ahead just to keep up with the music. The lines of dancers, which had been pretty straight at the slower pace, acquire some curious twists, dancers who were quite sure of themselves a few minutes ago begin to stumble a little, nobody seems to get to quite the right place at quite the right time. Rosemary claps her hands. Stop. Work it out. Try it again, at tempo.

Next, Rosemary takes a rehearsal of *Diamonds*, the third section of Balanchine's *Jewels*. She tries to get the girls lined up so that when they rehearse it with the boys, they will be opposite the appropriate partner. "Who has Peter Naumann? Who has Paul? Well, who had him last year?" The girl who had him last year has left the company, so Paul is assigned a new stablemate. It's very much an arranged marriage—the partners are not consulted. A very tall woman in the corps obviously requires a very tall partner, a fact not previously considered, so the arrangement has to be altered again.

The arrangement is not permanent. In a Balanchine ballet, the girl who starts at the front of the line does not necessarily stay there. Mr. B. orders too many expeditions out of the main body of his force for the deployment to remain unchanging. A short girl may start out at the front of the line and suddenly pop up in the middle. Putting the most experienced dancer up front is a good idea, too, but a few minutes into the ballet, the newest recruit may be leading the battalion. The developing pattern of the dance is a lot more important than any size-places game. Still, you need a starting place. Rosemary tries to keep most of the women in slots that are familiar to them—at least on the side of the stage that is familiar. The girls on the right side move left and those on the left side move right, and someone asked to do the opposite of what her kinesthetic memory tells her is correct can become very confused. Once the starting lineup is arranged, Rosemary begins to order the sequences and arrange the patterns of the dance. In *Diamonds*, the dominant pattern, logically enough, is a diamond. The corps girls must learn not only where they stand, but which other dancers they must watch as they move in order to maintain the proper distances and hold the figures in shape.

Something similar is going on in the main hall, where Sara Leland is conducting a replacement rehearsal for *The Goldberg Variations*. Sally Leland (she doesn't look like a Sara anyway) does for Jerome Robbins' ballets what Rosie does for Balanchine's. She rehearses them, coaches new dancers and tries to maintain the choreography. Probably, Jerry will polish it later, but he leaves the basic roughing in to Sally. She is training a new girl for the corps, using the mirror technique. Sally does a step, Stephanie Saland follows her. Once Stephanie knows the sequence, she has to fit the steps into the pattern, to do them at the same moment as the other dancers, to maintain the space between her and the girl in front, and to keep the line straight when Jerry Robbins drew it straight and curved just the right amount when Jerry designed a curve. Stephanie carries her long, pretty body with poise and style, but her full mouth and dark eyes acquire a look of pure panic every time she forgets a step—probably, she's thinking about Jerry.

Robbins has a reputation for insisting that every step be executed exactly as he created it. The dancers say that when he makes a ballet, he sets chairs to mark distances on the stage and says, "Move to three feet to the right of that chair," and he doesn't mean three feet, six inches. Balanchine, who works differently, says, "Move over in that direction. Go until it is comfortable. If it's not right, we change it." To the dancers, Jerry is the resident ogre. Stephanie is nineteen years old and trying to learn a very complicated ballet the ogre made, and she is just a little bit worried. Sally calms her down and talks her through it, then Stephanie keeps her big eyes fixed on the dancer in front of her and plays follow-the-leader, trying to remember exactly what she is supposed to do. She does it quite well.

Meanwhile, Jerry himself is rehearsing his three new ballets. There is a pas de deux to Beethoven bagatelles for Violette Verdy and Jean-Pierre Bonnefous, already made and now being polished, a suite of Prokofieff waltzes and one of Tchaikovsky waltzes. Nobody knows which of the three will be shown, or when, but they are taking up a lot of rehearsal time. Robbins shows up every day, his white beard shining in the artificial light—sometimes a purple shirt shining even more brightly—and locks himself away with his dancers. Nobody is allowed to visit his rehearsals. (A Balanchine rehearsal, especially on Sunday, has full bleachers.) Jerry's insistence on privacy does not help his reputation with the dancers. A lot of the chat in the lounge is about Robbins, and it is not complimentary. The dancers complain that he screams at them, snaps at them and makes cutting, sarcastic remarks. They find him tough and indecisive. They insist that he is not sensitive to the individuality of their bodies, as Balanchine is. You get the feeling somebody is overreacting. One of the young men storms out of a Jerry rehearsal, which is the way some dancers leave a Jerry rehearsal these days: "He's got me working with somebody short, and everything is fine when he demonstrates because he's six inches shorter than I am. Then I do it. He ends up with his arms around her waist, but I end up with my arms around her throat. Then he stares at me when it doesn't work for me the way it did for him, as if to say, 'How dare you be taller than I am!' "

The word is that Jerry's ballets are not working out the way he wants them to, and the word is spread sometimes with glee. People are overworked, the weather outside is lousy, the weather inside is unchanging, they're locked into the rehearsal rooms and The Submarine, and on top of that, they've got Jerry. He's almost as much of a hobby as crossword puzzles and movies.

Crossword puzzles get a lot of action in the lounge. There are pencil workers and ink workers, solo workers and communal efforts. There are a few experts, who knock off the *Times* in ten minutes, and a number of beginners, who have trouble largely because they are going far outside their frames of reference. "A Norwegian playwright," muses Heather Watts. "Is it Albee?" "No." "Ionesco?" "No." Heather never heard of Ibsen. Neither does she know the phrase "terra firma," and she has a tendency to confuse "A Greek god," Ares, with "An astrological sign," Aires. "And for this my parents sent me to private school?" Heather is pretty and in some ways quite sophisticated, but she is the sort of girl who thinks the three B's are Bloomingdale's, Bergdorf's and Bonwit Teller.

She's not alone. When you spend your early teens cutting class in order to go to ballet lessons, and your late teens dancing, when almost all of the people you know are dancers who also cut a lot of classes, you get to know a lot about dance, and about which expenses you can deduct from your income tax, and which masseur is the best, but you don't have to think much about Ibsen. You certainly don't care whether you think about him or not. You are doing exactly what you want to do and, except for your debts, your family and your love-life, that's all that matters. There is no world but the company, no devil but Jerry, no god but Mr. B.

Thursday morning, after class, Balanchine works with Bobby Maiorano and Lynda Yourth on the pas de deux from *Episodes*. They know it by now, more or less, and he is drilling for execution and timing. Mr. B. reinstates a particularly nasty lift that Nicky had simplified, calling Allegra Kent in from the hall to show Lynda how she does it. Allegra was on her way out, ready to go swimming or tend the rose bushes on her terrace or enjoy her children. She has changed out of practice clothes, but even in clogs and faded jeans with yellow-embroidered bell-bottoms, her body shows its clear, extended line. Her cat's face is thoughtful, but relaxed, as she arches through the pretzel bends of the choreography. She explains the passage to Lynda in a gentle, almost inquiring voice, then watches Lynda try it, helping with her eyes. Finished? She takes her bag from the floor as neatly as she set it down, smiles to Balanchine and the dancers, and the embroidered bell-bottoms swish happily out the door. I defy any man sound of mind and instinct not to fall at least a little bit in love with Allegra Kent.

On Friday, Bob and Lynda practice a section in which they are entwined with four girls from the corps. The girls surround the couple and, one after the other, bring their arms down over the bent heads of the leads as if crowning them. Something is going wrong. No matter what he does, Bobby keeps getting hit on the head by four pairs of arms. Balanchine has left the rehearsal to look in at the main hall, and nobody is sure what should be done. They know that Maiorano should move his head back, they know the four women are to lower their arms, and they know that nobody is supposed to be hit. Delia Peters, proprietor of one of the head-popping pairs of arms, suggests in her dry manner that Bobby "be a little more nebulous." Nobody can come up with a better idea, so Bobby tries being nebulous. He still gets hit. Finally Jurg Lanzrein, who has been digging through his notes, discovers that Bob should be kneeling, not standing. Balanchine, returning, agrees.

The next rehearsal needs only two dancers and no supervisor. Susan Pilarre is learning the soloist's role in the first section of *Stars* from Carol Sumner, who usually performs it. Susie, known as Susie Pil to distinguish her from her dressing-roommate, Susie Hendl, looks like the puppy with eyes as big as saucers. She's dark and serious, with a neatly compact body and a pretty taste in irony. Susie started to study ballet when she was eight, joined the company in 1963 and was named soloist nine years later. By now, she knows what questions to ask: "Which way do I get down from pointe here? . . . I feel I should travel more here, how do I do it? . . . Do you end on eight or on one?" The answer to that last one is, "Whenever you can." Both women are professionals; they understand the method of attack. The show-stopper in the first movement of *Stars* comes when the soloist raises her working leg as high as possible, grabs her ankle in her outstretched hand and travels across the stage on one foot. Exactly how do you do it? "I do it in passé—as many as you can in passé—and make it look as hard as possible." Carol knows exactly what the audience wants: It wants dancing to look difficult.

Pre-literate cultures have an oral tradition; dance companies have a kinesthetic tradition. Susie P. is learning a role that currently is performed by Carol Sumner and was made, in 1958, on

Allegra. It figures. Any time you see a role in a Balanchine ballet that requires the dancer to get a foot behind her neck, or a leg climbing straight in the air, or an ankle in the vicinity of an earlobe, ask "On whom was this made?" The answer, almost invariably, is, "On Allegra." The role was invented to capitalize on her flexibility. A role in a play may be written for somebody—the actor need not be present while the playwright works—but a role in ballet must be made on somebody, because without somebody, there is no role at all. Some choreographers experiment first on themselves; others, like Balanchine, tailor the steps to the dancer with whom they are working. When another performer takes over the part, the role changes. Watch three different dancers do the leading role in a ballet: it will be different each time. Body and personality help mold one another, and both help form the appearance of the steps. No matter how strict and classical the passage, the spirit of the performer shows through. When a part passes from one dancer to another, the ballet is altered.

Out in the lounge on Saturday, most of the dancers are talking about getting away for the weekend. Tomorrow is Easter Sunday, a day off. They're off on Christmas, too. They get two paid holidays a year. A lot of the kids will go to Saratoga Springs, where the company dances every July. Some have homes there. Others just want to visit, to look for houses to rent for the summer season, to loaf in familiar surroundings.

Susie Hendl, Colleen Neary and Jean-Pierre Bonnefous are comparing dance floors encountered during summer tours. Blossom Music Festival, near Cleveland, has a cement floor—"Bring a good masseur along for your tendons." Even stages with wooden floors generally are too hard, because most theaters are not designed specifically for dance. A real dance floor is made of wood; it may be covered with asphalt tile, but the floor itself is wood. It is resilient, giving when the dancers jump; it is smooth; it is kept clean and dry—balanced on pointe and whirling, a dancer can slip on a bit of dust—and it does not have holes. Holes in the stage can twist an ankle; hard floors kill your arches, pull your tendons and send pains shooting up your legs; sloping floors ruin your balance; and outdoor stages make you a feeding station for mosquitoes. Summer is not the dancers' favorite season.

After two days off, everyone comes back talking about "What I Did On My Vacation." Susie Hendl, who is very fair, has taken a bit too much sun. Others have taken a bit too much food. That two-day pass was short, but it was the last break the company will get for several months. Opening night and an eight-performance-a-week season are only eight days away.

After class, the company stays in the main rehearsal hall for a union meeting, which has been called to decide whether or not the dancers should go to Germany this summer after their regular tour. A producer in Berlin wants to film some of Balanchine's ballets and has offered a contract that will give corps members $300 a week and soloists $600. Principals, as always, will negotiate individual contracts with management. A lot of dancers are not happy about that offer. NYCB is not a European ballet company in which the dancers are neatly compartmentalized. Here, some corps people do solo work, some solists dance in the corps. One of the soloists sums up the position: "The corps works harder than anyone else, and they're getting screwed. Soloists get more, okay, but not double!"

Besides, they are concerned about how many hours a day they will have to work, how much per diem allowance will be given for food and lodging, and whether or not they are to get residual rights. Some of the more businesslike point out that video cassettes are going to be popular soon. Just buy one and see your favorite Balanchine ballet. If these films were to be made into cassettes and sold here a few years from now, when a lot of the public has viewing equipment, that German producer is going to get very rich. What will the dancers get? "Screwed again."

Some of the dancers, especially the younger ones, the "kids" of the corps, want to go. They want to see Berlin, they want to dance, they know Mr. B. wants them to go, they are sure it is for the future of the company. Some of the older dancers, the soloists and the principals, are not so certain. They've been through negotiations before, and some have made films. Many suspect the work is going to be a lot more strenuous than it sounds right now, and think they should get a good deal more money for going through with it. Remember, a first-year corps member earns $6,ooo a year, assuming he gets forty weeks of work.

Before this rehearsal period began, there was a lot of proselytising, a lot of talking, a lot of convincing. In a vote regarded by the old-timers as a sort of miracle, the company elected not to go to Berlin. Previously, the company never had voted against Mr. B. on anything. Logically enough, management scheduled a second vote, to be held today.

Edward Bigelow, the assistant manager, comes to the main hall after class, substituting for Betty Cage, the general manager, who missed her train. Bigelow used to be a dancer with the company. Now, he helps arrange tours, sets up travel and hotel reservations, acts as liaison with Karinska's costume shop and drives Karinska to the eye doctor. He does what everyone else forgets to do, and somebody else takes care of the things he forgets. He strides into the hall, businesslike but friendly, wearing a Western shirt very much like Balanchine's, to tell the company to take the contract as it is, it is the best they can get, and it is fair. The dancers will work five hours a day, no more. The anti-Berlin faction retorts that if they are required to work only five hours a day, it should be so stated in the contract.

Edward Villella, probably the best-known dancer in the company, says he has done films before, and it is more likely to be a twelve-hour day, much of it spent waiting for the technicians to get the lights right. Villella is a short, dark man with muscles—his thighs are about the diameter of heavy-duty sewer pipes—and honest eyes. He is a powerful dancer, and a matter-of-fact businessman. As a principal, he will negotiate his own contract, or have his agent do it, but he has had experience in these matters and thinks the kids should know what they are in for.

A union representative from the American Guild of Musical Artists shows up, dressed like a small-time insurance salesman. He tells the dancers the contract is fair. However, Eddie Bigelow will call Berlin and try to have the five-hour clause inserted. Exit Bigelow and the man from the union. Enter Balanchine. He makes some jokes, starts everyone laughing, then tells his company that he will go to Berlin, even if they vote against it. He'll negotiate with those who want to go, then fill in the gaps with German dancers. Now, he wants his dancers to take a second vote, because they were "cajoled" the first time and really didn't understand the situation.

Eddie Bigelow and the AGMA man return, unsuccessful. They can't get a five-hour clause in writing before May. One of the union deputies in the company suggests that in that case, they should wait until May before voting on the contract. Somebody else suggests a vote on whether or not to vote and a ballot box is set in place. The vote-now faction wins. A second vote is taken. The company will go to Berlin. The score was fifty-three in favor, seventeen opposed.

The no-go group is bitter, especially about the second vote being demanded after they'd won the first round. "I give up on these kids," one says. "They won't listen. You can't make them understand how important it is to hang on to things like cassette rights, or even to defend themselves against overwork. We all want to dance, but we don't want to get injured."

One of the older men nods his head: "They really don't know what they're doing yet. I was like that at eighteen, too. It's all for the company. The company is the world. There is no light beyond the company. They'll learn, eventually."

A third dancer says simply, "They're scared. They can't help it. They want to dance, to be accepted by Balanchine and get parts. They simply won't defend themselves or worry about money or working conditions. They know Mr. B. wants to go, and they know that Mr. B. decides who dances what, and they know that Daddy knows best." As long as dancing for Balanchine is the most important thing in the world, you go where he wants you to go.

Later the same day, the cast list for the first week of performance is tacked to the board. Balanchine, with help from Rosie, decides the casting. They try to pair dancers who work well together, to make sure, when possible, that principals don't do more than one major role each evening, and that those who do dance two heavy parts get a bit of breathing time in the middle.

Ballets that have been rehearsed with the men's and women's corps separated are brought together, and begin to look a bit sharper. Rosemary starts drilling for precision. In *Diamonds*, she goes over one short section three times, making certain everyone reaches the right place on the right count, that everyone watches the dancer in front of him to keep the line straight, that everyone starts out on the same foot every time. She rehearses the finale of *Stars*, saying, "Keep looking downstage . . . keep the lines straight . . . don't get ahead of one another." The joke of the day has Colleen Neary standing in for absent Steve Caras, saluting and striding through the men's steps, laughing all the way. While Rosemary keeps trying to rearrange the men's line, the kids play gym games, pushing one another, leapfrogging and giggling. Little Elise Flagg shrugs helplessly: "Any time we do *Stars and Stripes*, this is the way we get. We've all been in it too long." The resemblance to a third-grade recreation period is heightened by Rosie's references to "big girls and little girls," meaning tall and short.

Rehearsals have started for *Symphony in Three Movements*, which will fill out the opening-night program, along with *Stars* and *Scotch Symphony*. Eddie Villella, in street clothes, is teaching his role to John Clifford. Villella stands near the edge of the room, watching John go through the steps, sometimes marking them easily himself, as if for the pleasure of it. Only three couples are rehearsing, but they work slowly, getting the complex counts and steps secure in their bodies. Johnny interrupts to ask Villella, "There was a kick somewhere—was it here?"

Later, Rosemary works with the corps of *Symphony in Three Movements*, arranging partners and groups. The dancers break rehearsal to step and count out difficult passages for one another. There's no horseplay in this session, the work is too demanding. Each team of dancers is working to its own count. One of the women turns to Rosie: "Is it one, TWO, three, four or ONE, two, three, four?" Rosie says it's either one or five, however you decide to count it. "Just keep it consistent." A bit later, as the couples are learning to follow "paths" along the floor, passing beneath each other's arms, she tells the whole group, "You have three nines and then four sixes coming back." Sounds like a poker holding.

Robbins keeps working three, four, sometimes six hours a day, making his new works and drilling the old ones. Reports leak out of the main hall that the *Tchaikovsky Waltzes* is not going well at all, and that Jerry wants Mr. B. to have a look at it. The more rehearsals Robbins calls, the less popular he gets. The weather outside continues gray, the Berlin vote bothered people, everyone is getting snappish. It's Thursday—we open in five days.

Balanchine guides Allegra and Peter Martins through the pas de deux of *Agon*. Stravinsky based his neoclassical music on old court dances; Balanchine, of course, did the same with the choreography. As Peter and Allegra dance the toes-in duet, Balanchine stops them for a moment. "You know what this is? Is actually very old rigaudon—like this." And he demonstrates the antique court dance that began even earlier as a peasant dance. As he moves, he seems to trade his denims for embroidered knee-breeches and his Western shirt for a wide-cuffed coat; he takes on the style of a more elegant time. Balanchine, the kids tell you, is the best dancer in the company. Violette Verdy, who is wise about a lot of things, says he "extracts the emotional essence of each movement." He does. He is secure in his body; he moves with absolute certainty and phrases each step as if it were a bar of music, giving it a start, a climax and a relaxation. Mr. B. never dances fully, never tries to compete with his twenty-year-old high jumpers, but as he sketches in the steps, the music, the emotions and the style and flavor of the dance suddenly are clear. He stops, and the rehearsal continues. "Don't travel at all," he tells Peter. "It's Ta-DUM, right THERE." He wants the hands "like waaaves," and he drags out the word along with the movement.

While Balanchine teaches Peter *Agon*, Milly Hayden works with Gelsey Kirkland on *Scotch Symphony*. Gelsey is the local *Wunderkind*. She joined the company in 1968. In 1970, when she was seventeen, she became a soloist and Balanchine's new *Firebird*, the youngest dancer in company history to have a leading role made on her by Mr. B. Two years later, she was a principal. She is tiny, with pretty red hair and pretty blue eyes, and even prettier technique. There are dance fetishists who claim that she has the purest ballet technique in the city. Violette Verdy insists that Gelsey knows, at twenty, what most dancers don't learn until forty—assuming they last that long. She was pushed, of course. Balanchine gave her roles for which she wasn't ready and she sometimes looked awkward, even with the technique. She survived, she grew into the parts, she became a dancer. Gelsey is a good deal less fragile than she looks, which is just as well, since she is not the most popular girl in the company. A seventeen-year-old star, a twenty-year-old principal dancer, engenders jealousy. And if the dancer is a bit cool, rather underemotional and constrained, it makes things that much harder. "People told Gelsey her dancing was too unemotional," one of the girls meows, "so she went out and got herself a boyfriend."

Melissa Hayden is thirty years older, with a son about Gelsey's age and a young daughter. A determined, direct woman who says what she thinks, and who thinks a good deal. She was brought up in an old-fashioned Jewish family in which "when we sat down to dinner, with my father at the head of the table, we didn't speak unless we were asked a question. So I didn't talk much: I thought a lot, though. After I left home I started talking, and I haven't stopped since." When Milly dances, her moves are beautifully economical—her leg takes the shortest route to its destination and comes home again the same way.

She is not a pretty dancer, the way Gelsey is, but she dances with conviction. She goes out on stage, this fifty-year-old woman with the overly strong jaw and too-prominent rib cage, and defies anyone in the audience to believe she is not beautiful, and in her defiance, she becomes beautiful. When she teaches a dance, she puts as much energy into the performance as if she were on stage. Others just step through it lightly and hope the new dancer catches on. Milly teaches full out, singing the whole ballet as she goes, chanting the names of steps, counts, and da-ya-da-yas. She thinks this is the only way to teach. "How else will people learn? I used to go home crying because people didn't really try to teach me—they just walked through it. If you're going to teach, you work at it."

She communicates her enthusiasm, she's quick and clear and Gelsey picks up steps as a magnet picks up pins. The two of them work like experienced craftsmen. Milly demonstrates a sequence, then steps back and watches Gelsey go through it. When Gelsey starts to dance, not just to feel out the steps, but to dance, the tension and sharpness leave her face. Suddenly she is lovely. Standing still, she is pretty enough, but still too self-conscious for beauty. Moving, she is glorious.

Milly does a march forward, as if she were going to her coronation. Gelsey repeats the step, looking more as if she were going to her (very expensive and she knows it) wedding. And, yet, as she keeps dancing, the wedding gets to be a love-match after all.

Outside the practice room in the lounge, Deborah Koolish is sitting on the brown sofa holding her small-boned ankle and trying to look calm. Debbie came down from a lift and landed on the side of her foot. It seems to be swelling. The kids tell her to use ice packs or soak it in cold water. Gloriann Hicks tells her to see a doctor. It is not an uncommon injury. A few years back, Gloriann landed that way herself: She fractured a bone "and tore up all the muscles." Debbie limps to the locker room to dress. She is the first major casualty of the season, and the season doesn't even officially begin until Tuesday night. A few days ago, Helgi Tomasson hurt his knee slightly, but he's dancing again.

On Saturday, Patricia McBride does not show up for class. Her knee, like Helgi's, just went "pop." April showers, of which we've had more than the flowers really need, don't help the joints.

Late Sunday afternoon, when rehearsal is almost finished for the week, Wilhelmina, the most junior corps girl, is being introduced to the "Theme and Variations" section of *Suite No. 3*. It's a very elegant ballet, a ballroom filled with spirited ladies and gentlemen glittering in their costumes and filling the stage with the grandeur of an era that never quite existed. Willie is dancing by herself in the main hall, with Rosemary her audience and a piano her orchestra. Watching, you realize how fast the music is, and how many steps there are to the inch. On stage, with a full orchestra, a corps and soloists, it seems fast, but the speed is logical. Everybody is doing it, so it must be right. In the main hall, just Willie is doing it, and it is much too fast for humans, especially seventeen-year-old humans who have just learned the steps and are wearing tired rehearsal clothes instead of Karinska's wonderful costumes, and who should be out enjoying Central Park on Sunday afternoon.

Wilhelmina is still at the school. She is the current student star, rehearsing for the annual workshop presentation in which she will dance the pas de deux from *Sleeping Beauty*. At the same time, she is the newest corps member of NYCB. In school, she is the best; here, she is a beginner. After each mistake, she swallows a lump in her long throat and begins again. She is getting the feel of the steps now, and running them together, but it is late and the room is empty. Her calf muscles distend the baby blue knit socks she uses as leg warmers; one bra strap escapes the white blouse she wears under a thin-strapped black leotard. The bones in her back and chest stand out clearly, the gold-dark skin twinkles with sweat, her thin face is sharpened by concentration. She seems to be following an endless imaginary thread around the room but the pattern is becoming clear, even as she tires.

It's late on Sunday afternoon. Almost everyone has gone home. We open Tuesday night.

3

Opening

At about 10:30 on May 1, Garielle Whittle, a tall corps dancer with
a thatched-roof cut to her blond hair, walks from the elevator to
her third-floor dressing room carrying *The Teachings of Don Juan*,
her season's reading, and a small brown vase filled with straw
flowers, her season's decoration. Dancers enliven their quarters as
best they can. Susie Pilarre and Susie Hendl put up wallpaper one
year—"after all, we virtually live here"—but it was gone when
they returned the next season. Management doesn't like wallpaper.

The principal women's dressing rooms on the stage level seem
to have been decorated by the people who furnish Holiday Inns.
They have the same look of antiseptic transience, with their small
dressing tables and their airline-compact baths at the rear. As a
rule, there are two principal dancers to a room. The rectangular
corps dressing rooms, where Garielle is going, are more crowded
and even less chic. They seem to have been decorated by the people who furnished your high school locker room. Mirrors look
down on dressing tables running the length of one wall. A dingy
cot sags against the opposite wall. You keep waiting for Father Pat
O'Brien to come in and tell the men to go out there and beat the
bejasus out of Sing-Sing: "Ya may be murderers, rapists and con
men, but you're the best softball team in the state." None of the
rooms have windows. Perhaps Philip Johnson, architect of The

New York State Theater, feared performers were accident-prone.

Now that the dancers finally can dress in their own barracks, they also can rehearse on stage. Technicians are in the wings, muscling opera sets out of the way. Gordon Boelzner warms up the backstage upright while brass burps from the orchestra pit. On stage, Rosemary Dunleavy is trying to arrange the line of girls that begins *Symphony in Three Movements*, so it looks more like a sharp diagonal and less like a winding road. John Clifford, neat in new grey knit tights, is stretching and bending, spreading into a split, moving around, "trying things." Dancers sit in the red orchestra seats and on the gray stage floor, doing the same things they did last week in the lounge. A lot of the talk is about money: "You picked a good season to visit—it could be the last one. . . . We had a short rehearsal time because City Center's in debt. . . . We owe Capezio a quarter of a million dollars. . . . There might be a musician's strike in the fall; they might cancel the season. . . . We may have to start doing shorter seasons." For now, they have their stage again.

It is huge. The dimensions are the same as those of the practice area of the main rehearsal hall, fifty-six feet wide by fifty-four feet deep, but with that army of red seats out front and black velour stage curtains dangling from a grid six stories overhead, it looks bigger than Shea Stadium. There is a mystique about empty theaters: they always seem larger than full ones. There is no place more lonely, except an empty department store. From the foot of the stage, standing under the fifty-one-foot-high proscenium arch, you look out at a small continent called "the house," designed to support a population of 2,779. The orchestra pit seems wide and deep enough to delight a family of dolphins. The aisle-less orchestra spreads to each side of you like a desert of red plush. Above it, five golden tiers, mounted with headlamp-shaped houselights, climb until they reach the maroon ceiling, as distant as a sunset. To the kids, the house is "ominous" and "scary-huge." They much prefer it when it is filled with audience, and the expanse is blanked out by the dazzle of stage lights.

From the third row of the orchestra, rehearsal looks very different than it does from a folding chair in the practice room.

Watching the dancers in the main hall, you can think, "we"; from the house, you must say "they." The limits of the proscenium arch frame them, the elevated stage exposes them, the intervening distance depersonalizes them. It is instantaneous divorce.

Robert Irving, music director and principal conductor of NYCB, a tall, rotund Englishman who looks like the world's largest pixie, looms up in the pit. He folds his jacket over the railing, neatly places his wristwatch on the conductor's table and calls the orchestra to business. On stage, Balanchine stands in the down right corner, with Rosie nearby. (Stage right is the dancers' right; audience right is yours. Downstage is toward the audience; upstage away from it. In the sixteenth century, an Italian architect and painter named Serlio designed a theater. Perspective was big news in sixteenth-century Italy, and Serlio wanted the settings in his theater to seem to move to a vanishing point, so he created a raked stage, one which slanted downhill toward the audience. An actor who dropped his cane at the back of Serlio's stage was likely to see it roll all the way into the orchestra, but raked stages became popular anyway, and their terminology came to be standard. Hence, upstage and downstage.)

Robert gives the signal for musicians and dancers to begin *Symphony in Three Movements*. The women on the diagonal bend suddenly from the waist, then uncoil, poised on their invisible line like impatient horses at the gate. Then the line breaks. As the dancers spread over the stage, Balanchine opens his arms upward and out, raising his elbows like Dracula spreading his cloak, a signal for the dancers to do the same. He does not interrupt the rehearsal. After the performers make their exits, they return from the wings and come downstage to him or to Rosie for comments. They do the entire ballet, working, for the first time in months, with the orchestra. In their moments of stillness, the dancers watch Robert Irving, who cues them as well as the musicians, giving the signal to step out with his baton or with a nod of his head. They dance hard, each watching his partner like a linebacker watching a receiver he is trying to match step for step; they burst onto the stage and back into the wings like runners breaking from their blocks.

Afterwards, Robert smiles at the orchestra. "Very good. I think that was very good. Now we're going to play *Stars and Stripes*, right?" As Balanchine talks with the dancers about *Symphony in Three Movements* on stage, the men and women in the pit brass-band their way through *Stars*.

Part of the corps gets up a mock rehearsal of *Stars* upstage, exaggerating the steps and doing biting imitations of the principals' dancing styles. Robert Weiss and Merrill Ashley work through a delicate passage of *Symphony in Three Movements* with Mr. B., but Gordon's upright is giving away too much weight in its bout with the orchestra. Balanchine summons the stage manager, Kevin Tyler. Kevin summons a stagehand. The stagehand lowers the asbestos curtain (a precaution against the spread of a backstage fire to the audience) to even the odds, but Sousa bullies his way through the thick material, brassy and arrogant, while Gordon tinkles and Ricky Weiss and Merrill try to count. Off stage the crew keeps clearing away souvenirs of the opera season.

Yesterday, while the company had its Monday, the stage technicians moved most of the opera's gear. The huge flats were taken away, the thick platforms removed from the stage. Painted drops were lowered and folded into canvas bags and ballet hangings replaced them on the pipes. The special dance floor was winched from its storage crate and laid over the stage. The floor is gray asphalt tile, the same material that covers the floors of the rehearsal rooms upstairs, the same stuff used on the decks of battleships. It is thick and resilient, and mercifully free of holes because it is taken up each season before the opera moves back in. Opera sets are fastened to the floor with stage screws—vicious-looking things with corkscrew bits and handles like brass knuckles—which can be wristed in or out in a few seconds, gnawing deep holes in the floor. Ballet uses little stand-up scenery and needs no holes in the floor. Ballet dancers certainly don't need them.

This morning, while the musicians and dancers prepare for their eight o'clock curtain, the crew continues its work. Ronald Bates, production stage manager, Kevin Tyler, stage manager, and Roland Vazquez, assistant stage manager, are the captain, executive officer and mate. Ronnie, tall and broad enough to be the movies' image of a captain, has everything efficiently charted; he knows just which drop will hang from each battan. He already has planned the sequence of work and given his orders.

There is a keep-it-in-the-family style at NYCB. All the relatives work at the store, so to speak. Ronnie Bates is married to Diana Adams, who was one of the company's finest ballerinas some years back. They have a daughter who looks like a Christmas tree angel. Kevin Tyler, Ronnie's chief lieutenant, is related to Balanchine by language—he speaks Russian. Kevin has been with the company since 1959: "Nobody is left from when I joined, except a few of the principals." He is a White Russian, educated in Shanghai, who owns a Great Dane, an attache case and seaman's collection of dirty jokes, which he trades with the stagehands and dancers the way kids used to trade bubblegum cards. Before performance, he often passes a few to the men in the light booth, by way of the bitch box. (Theater intercommunications systems are known as bitch boxes; the stage manager bitches and the technicians bitch back.) Kevin delights in his theater, and a slight tendency to fluster when things get tricky only makes him run it more efficiently.

Roland Vazquez, third-in-command, used to be an NYCB dancer. The role of Bottom, in *A Midsummer Night's Dream*, was made on him. Now, he is boss of stage left (Ronnie and Kevin command stage right) and master of the shoe room. When a ballet baby needs a new pair of shoes—and he needs about nine pairs a week—he goes to Roland. The shoe room, like its chief, is as organized as a compulsive's medicine cabinet. Roland travels the theater with long-legged strides that let him hurry without running.

Roland tacks neatly typed blue index cards, ordering the sequence of curtain calls for each of tonight's ballets, to the bulletin board in the corridor outside the entrance to stage right. Call cards and lighting cue sheets for all the ballets in the repertory are kept on file, to be pulled for use as the works are added to the schedule each season. Ronnie Bates, who is the theater's technical director and the company's resident lighting designer as well as production stage manager, watches the electricians as they connect their instruments (stage lights are known as "instruments," the bulbs are called "lamps") to the correct sockets in the patch panel. The patch panel relays the circuits to the appropriate dimmers of the lighting control board. Kevin lays out his cue sheets for the performance on the little stage manager's desk, and supervises the work of the stage crew.

While the twenty-two-man crew prepares the stage, the dancers are upstairs rehearsing. It is six hours until the opening curtain. The performers follow their schedule as usual. Mr. B. rehearses *Divertissement* from *Le Baiser de la Fée*. Rosemary rehearses *Episodes*. Robbins rehearses his waltzes. During *Baiser*, Balanchine scolds one of the girls: "You are late—late, late, late—not a lot, a hair late, but you have to prepare and be ready with the music." Then, as he steps back to the front of the room, he smiles at her: "Don't be upset." Helgi Tomasson and Patty McBride execute their variations at performance pitch, and win nods of approval from Mr. B. Helgi leaves the floor panting; nothing seems to tire Patty. Balanchine claps to interrupt the corps: "You have to *move;* it has to *travel*." By the end, everyone is panting—except Patty.

At the *Episodes* rehearsal, the dancers still are counting aloud. Will they count even during performance? "Of course we count on stage. How else could we do a ballet like this?"

Everyone troops down to the stage again, and Balanchine and Rosie put the team through *Stars* while electricians wrestle long, heavy metal standards to their places in the wings, clamp instruments to them and pay out cable. John Clifford and Violette Verdy try the *Stars* pas de deux as the drops for the ballet glide down behind them. Several stories up, in the fly galleries, men are playing the heavy curtains like fish. Drops and curtains hang from metal pipes suspended on ropes, called lines, which run around pulleys fastened to a "grid" (from "gridiron," which it resembles) fixed below the ceiling of the stage. The lines are controlled from balconies jutting from the sides of the stage, which are equipped with pin rails like those used on old sailing ships. Since the scenery flies up and down, those who control it are called flymen.

Having tested the scenery for *Stars*, the flymen steal it back as silently as they sent it down, and replace it with the backdrop for *Scotch Symphony*. Jacques d'Amboise and Allegra Kent, who will perform the ballet in about four hours, are rehearsing. Allegra floats her arm horizontally and lifts her partner's wrist with hers, leading him first one way, then the other. She turns on pointe, holding his hand for support. From the audience, it will look quite natural: the woman, reaching up like a subway straphanger, holds her partner's hand and turns. On stage, you see a different version. Sometimes, the girl holds one of her partner's fingers, turning her hand around it like a nut on a bolt. Allegra interlocks her entire hand with Jacques', and as she turns their fingers weave a pattern like threads on a loom.

The company dances *Scotch* and Balanchine touches up the work Rosie has been doing for three weeks. Allegra stands in the center of a group of corps men as Jacques passes in front of them, then crosses back again. The men turn their heads, watching him. "Look at him," Mr. B. tells them. "Your heads must move at the same time, so look at him as he goes. If you really see him, it will be right."

The three ballets for tonight's program have been rehearsed. There is no dress rehearsal for opening night as it would cost time and money the company cannot afford. The orchestra has been drilled, the drops hung from their pipes, the lighting instruments plugged into their sockets. The crew takes a break, after bringing a piano and music stand on stage, and the company continues its regular routine of rehearsal, of ballets that will be done on other nights. There is no sign of opening-night jitters. As Bobby Maiorano says, "We've been through it too often. We're not doing any new ballets tonight, it's just a performance. The people who do get nervous will be the ones who get nervous before every performance, and they won't have time to worry until we get much closer to curtain. Right now, we're too busy rehearsing for tomorrow night, and for next week."

Tomorrow night will be the season's first performance of Balanchine's staging of Stravinsky's *Duo Concertante*. Now, the choreographer is rehearsing it on stage. Gordon sits at the piano the stagehands have moved in from the wings. Near him stands Lamar Alsop, the orchestra's young concertmaster, with his bow arm cocked and his long-bodied Stradivarius under his chin. In the curve of the piano stand Kay Mazzo, dark-haired, delicate and glowing in lavender, and Peter Martins, blonder than ever in black.

Mr. B. is downstage center. In this ballet, he has made, in effect, a double duet. Two musicians and two dancers, each facing a series of difficult physical encounters, conduct complementary dialogues that expand to blend into a four-way conversation. Each of the four artists works at least briefly as a soloist, much of the time with his partner and, most important, as a member of a quartet. In the first section, the Cantilene, Lamar and Gordon play while Kay and Peter listen as at a concert. Then the dancers join the musicians in their work, retreat again to the piano while the music sings alone, and step out once more to dance through to the end of the score. By the end of it, the music is accompanying them, just as at the beginning, they were decorating it.

Within this elegant interlocking puzzle, Balanchine has made a dance of physical complexity and dramatic fervor: It is a love affair. The first sections are playful. The steps are quick, light, almost tentative—the dancers even pause in their play to listen to the music before going on. After the second duet for musicians alone, they move more slowly, more seriously. Peter offers Kay his knee; she refuses; he lifts her and she falls back leaning on him, her arms around his neck. Then they play again. Peter extends his large hand to Kay, who teases him with a shake of her head, then lays her palm on his and smiles. They romp like children on a picnic with springy, liquid steps, holding to one area of the stage as if it were their secret magic place. They pause again for a moment, hearing the music. Kay retreats, Peter pursues, the play grows into passion: He folds her to him, legs straddle, bodies seem to occupy a wider space. Kay's fragile neck and waist magnify the power of her response, and her emotions seem as strong as Peter's arms. Perhaps they are too strong; they frighten her; she retreats again. Circled in a spotlight, their arms and hands beckon one another, entwine, escape. He kisses her hand, kneels to her, rises to circle and approach her again. She takes one of his hands in each of hers and crossing them, places them on her breast. He, in turn, moves his hands to cover her eyes. (The lover with eyes covered, blind to himself and the world, is an image Balanchine has used before.) This time, when Peter kneels, Kay sits for a moment on his thigh. Then, as the lights brighten, she leaves him. Returning, she offers a kiss, and he kneels before her for the last time, head bowed, like a knight in a gothic carving bending the knee before his queen of the courts of love. In Balanchine's ballets, the man lunges and pursues, the woman retreats, abides, is lifted in triumph, but, in the end, who has submitted to whom? Or have both submitted to an emotion greater than either, of which we are reminded by the music? Mr. B. does not make pas de deux, he makes love songs.

In this morning's rehearsal, during an especially quick-running violin passage, Lamar has difficulty turning the pages of his score. Balanchine offers a solution: Kay will drop out of character for a moment, turn the music, then return to Peter. It will solve a technical problem while adding another move to the game. But Kay may not be able to reach Peter again in time, without rushing and tearing the mood of the dance. Balanchine discards the ploy. Perhaps he can use it, some day, in another dance. The floors of his mind would be littered with ideas that did not quite work out if he couldn't file them away and keep the place tidy and ready for business.

Kay gets a moment to rest. She tosses a tiny pink sweater over her shoulders with the same gesture used by a football player ready to settle his bulk on the bench. There is the same flick of the wrists, sail of cloth, expression of exhaustion and satisfaction.

Balanchine is working with Peter. "Can you jump a little higher?" he asks. "Not forward, up—both legs open." He takes a mild plié and erupts into the air, spreading his legs like dragon's wings. For a few seconds, the stage is filled with the menace of his presence. His mouth makes explosive sounds, illustrating the sudden quality of the movement. Then he walks quietly back to the edge of the stage, a medium-sized man dressed in denim, no more violent or dangerous than a puppy's shadow. Peter repeats the leap, soaring higher than Mr. B. did, opening his strong legs wide. His big young body, his understated determination of mind, give the step command and virility, but he cannot repeat the unassailable force, the certainty of spirit and movement that threatened the world when Balanchine jumped.

An hour before performance, at 7 P. M., ushers arrive at the theater to change into uniforms. Dancers, those who had the chance to leave the theater at least for long enough to snack, feed the cat, walk the dog or pick up the laundry, start to return about the same time. Some, of course, have not been outside the place since they arrived this morning to warm up for class. The wardrobe department already is at work, as are the stagehands. The asbestos curtain has been raised. At 7:30, the gold dress curtain is lowered, and early arrivals among the audience begin to enter the house. On the promenade level of the theater, Bob and the other red-jacketed bartenders have polished the glasses and are ready to pour.

All scheduled dancers and understudies for the evening's program are required to be in the theater at 7:35, half an hour before curtain. They come down the stone steps to the stage door, greet the guards inside, search the little metal rack at the switchboard for messages and the reception table for flowers, than take the elevators to their dressing rooms. The women paint on their cat's eyes and dress their hair, the men do their equally conventional but less exaggerated make-ups. On stage, crew members clean the floor with a dry mop. Flymen send in the backdrop for *Scotch*, and electricians set stanchions behind it, clamp the black metal lights to them, focus the instruments on the drop and slip metal frames holding squares of red gel in front of the lenses. From the house, it will seem as if part of the painted highland scene is warmly tinged in red.

Kevin, at the stage manager's desk stage right, gives the ritual salute to the men in the light booth at the rear of the house. "Good evening, gentlemen," he tells the intercom, "May I have Independent 1, please?" He leans forward, looking across the stage to be sure light is shining from the proper source. Most of the stage lights remain focused on one spot on the stage throughout the season. There are hundreds of them, hanging like bats from the pipes and heavy movable light bridges suspended from the flies. There is no way in which all of those instruments can be focused separately for each different ballet. Instead, they are set to provide general illumination of the stage at every performance. As Ronnie Bates says, "You turn 'em on and you turn 'em off. That's it."

Groups of instruments are connected through the patch panel

to different dimmers which are controlled from the light board. The cue sheets in the light booth tell the electricians which banks of lights are governed by which dimmers. If Kevin asks for "Cue 12, please," the man at the board knows which dimmer to activate and whether the lights are to be turned up or down. In the next ballet, the same dimmer may control a different group of lights. With replugging, although the instruments do not change their focus, they can be blended in different ways. Six spotlights may work as a group in *Scotch Symphony* and be divided among three other groups in *Stars and Stripes*.

On occasion, a few of the instruments will be aimed at specific areas of the stage. Most specific lighting chores, though, are delegated to the spotlights clinging to the tall black stanchions set in the wings. Others, with long, pointing snouts, are set on the floor. These special-use instruments can be refocused and fitted with different colored gels for each work on the program. They are controlled by dimmers independent of those used for the general illumination lights overhead and are called, logically enough, "Independents." Even more independent than the Independents are the cannon-shaped follow spots, set in a booth at the very top and back of the theater. They pick out the leading dancers as they enter and follow them through the ballet like wandering haloes, separating them from the supporting cast.

Before each ballet, the stage manager makes certain the Independents are allied with the correct dimmers and functioning. Independent 1 for *Scotch* answers the roll and Kevin says, "Thank you. May I have Independent 2, please?" A theater is the politest place in America. Mothers who despair of teaching their kids to say, "Please" and "Thank you" should apprentice them to stagehands. A technician hurrying by with two heavy spotlights in each fist and a thick hank of cable under his arm does not snarl, "Move, damnit," he says, "Clear, please."

By 7:40, the elevators are Yo-Yoing between the dressing room floors and the stage level. Each time one hits the bottom of the string, girls swarm out. They are elaborately made up, carefully coiffed, wearing rhinestone earrings and clutching the flapping fronts of their bathrobes, especially since they are not wearing bras. In ballets performed in the equivalent of practice clothes—leotards and tights—the women wear the normal complement of undergarments; however, in some costume ballets, such as *Scotch Symphony*, their bodices are boned and constructed for support, and bras would distort the line of both clothes and dancers. Hence, bathrobes.

Little, round-faced Meg Gordon sports a silver-gray prize-fighter's ring robe, with her name in pink letters on the back. Renee Estopinal flaunts a flimsy brown wrapper with an Oriental design. Delia Peters is super-sensible in a green terrycloth job that belongs on a slack-bellied housewife in Queens. She says she wears it to remind her of the glamourous life she leads. "Besides, I can't buy a new one until we get to Saratoga. That's the big excitement up there—shopping Jamesway discount store for a new bathrobe." Make-up, rhinestones, flopping robes—you might as well be watching a gaggle of apprentice prostitutes. Except that no self-respecting whore would rush at such a pace, or be so diligent.

In a curtained-off room directly opposite the stage-right door, Mme. Sophie Pourmel, supervisor of women's wardrobe, and her ladies-in-waiting take the *Scotch Symphony* costumes off hangers and hook them onto girls. About two weeks before the season's first performance of a ballet, Mme. Pourmel and her assistants remove the costumes from their storage crates and prepare them for use. On the day of performance, they lay them out, ready for the dancers. Upstairs, Ducky Copeland and Arthur Craig maintain and prepare the costumes for the men.

Mme. Pourmel is invariably in a hurry. She takes a rack of costumes up in the elevator and wheels another rack down. She sets complicated hats on a table and makes sure nobody sits on them. She bundles tutus off to the cleaner's. (It costs twenty-two dollars to clean a tutu.) She bustles bodices off the dancers. She presses pleats and sews spangles, packs and unpacks. Wherever you go in the theater, you are almost sure to see Madame, in gray hair and gray smock, rushing in a dignified way from one article of clothing to another. After all this, what do visitors say to her?—"You dress the girls, don't you?" And she answers, as a sophisticated Parisienne might reply to a tourist with an irreparable American accent, "Yes. I dress the girls."

Young women come through the robing-room curtain one after the other, the way impossible numbers of tramps used to emerge from a circus box car, and scurry on stage to begin the nightly ritual of the shoes. One of them, perhaps Delia Peters, pauses just inside the door to the stage, brandishes a shoe and slams it against the brick wall as if crunching cockroaches. WHOMP! WHOMP! WHOMP! WHOMP! She changes hands and punishes the other shoe. Several whomps later, the footwear has been softened enough to bend across her arches.

A small tray on the property table holds sewing gear, scissors, Elmer's glue and lamb's wool. A box of tissues stands by. The scissors are for the second act of the rite, the circumcision of the toes. Pointe shoes are covered in satin, almost invariably an awful shade of orange-pink. With the scissors, Delia makes a small tear in the material covering the box that will support her toes, then cuts out a neat circle. On stage, satin can catch on something—a loose bit of tape, a swirled-off spangle, a dropped hairclip—and a whirling dancer may trip, slip or wrench an ankle. Satin also is slippery, and even a speck of dust can send a performer sliding across the floor like a bowling ball.

Next, Delia walks to a large red fire bucket near the closed-circuit television screen—there's only one channel, the stage, and reception is none too good, but a dancer can grab a cue from it— dunks her Capezios in the water and swishes them around. Wet shoes mold themselves more securely to the feet. Back at the prop table, she sits on one of the high stools, takes lamb's wool and tissues and packages her toes even more carefully than she did this morning in class. Then she applies Elmer's glue to the insides of the shoes and the soles of her tights. (Since the dancer is Delia, this entire process is accompanied by an ironic commentary, probably about the fact that she is supposed to co-hostess a dinner for twenty tonight, and hopes the performance ends early enough for her to get there before both the food and the guests run out.) Finished with the Elmer's, Delia slides on her shoes. She draws tight the elastic strings, ties them in a bow and snips the ends close, so there are no dangles to trip over. She winds the ribbons around her ankles, ties them, squirts glue on and under the fabric, and snips the dangling ends of the ribbons. The rite is accomplished.

Dancers are held together with pins in the back and Elmer's on the feet and, in spite of all the work, they have been known to throw a shoe during performance.

Dressed and shod, Delia finally can step in the resin box, go over to the barre and begin work. She took class this morning, of course, and has logged several hours of rehearsal, but she still needs to warm up. Dancing cold, like doing any strenuous excercise cold, is dangerous. Muscles can tear, ligaments can rip. Each performer has a personal pre-performance barre routine, and a favorite place to work. Little Meg Gordon likes to tuck herself away in the shadows, holding on to the metal supports for the fly lines. Others, especially when the barres on both sides of the stage are crowded, rest hands on the piano. Delia takes a place at the stage-right barre. She does pliés, battements tendus, battements tendus dégagés—it is class all over again, but at a much slower pace, since it's advisable to save some energy for the stage. At the on-stage end of the barre, Allegra, thin-armed and beautiful in her pink ballerina's costume, is doing her incredible extensions. She pliés and talks at the same time, then reminds herself that she must concentrate and stares straight ahead, her face as solemn as that of a child doing a bit of required praying.

Over the Elmer's the girls are talking, mostly about why shoes won't fit properly. Around here, Capezio plays second villain to Jerry Robbins. Milly Hayden may try more than twenty shoes before a performance, sitting on stage with them gathered around her like fallen leaves, hunting for one usable pair. Shoes come with welts that are too deep and cut the feet, with toe boxes that don't match, with shanks that do not correspond to the dancers' orders. Some fit too loosely to hug the arch. Shoes are dancers' most important tools outside their own bodies, and they never seem to fit.

While flowers for the ballerinas are being unwrapped and placed on the property table, Rosemary, in a light brown dress in-

stead of a black leotard, is conducting an emergency rehearsal for
Scotch. Deborah Koolish is out of the lineup. Her foot is not broken
but it is "all mashed up and twisted" and, the doctor told her, more
painful than a fracture would have been. She is afraid she is not
going to be able to dance for some time. As it turns out, she is not
going to be able to dance all season. She works, she tries to rehearse, but the foot will not heal properly—probably because she
tries to work and rehearse. As the season goes on, her brown eyes
get sadder, her face less animated and more tense. Since the company is the world, an injured dancer is removed from her universe.
The sense of distance, of being cut off from the family, is stultify-
ing. If you can't dance, you are not a dancer, and if all your life has
been spent in becoming a dancer, the worst thing that can happen
is to be made into a non-dancer. Balanchine, Rosie, Lincoln, the
kids, everyone accepts injury, everyone makes it as easy as possible
on the wounded, but a dancer sitting in street clothes in the audience, instead of moving in costume on stage, thinks, like the rest of
us, "they" instead of "we."

Fortunately, understudies have learned the ballet. A quick run-
through of a few passages is all that is needed. The girls, already in
costume, mark the steps, just making sure everyone knows the
sequence and her proper station. It could have been worse. Rosie
says it usually is. "Somebody always misses opening night, and it's
usually somebody with no cover." An injury to a principal dancer
is less damaging than a sidelined corps member—another principal
almost always knows the role, but often there is no time to prepare
understudies for the corps. The problem, Rosemary remarks,
"comes when the injury hits someone in a ballet nobody knows,
and that almost always happens on opening night."

The corps girls of NYCB still are securing their toe ribbons to
their tights with Elmer's and warming up at the barres when Ronnie Bates puts his mouth to the bitch box: "Fifteen minutes, please,
fifteen minutes to *Scotch Symphony*." His calm voice makes a soothing contrast to the increasing chatter of dancers and the rising
hubbub on stage. Most of the boys in the corps have come downstairs by now; they smooth down their kilts and take their places at
the barre. Roland walks through the area carrying a program and a

red pen. As each dancer appears in the wings, Roland draws a line through his name. Any name still legible at curtain time means a missing performer.

The company knows there is competition in town; nobody expects a full house or full press coverage. They know there are three major dance events tonight, and the only paper in town with three dance critics is the *Times*. NYCB is not offering a premiere. It is not showing a new star. It has not been off the boards for several years. It is just coming home, as it does every fall and spring. There's more news when the swallows come back to Capistrano. Clive Barnes, the leading dance and theater critic for *The New York Times*, is not here tonight. Many people think he is a very good critic, others insist he is a very bad critic, but nobody denies that he is a very important critic, perhaps the most important in the world. If you were first-string dance critic for *The New York Times*, you would be the most important dance critic in the world, and NYCB would very much like to have you at its opening night. Clive hardly ever can attend an NYCB opening, though, because there almost always is something else going on that takes priority. Frequently, he must cover the first night of a season too short to delay review.

At 7:55, Kevin calls through the bitch box, "Musicians to the pit, please, musicians to the pit," and pushes a white button on a panel near his desk, ringing a bell downstairs in the orchestra's lounge, thus breaking up the card games. Ronnie calls the dancers: "Five minutes, please. Five minutes to *Scotch Symphony*." Robert Irving, resplendent in his tail coat, joins the group at the barre for a few minutes, gracefully waving a big, beautifully polished shoe in his own version of battement tendu jeté. The audience is chattering its way in, tripping over one another to take seats in the orchestra without a center aisle, then leaning back to leaf through the program with its cover sketch of Milly Hayden as Eurydice in *Orpheus*. It's a middle-class, middle-aged audience, with a few young people scattered in like the almonds in a mixed nuts assortment. A comfortable audience, accustomed to being here, not expecting too much from opening night except a pleasant time.

The program gives everyone a chance. Villella isn't dancing, nor is Milly Hayden, nor Patty McBride, but they get Allegra and Jacques in *Scotch*, Helgi Tomasson in *Symphony in Three Movements*, and John Clifford and Violette Verdy in *Stars*. Pretty costumes in two of the three. Familiar music, familiar steps. Two old favorites flanking a recent Stravinsky ballet the critics loved. "Were you here for the Stravinsky Festival last year? It was wonderful . . . Have you seen Nureyev yet? . . . When is Esther going to be married? . . . What the hell is wrong with the market? . . ." An NYCB audience, but not a full house.

At eight o'clock, official curtain time, the theater is as crowded as it is going to get. Unofficial (actual) curtain time is set for 8:05, to give the subway-stalled and the parking-place hunters a chance to reach their seats. Ronnie Bates, tuxedoed for the occasion, calls, "Places, please. Places for *Scotch Symphony*." Most of the dancers already are on stage, stretching, chatting, giggling. A few more leave the barre, anoint themselves with quick squirts of cologne or perfume, and hurry out of the wings to join their colleagues. On stage, they prance and run in place. Some quickly sketch in a few steps, just to be absolutely sure. They strip off their leg warmers, toss them into the wings, and, joining their assigned groups, take their opening poses.

Kevin, speaking through the red telephone receiver mounted near his desk, asks the light booth, "May I have the opening preset for *Scotch Symphony*, please?" and the electrician pushes his buttons, bringing the lights to opening intensity. On stage, it feels as if someone had switched on a giant sunlamp. Kevin nods to Robert Irving, standing nearby, already beating time for Mendelssohn, bouncing his wrist as if dribbling a basketball. "Maestro Irving, if you please." Robert takes a keyring from his pocket and begins the long journey from backstage to the podium. His trip to the pit is almost as complicated as Dante's—he must pass through seven doors, which explains the collection of keys.

The dancers, restless as horses, still are talking and giggling. They touch the fingertips of both hands to their mouths, then dab the bare shoulders of friends in a good-luck ritual, wishing one another, "Merde." Merde is "shit" in French, and a traditional stage blessing. It is considered dangerous to be told "Good Luck" in a theater; superstition insists the wish will bring the opposite. Actors generally tell one another, "Break a leg," but in ballet, that is carrying reverse superstition a bit too far. People really do break legs in ballet. So dancers wish one another shit. In French.

Hank, a large man in a brown shirt and a one-day growth of beard, leaves his newspaper in the patch panel cubicle and strolls over to stand next to Kevin. He rests his forefinger on a red button bulging from a wall panel. Balanchine, who has been chatting with dancers, with Rosemary, with the company doctor, now takes his place just out of the audience's sight behind the large flat down-stage right. The dancers, on stage and in place, keep talking and bobbing up and down, flexing knees and stretching feet. Kevin, the red telephone at his ear, steps past Mr. B. onto the stage. "Ready on stage, please. Quiet, please. Ready on stage." The kids quiet, give final smoothing slaps to their tutus and plaster on performance smiles. A few practicing Catholics bless themselves. Applause pierces the curtain, recording the success of Robert's march through seven locked doors to his place on the podium. Kevin steps back to his desk and rests his hand on Hank's shoulder. "Warning houselights for curtain, warning Cue 1," he tells the red phone. Out front, the headlights on the tiers dim and go out. At 8:09, four minutes late, Kevin slaps Hank's shoulder; Hank slaps the button; the gold curtain glides up and settles in place with a little thud. "Curtain going up; Cue 1; Go," Kevin calls. "Stand by to pick up the Girl in Red, stage right." That last order is for the operator of the follow spot. The orchestra, following Robert's baton, flirts with Mendelssohn. The dancers step out into the music, and into the fifty-eighth New York season of The New York City Ballet.

Looking down from a seat in the first ring, it is much easier to see the mosaic of the choreography than it was in the rehearsal room, but the individual tiles are indistinct. With an audience in attendance, a full orchestra, with costumes and lights and back-drops, the dancers are even less familiar than they seemed from the third row of the orchestra. Distance plus proper lighting equals beauty: The ravishing creature at the other end of the restaurant turns hag as she passes your table. The space between the first ring and the stage transforms a group of moderately attractive young women into a pageant of loveliness. They are infinitely more devastating than the girls you know, the ones you saw primping and giggling on stage before the curtain went up.

Their first exit is a bit ragged as usual, the lines squiggle a bit reminding you they are human after all, but Allegra's entrance alters the perspective again. You forget Kevin calling cues into the red telephone, forget Hank, gone back from his button to his newspaper, forget the dancers warming up for the next ballet and whispering in the dark. You even forget Balanchine, watching from his post down right. Now you are seeing dance, not dancers. Something has happened to them, anyway. Suddenly Jacques, with his familiar smell of linament and hoarse voice, is JACQUES d'AMBOISE, the famous dancer. He is doing the same steps he did this afternoon, but they are more compelling now. His boyish enthusiasm has become professional boyish enthusiasm, his long-legged jumps are even more casual and supple. He spins, drilling a hole in the air around him, and you don't think of the perspiration whipping off his face to land twenty-five feet away on Balanchine's hand. You don't even think he is sweating. Jacques may perspire; JACQUES d'AMBOISE never does.

Suddenly, too, Allegra Kent is ALLEGRA KENT, not a delightful young woman, but an international star, someone people pay money to watch. She looks even more fragile on stage, but in a more artificial way, even more desirable, but less real. Her own femininity has become a conventional stage commodity, but it is amplified by convention. You can't see her face clearly, but you know it is beautiful. On that stage at that moment, ALLEGRA KENT could not be less than beautiful, even if Allegra Kent were. In rehearsal, you watched dancers, now you are watching DANCERS. Their art makes them artificial; their skill turns them into athletes. They have been enlarged by the glasses of our minds, as dolls are magnified by a child's imagination.

Allegra stands amid her kilted guardians as Jacques passes back and forth. The men look at him as he walks, and their heads turn in unison. When Allegra allows him to support her as she turns on pointe, you see a woman wooing a man, and give no thought to the complicated game of finger-folding that permits the turns to be so smooth. Allegra is carried high; she floats like a pink feather. The dancers form a circle, extending their arms like Maypole ribbons, and then London-bridge out under one another's arms. Very quickly, it is over. The company bows. The curtain falls. The principals come through a slit in the curtain onto the apron of the stage and bow again. Then, they step back into a void. The house-lights come on. Somewhere, people named Allegra and Jacques are talking with someone else named Balanchine about a ballet they have danced, but ALLEGRA and JACQUES no longer exist. They have been tucked into their places on the toyshelf, to wait there while we sleep.

On the first ring promenade of the theater, the spectators sip coffee and domestic champagne and talk. If the backstage area resembles a locker room or a convent, the front of the house looks like a very exclusive brothel. A bar follows a long curve across the back wall. Looking up, the drinkers can see elaborate wrought metal railings trimming the higher rings. Glass doors interrupt a glass wall and lead onto a balcony overlooking the plaza with its fountain. Hanging down the glass wall, gold bead curtains dive the length of the building. A favorite sport of those in the upper levels is jiggling a strand of beads and watching the ripples snake downwards. At each end of the promenade, a pair of stairways is separated by giant alabaster sculptures by Elie Nadelman—two melting Wagnerian heroines to a sculpture. Towering and white, they stand like Brobdingnagian soap ads, or the sort of bric-a-brac bookends God would put in His study, if God had poor taste.

Small fat ladies meet their husbands at the bases of the tall fat ladies. Klein's-clads eye Bloomingdale's-bedecked. Dating couples lean over the balcony, despite the damp and the chill. Very young girls, their backs straight, their hair in buns, model their extra-long slacks; they do not quite wear signs reading "I Am a Dancer." The gay crowd stages its private parade. Over near the stage-right stairs, the regulars, the people who will be here every night during the season, compare notes on the performance and speculate about the next one. They laud their favorite dancers and villify their goats as vociferously, if far more articulately, than the bleacher-warmers in Yankee Stadium carry on their duels. "Wasn't Allegra lovely . . .

Jacques is past it . . . Jacques always has been past it . . . When's
Patty's first this season? . . . Look, that figure is one of Balanchine's masterpieces, I don't care what anyone says . . ." They
know what they are talking about. They really see what they are
watching. Nearer the bar, critics talk to other critics about the difficulties involved in trying to be in three places at once, and what
are you doing next week when it really gets busy and have you
seen anything interesting lately? The bells tinkle the end of intermission.

The curtain goes up on *Symphony in Three Movements*, exposing a
long diagonal of girls in white. The line is fairly straight—a tribute
to Rosie's work. The women uncoil forward and contract back,
sharp and hard, even more violently than at rehearsal. Their knees
are bent, their hands claw air, their feet drive into the floor. Suddenly, Helgi Tomasson bursts onto the stage. His small, beautifully proportioned body inks Balanchine's calligraphy on the air.
He covers ground like a hungry infielder and every step is classically perfect. This is pure classroom technique on stage, cool and
underemotional, but stunning in its precision.

The passage Ricky Weiss and Merrill Ashley worked on this
afternoon, while the orchestra serenaded them with Sousa, is fine.
Merrill's dark horsetail of hair swishes, adding an accent to her cool
body line. Her determined jaw underlines her smile. Ricky, his
upper body a bit tense, as usual, jumps high and lands cleanly,
feeling the stage under his feet. There is applause. The black and
white costumes, the black drapes that form the only setting, are
stark after the kilts and pink tutus of *Scotch Symphony*, but this is
Stravinsky, not Mendelssohn. Balanchine is famous for black and
white and the fans, even those who revel in "the pretty colors," expect it. The lyricism is moving, the athleticism is thrilling. Even
people who come from the ballet saying, "Ooh, wasn't it lovely,"
are excited by the power and physical excitement of this style of
dance. They insist on the energy, the madness, the speed. They
want to see how high their favorite man can jump, how fast their
woman can spin.

Watching dance, like watching sports, is feeling as well as
seeing. It involves kinesthetic echoes. A favorite livingroom pas-

time when I was young consisted of watching my father watch boxing matches on television. Dad ducked every punch, and when a good right landed he rolled with it. Dad has good kinesthetic reactions. At a football game, the crowd stretches with the receiver and leans forward with the impetus of a downfield run. At the ballet, the echoes are not as obvious, but they happen. The eminent dance critic John Martin and other writers long ago described the action and theory of kinesthetic echo, the miniscule movement of spectators' muscles in sympathy with the larger moves of the dancers. Ballet buffs learn this, in time. The idea is not new, but every child must discover on his own that grass is green. Personal experience converts truisms into truths.

The audience in The New York State Theater, would-be dancers, suburban stockbrokers and spouses, the ladies from Queens and the boys in the band, all, to one degree or another, feel the dance inside themselves. Some are hardly aware of it. Those who are fairly relaxed, who come with few preconceptions, who can forget the stock market and tomorrow's exam and Esther's wedding to concentrate on the stage, see the performance more fully and feel it more intensely. They are jumping with Helgi the way my father used to bob with Sugar Ray, the way he still fades back with Namath, and they are gaining the same kind of enjoyment. Unfortunately, most people who attend ballet can't forget they are seeing "art," just as most of the crowd at football games is always conscious of being "fans." The tutus and the pennants remind them of everything they were taught in childhood about "enjoying" an event and get in the way. We lose our pleasure to a set of conditioned mannerisms, we play at being what we think balletomanes or football freaks ought to be and forget to attend to our muscles.

A fair number of people at any performance have trained themselves to sit back and "appreciate" it, and get so tied up in appreciation they don't enjoy things very much. They are busy watching technique to the exclusion of everything else, or deciding what to say to their friends at lunch tomorrow. They're like the Martian who tried to send home a description of Earth water after spending six weeks contemplating a glass of the stuff, but never tasting it or trying a dip in the pool. Others, self-styled estheticians, the "I'm-

so-sensitive-I-melt-in-the-sun-" crowd, try so desperately to submerge that that they conjure up a mirage on the beach and never see
the sea at all. Then one day, filled with well-being or just dead
tired, they forget Esther's wedding gift and the price of gold in
Zurich, they drop the personae usually worn to these fancy-dress
parties, and quite accidentally, start watching the stage. Suddenly,
as they see the movement, they feel it. After that, it is possible to
understand how Balanchine, looking at Helgi, can create movement to suit his body perfectly, and how Helgi can communicate
that movement to the audience.

Movement and emotion are mutually evocative. Whatever it
was that Balanchine felt as he listened to *Symphony in Three Movements*, he translated into physical action for his dancers. It is not a
conscious process, but a subconscious mutation of felt emotion into
visualized emotion. The music, and the body of the dancer on
whom he is working, stimulate the choreographer's kinesthetic
sense. Balanchine is famous for abstract—plotless—ballets, which
have no story lines to provoke emotional response. Instead, he
trusts to the structure of the music, and to that of his resultant
choreography. Whatever mood the music breeds in him is turned
by that mysterious function called "the creative process" into patterns and actions. When Balanchine looks at a dancer, then closes
his eyes, he seems to be giving himself up to the music; when he
begins to sketch out steps, he seems to be moving on the instructions of the score.

The chain of dance connects music and movement, movement
and feeling. The old white ballets evoked emotion with silly stories
of betrayed peasant maidens and enchanted swan-girls, with great
romantic *liebestods* and stylized gestures—hand on heart in love,
hand to brow in horror—that called up conventional responses.
They still do. Balanchine's genius eliminated the fairy stories and
conditioned responses, leaving the basic elements of music, action
and feeling flowing through us like an electric current. When the
curtain falls, breaking the connection, the last bit of energy is dissi-
pated in applause.

Applause is the tension-dissolving orgasm that allows the performers and spectators to separate. It can be overly loud and self-

convincing, "Oh, that was MARVELOUS,"—an hysterical response—or so restrained as to be merely a gracious formality, a
frigid response. Once in a while it is spontaneous and healthy.

Dancers hate to perform for benefit audiences, because the
spectators, filled with pre-performance dinner and awaiting post-
performance parties, "sit on their hands." As soon as the curtain
falls, they patter their palms politely and go away until the next
benefit. The performers think they have wasted their efforts, and
maybe they have. To dancers, applause is a necessity. Even an
hysterical breaking is better than pitter-patter. Dancers are perfec-
tionists; they know when they work well and when they don't. But
they have driven hard to satisfy us and if we cannot respond, they
are hurt, angry, frustrated, and sometimes cold in the next encounter. They don't expect bravos for mediocre efforts, but they do
look to be requited. There is no sense in striving alone; performance requires a participating partner. Tonight, as the curtain
falls, the response is there. The dancers can build their energies for
another bout.

Backstage, the girls are rushing from the stage into the curtained room. Mme. Pourmel and her ladies help them out of the
white leotards and into their bathrobes. The dressers hang the
clothes neatly while the dancers whisk into the elevators and go to
freshen their make-up and, if necessary, fetch fresh shoes. The
men dash for their dressing rooms, where Ducky and Arthur help
them to change.

A stagehand is dry-mopping the floor as Roland calls, "Fifteen
minutes, please. Fifteen minutes to *Stars and Stripes*." The patriotic
drops fly down. Electricians remove the gels from sidelights and insert new colors, reaching up with long poles the way the corner
grocer used to fetch cereal boxes from the top shelf. Dancers who
did not appear in the last ballet are finishing their barres, soaking
their shoes, gluing their ribbons. The girls are downstairs and dressing again. Madame and her associates hook them into *Stars* costumes, and they burst through the curtains tugging on obstinate
white gloves. Kevin calls for Independent 1 for *Stars*. The property
men assure themselves that Carol Sumner's baton and Gloria
Govrin's bugle are in their proper places. Roland calls five minutes.

On stage, John Clifford is jumping. Carol Sumner is doing a few steps on pointe, testing the balance of her shoes. She will lead the first movement of the ballet. Carol still thinks, before going on, "I do this, but if it doesn't work, if someone makes a mistake, I'll have to do that so the audience doesn't know anything is wrong."

Kevin dispatches Robert on his voyage of the seven doors. Roland calls places, and takes his stand stage left, ready to note in his program the time at which the music starts. At the end, he will write down the time it finishes. If a ballet consistently runs over or under the appointed time, something is wrong, probably with the conductor's choice of tempi.

In the wings, Carol Sumner sets her costume right and shakes. Her hands, her legs, even her lips in their wide red-painted smile, are trembling. Thin, blonde, intense, gentle Carol has been doing this for fourteen years, and still, she shakes. Once the curtain is up and she has given herself to the music, it will stop. Other girls are spraying themselves with cologne, or dabbing themselves with perfume—it's cooling. Perfume is the women's annual Christmas gift from Mr. B. He says he gives it to them so he can keep track of comings and goings in the theater. "I smell the air," he says, wrinkling his nose like an inquisitive rabbit, "and I say, 'Ahhh, Arpege—Kay is here.' "

Kevin, still smiling, still tied to his umbilical telephone, calls for the opening preset and warns the dancers to be ready. They slap down their tutus and slip on their smiles. Mr. B. is ready at his wing. Hank is ready at his button. Kevin glances at his cue sheet, calls the warning and slaps Hank.

The girls smile as they step and strut. Carol prances on with an even bigger smile. It's an old tradition in ballet: Whatever you do, smile. Dancers don't feel dressed without a smile. From the front, it looks entrancing. You can't see faces very well but you see all those teeth and you know that everything is all right and all the girls are gorgeous. From the wings, it looks as if they're wearing plastic masks. The smiles press up so hard their cheeks quiver. Most of the eyes are set and dead. Hands are tense. Nobody seems to be breathing. Nevertheless, they smile. Sometimes, when the girls turn around, their mouths relax for a moment, but as soon as they face front again, especially if they are standing still, on goes the smile.

The smiling does serve some practical purposes. A smiling dancer can count out loud or ask her file-mate, "Where to now?" without letting on to the audience. If you are not quite sure what you do in this ballet, keep smiling. If you think you just sprained your ankle, smile even more. And you can absorb quite a bit of nervous tension in the muscles around your mouth, so smile, smile, smile. Carol twirls her baton, Gloria tootles her bugle, Deni Lamont shows his elevation. John Clifford and Violette perform the pas de deux. They have not done it in months, except for a quick rehearsal this afternoon. As usual, Hollywood John is off and running at the gun.

Leaping high and soaring wide, Johnny pounces on every step like a cat playing with a cockroach. He sells the ballet the way the star man in a credit operation sells furniture, with as much confidence and panache, and as many tricks. Balanchine should choreograph "Peter Pan," and make the title role on John. The audience loves him.

Johnny really isn't pushing Borax, though. He stands behind every sales. The spectators love him. Because he loves what he is doing. He wants so much to be liked that he makes you like him, needs so much to succeed that he drives full-speed all the time. Johnny is out there selling, but he gives value for money. His dancing sometimes is superficial, but it is always fun and frequently exciting. He may not want to grow up, but no schoolboy ever worked harder for his "A." Johnny jumps and spins and flies through the air with the greatest of ease, carrying the whole theater with him. He flashes across the stage as brightly as the brass buttons of his costume.

Then it is Violette's turn. "When you dance with John," she once pointed out, "you have to start early to keep up. He really is a very good partner, you know. He is not so strong but up here (she taps her head) he is very good. Very agile." Tonight Violette starts early, letting her frisky feet do their act. She nibbles her fingers in terror as the feet start to run away with her. She looks down at them, trying to figure out what they are doing. As a matter of fact,

Violette knows exactly what her feet are doing; she has worked for years to teach them to do it. Her idea of a barre is a two-hour workout.

Violette is the company's French maman, everyone's beloved older sister. Her hello kiss is as warm as a great Chateau Latour. "You know, after a while, you tend to become not what you are, but what people expect you to be. Everyone expects me to be very French, so somehow I am always very French." She is—with warm French humor and common sense. Her mind is at least as fast as her feet. She talks frankly, and she talks sense. Violette is a complete professional who dances with the élan of an amateur, and she gives Johnny Clifford a good contest. The audience loves her, too.

John and Violette tease their way through the pas with salutes and runaway feet, arabesques to an euphonius euphonium, balance with bravado and work in the whole armory of athletic nonsense. A classical pas de deux, complete with adagio love song, to Sousa marches—who's kidding whom? But what fun it is.

After their exit, Violette and her partner indulge in one of the prettiest and politest of ballet traditions. "Thank you, John." "Thank you, Violette." The ballerina thanks her cavalier for his support; he returns the honor. No matter how out of breath the dancers are, they always have enough left to pant their thanks.

In the end, Violette, John, Carol, Gloria and Deni lead the corps in a triumphal, swooping finale as the American flag rises from the floor behind them to form a streaming backdrop. High patriotism or high camp, it can't miss.

Hank pushes the button to drop the curtain, then the other button that sends it up again as the dancers take their bows. Each time the curtain falls, they wilt. Knees fold, arms dangle, chests heave as they try to catch up on their breathing. Each time the curtain rises, they revive, smiling and bowing. "Call Robert," whispers Kevin from the sidelines, "Call Robert." Violette takes a few steps toward the wings and extends her hand to Maestro Irving, who beams and bows with the best of them. A flower boy brings Violette her bouquet. Roland scurries from stage left to pull back the flap of the curtain as Kevin urges, "Front please. Quickly, please."

Quickly, before the applause dies. They pass through the slit in the curtain and bow again. Returning, they do their wilt-and-blossom routine. Finally, Kevin calls for the houselights. The girls crowd into the curtained room offstage to undress for the third time. Electricians remove the light standards from the wings. Kevin says, "Thank you, gentlemen," to the red phone and hangs up for the night. Visitors are coming back to see Violette. Roland grabs his jacket and his newspaper, locks up and heads for home.

It is 10:21.

4

The Corps

Degas didn't lie after all. His paintings and statuettes, at first glance, seem to show the corps girls of myth—fragile and lovely, undoubtedly the *petites amies* of noble lords who ogled them from the boxes, then fell desperately in love. The soft colors of the paintings, the curves of the sculptured pieces, make it all so easy to believe—the glamour, the beauty, the richness of *la vie de ballet*. Walk through the gallery again. Look at each painting. Look closely. In this one, underneath the gauze, that lovely waist is beginning to thicken, the soft thighs seem overused. In another frame, under the make-up, faces are hard and bored, and not quite as young as they first appeared. As you stroll the exhibition, sylph-thin bodies begin to look merely undernourished; that expression in the eyes is less likely to come from romantic passion than realistic poverty. And, in the weight of the bodies, the pull in the muscles, the set characters of the features, the slightly threadbare appearance of the tutus. Degas delineated the reality that haunts the life of a dancer—stress.

There is physical stress: speed, pain, the arbitrary acrobatics of their profession. There is emotional stress: the quest for perfection, the drive of ambition, the need to succeed here, in this theater, because no other arena of life exists. Meals are irregular, circles of friendship are limited, work is taxing. In the spring of 1973, there is concern because City Center is having financial difficulties and the orchestra may strike. Will next season be shortened, or even dropped? Will the company be pared down? Short-term stress is stricter: Someone is injured and must be replaced in tonight's performance, can I learn the steps in time? Will I get a major role this season? Will I be allowed to drop a role? The stress, like a familiar ache, can become so much a part of life that you fail to notice the warning in time. And always and forever, there is the danger of injury. At any ballet performance, it is a safe bet that one of the people on stage is working with a torn ligament, a twisted ankle, a pulled muscle, a bad cold. The more dancers who are hurt and need to be replaced, the more the others have to work, and the more chance they have of being injured in turn.

If a principal is unable to perform, Roland Vazquez makes an announcement to the audience, or a quickly printed insert is slipped into the program. If a corps dancer is hurt, nobody out front knows. The program for a typical NYCB performance sets two names at the top of the cast list in reasonably large capital letters. They are the principal dancers, and even the benefit audiences recognize them. Then come three or four names in slightly smaller capitals: Those are the soloists, and the subscription audience knows them. Below that, in still smaller type is a long list segregated by sex—first women, then men—arranged in alphabetical order. That is the corps de ballet. Nobody recognizes them except their mothers and the dance freaks. No announcement is made if an injured corps dancer is replaced by another member of the ensemble. Your program lists Lilly Samuels but you're seeing Polly Shelton. Does it matter? Would you know, even if you were told, that the third girl from the left in the second movement of the first ballet is Polly, not Lilly? You can't tell the dancers even with a scorecard.

Corps dancers are, by convention, anonymous. They are paid, like soldiers, to subdue their personalities to their uniforms. You are not to know, or care, that Lilly is soft-faced and suffered with a foot injury all season and that Polly is sharp-faced, terse and efficient. To you, in the audience, it doesn't matter at all that Bonita Borne's boyfriend is a dentist in Los Angeles, that Suzanne Erlon's

husband is interested in politics and plays bridge, or that Kathleen
Haigney is married to soloist Ricky Weiss. Delia Peters plays tennis
and Richard Dryden does fine needlepoint. Debra Austin is seventeen and Michael Steele is thirty. Donna Sackett is learning choreology from Jurg Lanzrein and Alice Patelson is trying her hand at
choreography. Victor Castelli is from New Jersey and Danny
Duell from Dayton, Ohio. None of these things matter to the critic
in the first ring or the high school student in the fifth, and there is
no reason they should. The knowledge would distract them from
seeing the corps as an organism, a beautiful, not-overly-bright animal trained with carrot and stick to dance Balanchine's ballets and
not get in the way of the choreography.

They—the members of the ensemble—are the heart of classical
ballet. The principals may do the great leaps and lovely balances
downstage center, but you can't have *Swan Lake* without swans, or
Giselle without Willis, or Balanchine's *Symphony in C* and *Tchaikovsky Concerto No. 2* without an ensemble. The NYCB corps is
made up of fifty-three dancers, eighteen men and thirty-five
women. They are young, dedicated, overworked and underpaid.

First-year corps members earn $ 150 a week. They are guaran-
teed thirty-two weeks of work a year, which means $4,800. They
are more likely, it is true, to have forty weeks of work, which multiplies out to $6,000. Of course, first-year corps members are very
young, so presumably it doesn't matter. When they get to be
fourth-year corps members, the top of the ensemble salary scale,
they earn only $75 a week less than soloists—$275 a week, or $11
grand a year if they do forty weeks of work, $8,800 for 32. That's
more like it, right? The only catch is that a fourth-year corps
member who does not make it to soloist—and most of them don't—
goes without a raise until he leaves the company. Eventually, a
new contract will bring them more, but not much more, because
the company can't afford to pay much more. There is overtime,
and some dancers work for other companies when they can, but
most of the outside jobs go to principals and soloists, dancers who
have been around for a while. Most of the corps dancers live in
Manhattan, which is costly, and their earning years are relatively
few.

Dancers generally join the company between the ages of sixteen and eighteen, although there are exceptions. A few began even younger, and some of the men came to ballet in their late twenties. As a rule, though, dancers start young and finish young—their average working life is ten years. Again, there are exceptions, but for most, at twenty-six or twenty-eight, or at the outside, thirty, it's all over. A performer who has not been promoted out of the corps by then never will be, and promotions are infrequent. They depend on talent, technique, style, hard work—and Balanchine. The odds are against the dancers.

When the company toured Eastern Europe in the early fall of 1972, most of the kids got a few surprises. They learned that, generally, corps dancers in the great Soviet companies don't expect promotion. They graduate from a State school, are assigned to a company as corps members—and civil servants—and remain corps members until they retire, still young, on a pension. Dancers at The Royal Danish Ballet receive their pensions at thirty-five. These national companies recognize as a matter of policy that ballet, like most other athletic events, is work for the young. Balanchine once asked, "Shouldn't we have a pension plan for the dancers?" Unfortunately, as an AGMA representative later pointed out, most dancers do not work long enough to make a significant contribution to a pension fund. There are artists in both Denmark and the Soviet Union who continue to dance well into middle age and add maturity to technique in their portrayals, but they are principals, not corps dancers. And, in the U.S.S.R., the two categories are separate from the beginning.

There are other differences between Soviet and American companies, as the NYCB performers discovered on their tour. Bolshoi Ballet dancers don't rehearse on the day of performance, they don't give eight performances a week, they don't perform forty or fifty different works in one season. "And," the NYCB corps kids say, "their corps work is so easy. They do the same steps over and over again—not the complicated patterns Mr. B. gives us—and they even stand still once in a while."

The kids are right, of course. In white ballet, the leads and featured dancers do all the fancy stuff. The corps does relatively simple steps, but does them absolutely in unison. In American ballet, especially Balanchine-NYCB ballet, the corps executes complex steps and performs them very quickly. Every so often, a dancer slips out of the mass like a pseudopod extruded by a microorganism, presents a short solo and melts back into the amoeba again. Dancers who are asked to do this often enough may be on their way to promotion. These solos are one reason that when the choreographer does demand absolute old-world precision, he usually doesn't get it: The corps is not trained as a Russian-style army in toe shoes. The other reason, of course, is that the rehearsal and performance schedules of NYCB probably are unique. Peter Martins, who was trained at, and still is affiliated with The Royal Danish Ballet, says European dancers are convinced the Americans are nuts. Fifty-four ballets in a nine-week season? Eight performances every week? Six rehearsal days every week? Dancers doing three different ballets in one evening? Of course they're nuts. During the first week of this season, the company rehearsed twenty-three ballets and performed fifteen. No wonder the corps looks sloppy much of the time. Besides, in a twenty-five-minute ballet by Balanchine or Robbins, the corps dancers may do as many steps, and as difficult ones, as the leads do in the four acts of *Swan Lake*. In the regular routine, NYCB principals rarely dance more than one ballet at each performance, but corps dancers must accept multiple appearances as a normal part of their work.

To make life more interesting, the kids explain, "there are corps dancers and corps dancers." Some members of the ensemble don't merely flow out of the organism now and then but work more or less regularly as soloists. Merrill Ashley and Colleen Neary do a tremendous amount of solo dancing, but are working, listed and paid as corps members. Bart Cook and Bryan Pitts are only two of the corps dancers who have had roles made on them by Jerry Robbins, who looks for promise among the younger members of the company and builds on it. Sometimes, the kids are presented not merely as soloists, but as principals. Christine Redpath and Renee Estopinal have learned and performed leading parts in *Jewels*. Elise Flagg does roles usually executed by Gelsey Kirkland. When Elise is being Gelsey—when she is performing as a principal—she is expected to act the part; to dance with individuality and panache. When Elise is being Elise—prancing about in the corps of *Stars and Stripes*—she is supposed to blend into the ensemble. The little dancer may be on her way to promotion, but she also may be working her way up to a split personality.

Dancers are given billing according to the roles they are performing, not by their contractual status. Renee, Christine or Elise may get big capital letters one night and alphabetical order the next—or even later the same evening. The program contains no company roster divided by status. Balanchine, although in politics he seems to be slightly to the right of Ivan the Terrible, believes in a company structured according to the old communist idea of a classless society in which promotion depends on merit. He also wants people to come to the theater to see the ballet, not to cheer a favorite dancer. He does not encourage a glittering personality to stand between the audience and the choreography. To the dancers this means that, in theory, any little girl can grow up to be an NYCB ballerina, just as, in theory, any little American boy can grow up to be president. In both cases, theory differs from practice. "So much depends," one young woman says bluntly, "on whether or not Balanchine likes you." Still, there is hope. Of the company's eight female principals, all but Violette Verdy and Melissa Hayden made the Horatio Alger trip up from the ranks. And every dancer joins the company with the hope, if not the expectation, of principal status.

They began very young, as early as seven or eight, in places like New York and Los Angeles, Schenectady, Tacoma, Washington, and Dayton, Ohio. They started because their friends were taking class, or their mothers wanted social status, or their posture needed improvement or sometimes because they had seen a ballet performance and fallen in love. They kept on studying, out of love, or pleasure, or simply inertia and suddenly they were being scouted by the big leagues. The School of American Ballet (and hence, NYCB) has a farm system. It keeps on good terms with teachers throughout the country and stands a close watch on their pupils. Violette Verdy is one of the scouts. While on a concert tour she uses free time to visit ballet schools. Sometimes she makes special trips. Violette knows ballet schools the way a major league scout knows high schools. "You know, you have to do a very thorough detective job," she says. "You have to know the teacher—is she doing it for prestige, or for art or for community vanity? Is the teaching realistic—does it educate people to ballet? Does it achieve at least a 'high intermediate' level?"

After checking out the franchise, the scout goes on to examine the talent. "You look at very young children—you know, nine or so—and make notes. Then you return the next year and look again. You look at the body. You look for intelligence, talent, technique, a capacity for work. Usually you can't bring them to New York until they finish high school—sometimes you can—so you bring them in for summer classes at The School. Then, suddenly, between one summer and the next, they grow much too tall or much too lanky, or hurt themselves doing sports programs or baton twirling."

The ones who *know* they are going to be dancers don't go in for sports programs and baton twirling. They haven't the time. They're too busy going to school and then going to class. New Yorkers, or those who do come to town before finishing high school, generally are enrolled in The Professional Children's School, to get the education required by law, as well as in The School of American Ballet, to get the education required by Balanchine. Classes at PCS are so scheduled that the kids have time to act on Broadway or study ballet. As far as the children are concerned, professional studies take priority. Delia Peters and Susan Pilarre, both PCS graduates and both bright young women, report, "It's a very good school if you bother to go to class. Most of us didn't." Not all the students at The School of American Ballet attend PCS— Allegra was an "A" student at The Rhodes School, but that's Allegra —but it is the norm. And no matter what PCS does, it is hard to make students take the interest in algebra they do in adagio. Dancers don't need algebra anyway, and these kids know they are going to be dancers. They are, after all, students at The School. Some were there only for a year or so, others learned all of their dancing there. Eventually, the top few, the stars of their year, those with the look and the drive, the technique and the style—and the ones who appeal to Mr. B.—join the company.

DEBRA AUSTIN is seventeen, the only black dancer with NYCB, a sweet, voluptuous teen-ager with a big soft smile and big soft breasts. She began ballet lessons at ten "because everyone in the neighborhood was doing it" and decided she wanted to dance, "not as a professional, you know, just to dance." At thirteen, she auditioned for the school. Just turned sixteen, she joined the company. After one year with the troupe, of course she's not getting solo work, just being part of the amoeba, but she has hope. At thirty-five, she says, she'll still be dancing. "I want to be like Milly Hayden." Sweet and warm, with a tendency to giggle now and again and a smile that, even on stage, is joyous, Debbie is a bit young for her years in some ways, slightly old for them in others. There is a quality of innocence about her that would shock a lot of her non-dancing coevals. She's happy to be dancing, to be with the company, to be doing what she knows in an atmosphere she understands. But what if she isn't still dancing at thirty-five? What if she's not another Milly Hayden? What if she's not that talented, or that durable? "I haven't even thought about it," says Debbie. And giggles.

In the company, as in the army, you don't have to think. People tell you what to wear, and where to go and what time to show up. Balanchine offers advice on diet (protein), pets (cats) and hobbies (plants and cooking). He gives the girls perfume for Christmas, so that they don't have to worry about that choice. He has been known, at least to hint about love, marriage and pregnancy (don't). So all a dancer really has to do is dance, try for roles and aim at advancement inside the company. When you are seventeen, there is no outside. The important thing is to dance. The next important thing is to be sure that Balanchine likes the way you dance. Twenty-year-old Meg Gordon says that if she wants a career, she'll have to move to a smaller company. "They think I'm good enough to be in the corps here and to do roles in some ballets, but I'm not really going to get anywhere—I'm not tall and slim."

Height is not an absolute requisite for success, but it does help to be thin. When Bonita Borne joined the company, she was a few pounds overweight. "I want to see bones," Balanchine told her, prodding like a conscientious housewife at the chicken counter. "I want to see bones here and here—your chest and your neck." His suggested diet includes fish, chicken, meat and a few vegetables. Fruit produces excess sugar; bread obviously is off the menu. The man wants to see bones. A night club pallor also helps. When dancers manage to get a bit of sun on their days off, they powder down carefully before the next performance. The man does not like sunburns, or even suntans, on stage.

It is important that the man gets what he wants. Toward the end of June, one of the corps girls was saying how little she looked forward to Berlin, how much she wanted to go home, to rest, to see her parents, her friends, her beau, to not be a dancer for a month. But she had voted in favor of going to Berlin—was she changing her mind? No, she had known in April that she didn't want to go. "But even though it was a secret ballot, Mr. Balanchine would know how you voted. Somehow, he knows these things. And if you wanted to get roles, you voted 'Yes.' "

One difficulty with playing up to Balanchine is that there is no obvious way to do it. Being obvious, in fact, is a serious mistake. One of the girls once went to the company's director, Lincoln Kirstein, nearly in tears, saying, "Mr. B. doesn't like me." Lincoln assured her that this was nonsense. "He can't not like you," he told her, "he doesn't know you're alive." Meg Gordon has been with the company for two years, and worries because Balanchine doesn't speak to her outside of class. She's not at all sure he knows her name. You are not going to get far in NYCB if Mr. B. doesn't know you exist. Since the choreographer has a reputation as a connoisseur of old wine and young women, it sometimes is assumed that the girls who make it, make it. It won't wash.

First off, Balanchine is a gentleman of the old school with a sense of fitness and order. One look at his love songs will tell you which sex is supposed to do the pursuing. Secondly, Balanchine's wives have been women of beauty, talent and independence. (Maria Tallchief can hardly be described as a clinging vine, and Tanaquil LeClerq has proven herself a remarkable woman as well as a remarkable dancer.) Balanchine may have, as it is said, molded young dancers into wives while making them ballerinas, but he does not see every young corps girl in those roles. An eighteen-year-old would-be ballerina wouldn't have a chance, unless she could offer a good deal more than an eighteen-year-old body, in which case, she could prove herself in a lot of other ways. Nobody checking the list would suggest that Balanchine's sex life and professional life are not intertwined, but the fact that they are is not going to be of much help to the girls in the corps. For one thing, Mr. B. has a reputation for loving one woman at a time.

Balanchine's influence is far more subtle. He simply sets a pattern of life, and people follow it, out of respect, or ambition, or both. In any closed world, it is important to conform to the patterns of the community, and to follow the style of the leader, unless you either are of great importance to the group or do not care whether or not you are accepted. You don't wear your hair long at the Harvard Business School, you don't cut it short on tour with the Rolling Stones. You don't let yourself gain too much weight at NYCB; you don't get pregnant at inconvenient times; you don't ski; and you don't buck the system. At least, you don't do it so it shows.

BONITA BORNE is nineteen, too young to wear the sharp face of tension, but she does. Bonnie is a frisky girl, obviously raised to be a middle-class housewife. Her father is a composer and music director in Hollywood. Her younger sister, Elyse, dances with NYCB. Her dentist beau lives in California, "and there are certain things you can't do on the phone." If she were in college, Bonnie would be husband-hunting. In the ballet, her hunting ground is limited. "In the beginning, I was afraid of what would happen if Mr. B. saw me with a boy. Now, I don't worry about it, but I just know he wouldn't like it. He doesn't approve of relationships." Whether that says more about Balanchine or Bonnie is hard to say, but what Bonnie believes about what Balanchine thinks pretty much determines her life. She teases and jokes and flirts and worries her way through it. The older girls, the ones who get to make television commercials and perform with touring companies, have a chance to meet people. Bonnie lives in a hotel near the theater, and gets to meet dancers.

It is a circumscribed world, with very definite rules. Unlike ballplayers, dancers are not fined for breaking curfew or training, although prolonged disregard of the code can result in being expelled from the company. They are not bound by vows, like cloistered religious. Still, the rules and vows are there, unwritten and often unspoken, but universally acknowledged. The first of them is to disregard the rules of the world outside, and to promote a Chosen People mystique. Corps members, especially very young ones, define themselves as NYCB members first, dancers second and human beings third.

The physical training and mental discipline of ballet require that those who would be dancers make themselves different from other people. The most obvious difference is that they can stand with their feet making an angle of 180 degrees, but that's the easy part. The biggest difference comes from a knowledge that they are different. All chosen peoples have histories of suffering, deprivation and private and particular laws which must be obeyed. They are chosen because they have the laws, and obey the laws to remind themselves they are chosen. In any segregated society, whether segregated by force or by choice, the underlying assumption is, "It's us against them."

Like the thoroughbreds they resemble, NYCB dancers wear blinders to keep their eyes from straying to temptations or sources of fright on either side of them. Their main concerns are their work and their bodies, and they are hard on themselves. Compliment a dancer after a performance and he nearly always will tell you what was wrong with it. Dr. Louis Shaw, dancer-turned-psychiatrist and author of *The Bonds of Work*, blames the syndrome on "a let-down, like post-coital depression. You've been so high and there's no way to follow through, so you drop." (It is interesting to note that some psychiatrists maintain that post-coital depression results not from satisfaction, but from a lack of it. Too often the emotions driving the sex act are anger and fear, emotions which must be repressed. As a result, orgasm cannot be a true release, and depression follows. Dancers on stage also often are driven by emotions they do not recognize in themselves, which stand between them and complete release within the music.)

There also is the problem of a conditioned demand to achieve the impossible. Years of training in class have stressed the neccessity of perfection of technique, yet perfect technique at every moment of a performance is almost beyond possibility. Year after year of classes, with teachers pointing out the most minuscule of errors, have schooled the kids to search their bodies for impurities even at the moment of achievement. George Jessel used to tell the story of a cop who caught a small boy heaving a brick through the window of the local grocery store. "Why did you do that?" he demanded. "Well, officer, I'm on my way to confession and I'm a little short of material." Dancers always are on their way to confession and short of material. When you are required to reach perfection, when you know only one society and one set of rules, it is easy to satisfy the need for self-castigation and to turn pecadillos into venial sins. Under the banter, a dancer is not saying, "I goofed," he is chanting, "Mea maxima culpa."

COLLEEN NEARY, black-haired and striking, has legs as long as a Russian novel and as much endurance as its readers. She has the line, the stretch, the speed to be a "Balanchine dancer," and Mr. B. made a variation for her in his new ballet. On evenings when she does not perform, Colleen spends two hours or so in the rehearsal rooms, "working by myself." She works on her variation; she works on her technique; she practices balances until she can stand unsupported on pointe for nearly half a minute. Colleen's sister, Patricia, was a principal dancer with the company, so there is family tradition to maintain. Colleen has been noticed by critics and the audience, so there is reputation to maintain. She has been noticed by Balanchine and given roles, so there is a career to maintain. Colleen is stunning in her cool, detached way, with clear skin and dark eyes, but her lithe body seems more instrument than animal, more a driven vehicle than a running mare. She laughs and romps with the others, but the coolness, the drive, the aim, never leave her. Whenever Colleen is not dancing, she's dancing. She is consecrated.

The dance theater is not far removed from the convent. There is the same mortification of the flesh, the same adoration of saints—the canonized great of the company, whose roles now are executed by others—the same conditioning of beliefs, the obedience to superiors, the absolute knowledge that one has been called to serve an ideal beyond the power of those who remain outside the walls. And often, as in all limited groups, there comes a sense of superiority to those outside, a knowledge that we can do things they can't. The knowledge is correct, the superiority justified. Yet, it must be admitted that they can do things we can't. Self-deprivation breeds self-righteousness, but it also breeds jealousy. The one can be used to cover up the other. It has to be. The corps of NYBC is a religious elect, but so much must be abandoned at the door of heaven. So many pursuits must be relegated to the short time spent outside the walls each day.

The dancers often have an insatiable craving for approval—another heritage from years of class—and a tendency to see themselves through other's eyes. As they grow older, as they advance in the company and spend less time in the theater, the tendency lessens somewhat. All performers hope for approval from the audience—it is one of the many reasons they become performers—but more important is the estimation of one's peers. The child's "gang," the collegian's fraternity or political group, the socialite's clique, the businessman's commuting companions—these are the people whose approval counts, because "they really understand what is important," and because through them, one can advance in status. At NYCB, it is important to be accepted by the dancers and crucial to have the approval of Balanchine.

They have so many opportunities to earn it, and to remind themselves that other people, those outside the group, need not worry about it. Carol Sumner, dressed to leave the theater in neat blue dress and high-heeled shoes, looks in the mirror and remarks, "We don't look quite human in practice clothes. Of course, ballet dancers aren't quite human." It is not only the practice clothes, but what they do in the practice clothes that reminds them. Dr. Shaw asserts: "Dancers think they know their bodies, but they don't." Dancers know their bodies in the sense that they know what their muscles can do; they feel the pulls and stretches, they are aware of pains and warning signs; they sense balance and the actions of movement, but they know their bodies as outside observers, not as integrated beings.

Most humans have the misfortune to think of themselves as compartmentalized trinities—mind, body and emotions. Few people can think, feel and act spontaneously and all at once function as a complete organism. Their training makes dancers even more divided than most of us. Dancers are body-aware, but the majority subconsciously see their bodies as tools. They live in their bodies, not with them. On stage, a few can go beyond the stage of three separate segments and move as total beings; they often end up as stars. Even they, however, seldom continue to function totally once off the stage. Of all the people in the theater, only Balanchine seems capable of doing something totally; it is one of the secrets behind his magnetism and presence. The dancers, although they feel the stretch of an arm muscle, do not recognize the thrilling in the bicep that is a sign of anger.

The company acts as a giant, exterior superego, driving the dancers with deeply engraved "Thou shalt's" and "Thou shalt not's." Under its rule, the individual egos are subdued, emotions are sublimated. The dancer of ballet expresses emotion, but he does it in prescribed ways. The same is true off stage. A dancer suffering from pre-performance jitters can't very well scream out his fear, run away, or throw things. He can merely tremble, grow rigid, or become snappish. Schoolyard joking is an approved way of expressing boredom; leaving the rehearsal is not. Nobody has complete freedom, but for dancers, the discipline and the all-seeing superego are more obviously present than they are for other people, and the armoring and the repression of emotions become more manifest.

Partially because of this, while dancers are physical creatures—heaven knows they get enough exercise—as a species they aren't terribly healthy. They tend to spend Monday patronizing the masseur or the chiropractor. AGMA's medical plan has had to limit non-disabling doctor visits to twenty-four a year, in order to keep the premiums within reason. Some of the need for treatment is caused by physical strain, the penalty exacted for forcing one's body to perform unnatural acts. A good deal of the masseurs' work, though, is the simple loosening of muscles knotted by tension. There are nineteen-year-old girls in the company with lumps as hard as lumber in their shoulder muscles, their back muscles, their jaw muscles. Physical tension mirrors emotional stress; there is a long history of anger, frustration and unhappiness knotted into those muscles.

Late in the season, Bonnie Borne is slashing her toe shoes with scissors; a bone spur has made it impossible for her to get them on any other way. She dances anyway. Jerry Robbins lends her a bottle of ethyl chloride—the chemical used by athletes to freeze and anesthetize an injury—and she dances. Bonnie knows she needs an operation to remove the spur but with rehearsal period, the regular season, the tour and Berlin, she doubts she'll have time. Of course, she simply could stop dancing for a few weeks, but "they wouldn't like that much." Besides, an injured dancer gets paid for three weeks; after that, she has to show up to collect. The company tries to help. Walk-on parts that don't require much dancing bring the program credit needed for payday. And the pain of not dancing is greater than the pain of dancing, even with an injury. If Balanchine thinks it important that you dance, your own importance is confirmed. You dance.

Physical ease is not the only possession left at the door of heaven. "Don't I have a right to a life of my own?" Lincoln Kirstein mimics the dancers. "Don't I have a right to do what I want, to play ball, to go out, to have children . . ." And he answers his mimicry with violence: "No, you don't. Not if you're going to dance." As far as Lincoln is concerned, there is no God but Balanchine, and NYCB is his prophet. "It takes years to make one of these dancers into a ballerina, six or seven years of hard work. And after George teaches one of them, she wants to go away and get married and have babies. No, you do not have the right to do that. Not if you want to dance."

> CHRISTINE REDPATH, another up-and-comer, has a long, sweet face to go with her long, sweet body. Blond, sophisticated, witty and aware, she has a sense of style and is taking on bigger roles. Her father is an editor at *Time;* she's read a book. Her mind is a lot less limited than her universe. She jokes about "the need to raise hell once in a while, to go out to dinner, to find someone to take me out to dinner." Should be no problem—bright, pretty, clever Chris should have no trouble finding someone to take her anywhere. "Who in hell wants to wait around to start a date at 11 P.M. when I get out of here?" After her "need to raise hell" speech, Chris goes home to watch Fred Astaire on the late movie.

Home, to the corp kids, usually is within walking distance of Lincoln Center. West 69th Street seems to be populated entirely by dancers. Some live in a hotel directly across from the theater, and convenient to O'Neal's, the favored pub. Dancers tend to live with other dancers usually, but not always, from the same company. (Renee Estopinal shares lodgings with Starr Danias of the Joffrey company.) Possibly only dancers can put up with other dancers as roommates. Then again, perhaps dancers like to think that only other dancers can put up with them. "I have friends who have known me since I started," Bruce Wells remarked, "and they still don't know how much work is involved." Besides, young dancers don't get to know too many people who aren't dancers. The home becomes, in effect, an extension of the theatrical hothouse, where performers can live under glass, protected from the elements.

Interestingly enough, dancers who live with lovers—of the same or the opposite sex—often choose partners from outside the company; frequently, they select non-dancers. One of the older men in the corps insisted that choosing a lover from the company would be "like sleeping with your brother or your sister. You see them all day; you work, talk, eat and dress with them—you don't want to live with them, too." The women in the company outnumber the men by a goodly margin, and they outnumber the strictly heterosexual men overwhelmingly. A girl had better look elsewhere. Furthermore, long-term relationships generally come to the slightly more senior dancers, those who not only have the opportunity, but the desire to look elsewhere. Even a hothouse needs windows.

Still, the corps tends to live in the same area, if not the same buildings, eat in the same restaurants, drink in the same pubs, shop at the same stores. They always know who is doing what and with whom.

As the dancers get older, the world outside the walls begins to look greener, and no lightning strikes if they graze in it. Some come to understand the problems of wearing blinders, wondering if the restricted view doesn't limit their dancing instead of advancing it. "The future of ballet isn't with this company," one girl says. "It may not be with any company going now; I don't know. But I do know it doesn't have to be like this. It doesn't have to be a choice between dancing and living. You dance better if you live, if you experience more things. Maybe in the old days, when Mr. B. was trained, they thought cutting yourself off from everything made you a better dancer, but we're learning that it isn't so. You can't let one man dictate the way eighty people should live."

The New York City Ballet is not a democracy but an autocracy, a feudal fiefdom. Classical ballet is not a democratic art; it demands absolute adherence to arbitrary rules. It originated in monarchy, and reached what many consider its apogee under the tsars. The great Soviet companies, often considered the best in the world, are part of a state-dictated society. Britain, too, has a tradition of caste and class. Balanchine and Kirstein have custom-built an ordered hothouse to sustain the ideals of the art, but their world order is becoming difficult to sustain. America holds its citizens in their places by more subtle means than does the U.S.S.R., and our aristocracy derives more from lucre than from lineage. The middle class, at least, is encouraged to believe in freedom, and during the decade just past, many citizens began to take the freedom-talkers at their word. Human rights movements developed among blacks, Indians, women and other groups. Baseball players revolted against the option clause in their contracts. Military servicemen formed a trade union. And young, middle-class Americans began to say "No." Now, dancers are saying it, thinking about joining less regimented companies, or even about forming their own companies.

Perhaps, several years late, while it is petering out elsewhere, the youth rebellion of the 1960s is catching up with ballet. The people who dropped out of Harvard, who didn't want to work for IBM, who had no wish to make the gross national product ever grosser, looked for alternatives. Some came to value creativity more than productivity, some tried to get the system out of their systems, some just got lost. Dancers are artists. They have, according to the myths, creativity, freedom of movement, strength of body and soul. But ballet dancers work within the discipline of the art, under the discipline of the company. They, too, confront an Establishment, and it is older, and even less yielding to the forces of time than ours. They, too, are chasing alternatives. They want freedom to dance, and freedom from the restrictions dancing, especially NYCB dancing, entails. The seventeen and eighteen-year-olds don't feel it. They are doing something they love; they are getting paid to do it; they have achieved success. The older people, those in their twenties, are not so sure of themselves.

DELIA PETERS has been with the company ten years, long enough to develop a wry perspective. She's a good dancer, but has never made it to soloist. She lives more outside the theater than in it. Younger dancers do things the other way round. Delia has her tennis, her parties, her friends who don't dance. She'll absent-mindedly sit in a split at a party, stretching her thigh muscles, but she's probably the only dancer at the party. She's devoted to the company, but could not love it, dear, so much, loved she not Delia more. She is a dancer, not A DANCER. It's easier that way.

Delia is a realist. Her world is less than realistic. Classical ballet is an artificial art. NYCB is an artificial state. It is aligned into a definite hierarchy, arranged like a medieval order of angels. As long as the lower orders accept their places in the scheme, as long as they accept the scheme, it survives. But what if a new generation of angels decides they don't want to be cherubim shooting for seraphim? Suppose they just want to be people? Suppose the strain of celestial self-discipline becomes unbearable? Right now, there is no war in heaven, but there is a certain amount of murmuring. Today's teen-agers are not quite as docile as those of years ago and a national change in attitude will, sooner or later, affect the corps de ballet.

VICTOR CASTELLI became a ballet dancer somewhat by accident. He started studying, and kept on studying, and suddenly he was a member of the company while he still was trying to decide whether he wanted to do ballet or jazz. He still has not quite decided, but he has a good job among congenial people and he is held in place by the laws of inertia. Watch Victor in class. He works, but he seldom gives his work that deadly serious expression that is the sign of a young man going places. He can't quite convince himself, despite his phenomenal extensions and breezy personality, that this is the end of the world. He really doesn't know what he wants to be when he grows up.

Dancers, sooner or later, stop being dancers, and that can cause problems. Athletes can always sell insurance or real estate when they retire. The famous ones can franchise their names or open bars. Dancers don't get famous enough to inspire anybody to buy a hamburger or to add ten grand to his life insurance. Athletes who don't achieve the status of national monuments often wind up teaching physical education; dancers end up teaching dance.

After a stint with NYCB, a dancer has sufficient credentials, within his profession, to move to East Cupcake, Nebraska and start a school, or to get a job with an already established plié parlour. Better, yet, he can hook up with a college dance department, or a civic ballet company, where he's more likely to make a living. Retired opera singers, if they're celebrated retired opera singers, can hit private pupils for fifty dollars a lesson and better. Student dancers don't pay fifty dollars an hour for lessons.

The girls, of course, can marry—a few are married already, the others will get there in the course of time. Society does not provide a similar way out for the men, who sooner or later will have to go to work. Some may find jobs within the company, or with other companies. Some have skills or interests outside dance: Richard Dryden could be an interior decorator, if he put his mind to it. Soloist Bruce Wells owns a piece of a snail-sized crafts shop called "By Hand"—it's in the neighborhood, of course. Some of the older dancers, soloists and principals, try their hand at choreography, as does corps dancer Richard Tanner. Choreography, though, is an amazingly elusive talent—there are fewer great choreographers in history than great composers—and only a few will be good enough even to turn out hack-work for a small regional company. Most of the members of the corps, especially the young ones, don't have the vaguest idea of what they will do when they retire. Most of them can't imagine the time when they will retire. When you are eighteen, twenty-eight seems light-years away. In most cases, it's not a case of seizing the day, either. They just don't know of any other way to live. "What would you like to do when you retire?" "Anything I can do sitting down." It's as sensible an answer as most people could make.

5

"I Made it for Melissa"

Creation of any kind begins with nothing; empty space and empty time, and the need to fill them. There is an infinite choice of fillings—far too many choices, in fact. No matter how strict the conventions of his form, the artist still looks out over a nearly endless landscape of possibilities. He glares at his empty space, listens to his empty time, procrastinates, and toys with themes until, finally, he must make a choice, hope it is a good one, rear back and begin, as Balanchine says, to "put the pieces together."

A choreographer's choices are based on the space, music and bodies available to him, and limited by the conventions of dance. Some begin with one, some with another. Balanchine nearly always starts with music. To him, it is the foundation of ballet. "The music dictates the patterns," he says. "The rhythm gives us the floor on which we can dance. The composer is the architect of time." Music is his second religion, after Russian Orthodoxy, and by far the more public of the two. Devotion to his church is a private matter, but music is one of the few subjects Balanchine will discuss at length with strangers. "Idiots," he snarls, when the audience begins to applaud before the orchestra has finished. "Idiots. They don't know what they are hearing. They don't know anything. The critics are idiots, too. They don't write about the music. How can you write about a ballet without writing about the music? How can you look at a ballet without listening to the music? But as soon as the dancers stop moving, they clap, whether music still is playing or not. They don't know; they don't listen; they just clap. They are idiots."

His criticism of other choreographer's dances often is based on their choices of score. He does not like Jerry Robbins' *In the Night*, danced to Chopin *Nocturnes*, because "the music is boring." He tells John Clifford that a ballet the young dancer-choreographer made in Los Angeles would be better with different music, and he sometimes suggests scores for Clifford to set. A work he saw recently failed to hold his attention because, "the music never changes key—how can you make good dancing to such uninteresting music?" And one piece offered by the Stuttgart Ballet at the Metropolitan Opera House absolutely infuriated him because, "The music was made to listen to, not to look at. Some music you don't dance to, you just listen, and to use it for ballet is worse than a crime, it is a sin. Nixon and some of those others, maybe they are criminals, and if they are, the law can punish them. But the composer is not here on earth any more and to use his music without thinking about it is a sin, because he is not here to defend himself. It is like taking a hundred-dollar bill and using it to clean yourself after you go to the bathroom." (For Mr. B. to use so crude an image, he must be violently disturbed.) "To show disrespect for music, and for composer, is a sin."

In class one morning, emphasizing a point of technique, Balanchine asked Jean-Pierre Bonnefous if he played an instrument. He asked if any of the other dancers played. One girl said, no, she didn't, but her father was a violinist. "Ah, your father," said Mr. B. "That doesn't help you. MY father was a *composer*. Fathers don't matter." The gifts of the fathers are not visited upon the sons; it is only what you can do that matters. There was reverence, almost envy, in the word "composer." (Balanchine had studied composition, before turning to dance-making.) The high priest of choreography might well have preferred to be an acolyte of music. Balanchine's father and brother, both writers of music, never will be accorded the honor he has achieved, but he reveres their craft above his own. Perhaps that is why his ballets have gone beyond respecting music to illuminating it. Perhaps it is part of the reason for his long, close and fruitful friendship with Stravinsky. Certainly, his reverence and his musical studies have brought him to the point at which Robert Irving, who has had wide experience, can say that no other choreographer understands music as well as Balanchine.

His office is furnished with a grand piano and a small stereo phonograph. He plays through scores (he once considered a concert career), reads through others and listens to recordings. One of the practice room scores for *A Midsummer Night's Dream* carries the note: "Mendelssohn. Sinfonia IX—Transcribed for Piano Solo by G. Balanchine." Often Mr. B. chooses to make a specific ballet because there is a piece of music he wants to work with. This season, his office music library includes a new work by Nicholas Nabokov ("brother of 'Lolita,' " says Mr. B.—actually Nicholas Nabokov is a cousin of the novelist Vladimir) who wrote the score for the choreographer's version of *Don Quixote*, and the company is excited by a rumor that Balanchine is thinking of making a ballet to music by his own brother.

His new ballet for this spring season is being built on a score he has used several times in the past, Alexander Glazounov's *Raymonda*. He used music from the full-length Russian ballet in 1946 when, in collaboration with Alexandra Danilova, he made *Raymonda*. He returned to it in 1955, for *Pas de Dix*, and in 1961 for *Raymonda Variations*. By the time he finishes the newest version, he says he will have "used all the parts of the score that are danceable." Balanchine has used this score more often than any other. Oddly, he has set no other work by Glazounov, while he has made twenty-six ballets to music by Stravinsky (including two versions of *The Firebird*), twelve to scores by Tchaikovsky and seven to works of Mozart.

Some of the music in the new *Raymonda* was used in the older treatments of the score, and some of the choreography has been carried over into the new version. For this ballet, Mr. B. chose the music to suit a dancer, instead of selecting performers to fit the music. Melissa Hayden has told the company that she is retiring to become artist-in-residence at Skidmore College. Milly has been, in

Lincoln Kirstein's words, "the nearest thing to a 'star' in our starless company." She has danced Balanchine's ballets for more than twenty years. She began as a Radio City Music Hall Rockette, was a star of American Ballet Theater, a creator of roles, a pillar of the art. She has a following. If a New York mugger accosted a twice-a-year ballet-goer, demanding, "Give me all your money or name an American ballerina," the muggee probably would stammer out, "M-M-Melissa Ha-Hayden." So, last winter when Milly made her decision, Mr. B. made his. In ten rehearsals during the final days of that season, he choreographed a ballet using material with which Milly already had achieved not only success, but identity. "I made it for Melissa," he said, and stuck to it.

Once that was established, and once the music was chosen, the rest fell into place. It was for Melissa, and it was *Raymonda*, and those circumstances helped determine the structure of the ballet, the sequence, the style of the pas de deux, the grand processional entrance of the leading couple and the star-centered adoration that closes the work. Other theorems also could be constructed from the original assumptions. Milly's partner, obviously, would be Jacques d'Amboise. Having Milly without Jacques would be like having half a Yo-Yo. They've been partners too long. Together they've danced *Stars and Stripes*, *Medea* and *Raymonda Variations*. They even joined the company in the same year, 1949. A lot of things fall into place once it has been decided that the new ballet is "for Melissa."

Many in the company feel the new ballet is not one of Balanchine's best efforts, certainly not equal to the pieces he did for the Stravinsky Festival last June, perhaps not even up to earlier incarnations of *Raymonda*. This, too, they say, is because he "made it for Melissa." Although Milly shows high respect for Mr. B. and he returns the compliment, a lot of dancers insist, "He never liked her— and she's not crazy about him, either." Milly, they say, really is a dramatic ballerina, a dancer whose emotional power and acting ability are as important as her technique, and Mr. B. has never had much use for dramatic ballerinas or dramatic ballets, either. Milly, they hint, always has been too independent to suit Mr. B.

Milly herself admits: "In more than twenty years with this company, I've always been Number 2." She was Number 2 to

Maria Tallchief, to Allegra, to Suzanne Farrell, to Gelsey Kirkland—to whoever happened to be Number 1 during an era.

Still, *New Raymonda*, as the rehearsal schedule calls it, is a highly skilled piece of work, a tribute to one professional from another, a gesture of esteem, if not of love. There are worse ways to say good-bye.

At the end of the winter, 1972–73 season, just before the layoff, Balanchine poured the foundation and erected the basic structure. Now, in April, 1973, although the steps and patterns have been set, a good deal of decorating, trimming and polishing remains to be done. From the start of the rehearsal period, *New Raymonda* becomes a regular part of the schedule. The first rehearsal is devoted to a stamping czardas, led by Jean-Pierre Bonnefous and Karin von Aroldingen. Jean-Pierre looks properly Gypsy with his tree-bole chest and a single thin gold earring, but he can't seem to alter the slight forward thrust of his head and shoulders that make him seem very French, no matter what he is dancing. While dancing, he is intensely concentrated; his eyes and mouth are fixed in their places as if they had been glued there. Off stage, he is a relaxed, open young man with a smile of such warmth that any producer wanting to do a film about the Garden of Eden, pre-Serpent, would immediately cast him as Adam. He was a star of Paris Opera Ballet; he is a leading dancer with NYCB; he has been a guest artist with the Kirov and Bolshoi Ballets; and he is engaged to marry Patricia McBride, as delightful an Eve as anyone could imagine.

Karin is a tall, long-waisted young woman, slender but heavily muscled. She says the thick, bulging muscles of her thighs are the result of incorrect dance training in Germany—"They did too much of the acrobatics"—and her rounded, clearly defined shoulder muscles have a look of the trapeze artist about them. Karin's movement has a solidity to it; in the wrong part, she looks clumsy. (When she performs the title role in *Firebird*, the corps kids rename it "Fire Engine.") In the right part, it adds tension and excitement. Studious eyes look out over a square jaw that promises serious things, but she often shows to best advantage in roles in which she can flirt and play. *New Raymonda* gives her the chance.

Now, Jean-Pierre is trying to remember the steps he learned last season. He stamps and swings his way through the steps, partnering Karin with strength and grace. Balanchine is revising the section. Dressed in one of his Western shirts, his turquoise-and-silver bracelet shining on his wrist, he stands with his hands at his sides looking down at Karin's feet, as if trying to imagine where they would like to go next. He turns his head toward the piano and listens. (As a general rule, Gordon Boelzner is Balanchine's rehearsal pianist; Jerry Zimmerman plays for Robbins' new works and Dianne Chilgren gets what's left. For obvious reasons, it's best to have one pianist do all rehearsals of a new ballet; it saves constant consultations about tempi and relieves the musicians of having to decipher one another's handwritings in the score.)

Gordon stops playing as the choreographer claps his hands. Mr. B. looks down at Karin's feet again, then closes his eyes for a few seconds. "Maybe give me your hand and walk left-right." He extends his hand to Karin, she takes it and they walk the step through. Jean-Pierre follows Balanchine, as if literally walking in his footsteps. "Yahm-yahm-yahm," Balanchine provides an accompaniment for the promenade with the nonsense syllables in which musicians talk to one another.

Now the step is sketched in again as Gordon plays the Hungarian theme of the movement. Karin and Jean-Pierre spring apart and together again as the corps, aligned behind them, tries to look Magyar. The principals are together down center when Mr. B. claps again. Everything stops. "Do this now," and he demonstrates a backing-up movement, unfolding his arms from mid-chest and spreading them as he skips upstage. They do it after him. Rehearsal is rather like a game of "Simon Says."

Simon Says to Jean-Pierre, "Very small on the floor," and shows with his hands the kind of steps he wants, neat, and closely spaced. Balletic effect depends not only on what kind of steps are used, but on how they are executed. The small, tighter steps Jean-Pierre is making now seem more in the spirit of the music than the larger ones of a few minutes ago, and they have an air of precision that fits well with the stamps he performed a bit earlier in the ballet. The dancer's feet mimic Balanchine's hands, placing the steps on the floor as carefully as a dowager sets teacups on a table.

The corps de ballet flows down and around the principals, amid some confusion as to which couple goes where. Karin and Jean-Pierre fade back as the corps rushes forward, and they have a bit of trouble finding the pocket. "You don't have to look back," Mr. B. tells Jean-Pierre, "They have to look out. Just take her back." He appropriates the place at Karin's side and escorts her backwards through the crowd. The audience is to see a cavalier leading a lady, not an unrelated brace of dancers.

Now that the footwork for the principals has been defined, Balanchine lays out a right of way for them. "How should it be?" one of the corps men asks. "How should it be? Didn't I show you already?" "Yes, but that was last season."

He shows them again, changing the choreography a bit in the process. The work takes surprisingly little time. Balanchine steps into the sea of dancers, which parts for him the way the waters did for Moses. He points out paths for the couples to follow, and they prance downstage as Karin and Jean-Pierre sweep up. The steps are small and sharp-edged, like the ones Mr. B. laid down for Jean-Pierre; the style makes you think of Technicolor gypsies.

The stamping czardas is made of "character" steps, those not part of the classic balletic canon. Nineteenth-century Russian ballets, such as *Raymonda*, used stylized ethnic dances as a contrast with the more abstract, romantic passages of classical choreography. Much of the entertainment provided for the royal spectators in the ballroom act of *Swan Lake* and the closing act of *Sleeping Beauty* is composed of ethnic and character dancing. Originally, classical or "noble" dancing—defined by pointe work for the women and leaps with beats for the men—was reserved for the noble characters in ballet. The peasants got other assignments. In his *An Elementary Treatise Upon the Theory and Practice of the Art of Dancing*, published in 1820, the great ballet master Carlo Blasis divided dancers into three categories: Serious, Demi-Caractère and Comic. Serious dancers must be well-proportioned and of noble carriage, he writes. Comic dancers, on the other hand, are to be of stocky build, and they should study characteristic ethnic steps and learn to "imbue each step and pose with the style and spirit of the peoples whose dance they are performing." By alternating classical and character passages, the Russian choreographers gave the audience more variety than pure classicism could provide, and allowed the leading dancers a chance to rest between pas de deux. Balanchine's *New Raymonda* alternates sequences as did the original, evening-long Russian ballet, and the czardas now in rehearsal is a major character interlude. (Today, of course, especially at companies such as NYCB, the distinction between "noble" and "character" dancers is not made as it was during the time of Blasis—Jean-Pierre Bonnefous performs character steps with the technique of a danseur noble. In Balanchine ballet, everybody has to know how to do everything.)

As Mr. B. demonstrates the stamps and glides, you realize what a great soft-shoe man was lost to the world when he took to classical ballet. His knees are bent, his body seems light enough to float. His heels stamp out the rhythm, delicately but with great precision. It is taken for granted in the company that Balanchine is the best dancer here, that he makes the steps look right. In this passage, the flexing of his knees, the downward pressure of his heels, the slightly forward bend of his body all contribute to the impression that he is dancing on brown Hungarian soil, not on a gray New York practice floor.

As the dancers imitate his movements, the corps is divided into couples, with the men now behind their women, now at their sides. Balanchine claps his hands. "It looks as though you don't give a damn for your woman," he tells the boys. "You're dancing together, but you're alone. *Look* at her." He is insistent on this: the male dancer is not a sort of animated subway strap to which the lady can cling going around the curves; he is a cavalier, an escort, a lover. "You cannot do this and look in the mirror," Balanchine tells the boys. "It's very difficult to do the step when you look at yourself. The boys must look at the girls. You look at her THERE (he dances through the promenade), then you walk and look at her THERE, then you do like this and you look at her HERE." On "HERE," he slips very slightly back and to one side of his partner. He presents her to the audience as if displaying her to judges who will award the best-of-show ribbon at Westminster.

A slight man, elegant in casual clothes and bright eyes, comes into the rehearsal hall and rests a deck of drawings backed with cardboard on a chair near the mirror. Rouben Ter-Arutunian is the designer for *New Raymonda* and his oversized pack of cards is the collection of costume sketches for the ballet. Balanchine, calling a break in rehearsal, devotes his attention to the drawings. He and Rouben converse at length and in Russian, punctuating their talk by pointing fingers and tugging on one another's shirts and shoulders. Balanchine calls to Karin, compares her with one of the sketches, and gestures, making long flowing sleeves appear in the air around her arms.

At Christmas, while the company was performing its annual ritual of *The Nutcracker*, Rouben and Balanchine conferred about the costumes and setting for the new Glazounov ballet. By the end of March, before the season's rehearsals began, the designer had completed his sketches and surrendered them to Mme. Karinska, in whose shop they will be translated into cloth. The fabric already has been chosen, as have the colors; from the beginning, Balanchine insisted on green, white and gold. "That's how it was," he explains. "When we did *Raymonda* in Russia, when Petipa was ballet master, those were the colors."

Rouben, who has worked with Mr. B. often, finds that the choreographer usually knows what he wants, and has good reasons for his desires. "Sometimes, though, he wants you to feed him ideas—and he listens."

The work of making the costumes will keep pace with the making of the dance; both will have changed before they are completed, but the basic conceptions, which complement one another, are clear.

Having settled the matter of Karin's sleeves, Balanchine calls the dancers back to work. Casual chatter buzzes around the perimeter of the room. Mr. B., like a telephone operator, works amid ceaseless, stereophonic conversation. He doesn't seem to mind. The dancers who are neither talking nor working on the floor practice their steps, trying them on for size and style. Suddenly, one of the girls from the center corps crashes into her partner. The couple untwists itself immediately and catches up with the rest of the ensemble. As the performers whirl through the passage, Balanchine sits front and center, urging the dancers on with his eyes, encouraging them with the high arch of his nose, keeping his mouth patiently closed. His hands, folded in his lap, are as calm as purring cats.

Every time there is a break in the rehearsal, Ricky Weiss dashes over to his dance bag for a nibble of chocolate. He rewraps the bar, tucks it back into the bag and regains his place before his next cue. While Ricky augments his energy, Balanchine changes a move: the men are to hold the women with two hands instead of one as they do a deep bend and recover, "because it's faster—you may need that." Designing movements and patterns is the most easily visible part of a choreographer's work, but it also is essential that he make it possible for the moves to be executed and the patterns developed on time. That is the logistics, the traffic cop work, of dance-making. The dancers may need to save a fraction of a second in the transition from one step to another, and the choreographer must give it to them without disturbing the momentum of the dance or violating its style.

Lincoln Kirstein sails into the hall, his dark double-breasted suit filled out in front like a spinnaker in the wind. Balanchine and the company's director discuss plans for scenery, speaking in undertones and using their hands to hang imaginery drops from the flies, mark off stage depths and define dancing areas, just as Rouben and Mr. B. had constructed costumes in the air. When Balanchine sits to watch the dancers, he sits completely still, concentrating his energy on seeing the ballet. When he talks, his hands talk, too, gesturing punctuation and emphasis as well as description. Whatever Mr. B. is doing, he does it with his entire being.

Around the room, the conversations which were interrupted by the last bit of rehearsing pick up again. Chris Redpath sits in a full split, looking down under heavy-lidded, sexy eyes to read a paperback edition of *The Idiot*. Merrill Ashley is on the floor, her muscular legs folded under *The New York Times* as she studies the stock market listings. Renee Estopinal leans over the piano to half-flirt with Gordon, saying something about being invited to attend a Buddhist meeting. Gordon doubts Renee really needs Buddhism. Lincoln finishes his session of conversation and charades with Mr. B. and sails out of the room again, his eyes focusing on something inside his own mind, already considering another question.

Balanchine stands in the center of a group of four men—Ricky Weiss, Tracy Bennett, Frank Ohman and Victor Castelli—facing the mirror as they do. He leads them through a variation, making steps for them to copy and then working out the next sequence as they echo the one he has just completed. He hums the music as he works. At the very end of the sequence he turns to face the dancers and shoots his forefinger at each one in turn, cueing a sequential series of tours en l'aire.

Four slim young men are breathing hard as they start the variation a second time. They come together in the very center of the floor, then lunge like fencers at the four corners of the room. You can feel the pull of thigh muscles as they reach full stretch. "This one is to rest," Balanchine tells them, and they laugh. "Yes, it's made that way." His voice is serious, reassuring. "Take it easy—the hard one comes later." He performs the step, showing them how to relax into it and let the movement carry them forward. As usual, his dancing is calm and intensely energetic, but the step still doesn't look as if it had been made "to rest."

Now, he decides to alter the climax of the quartet. Two of the four boys—those on audience left—will perform their tours to the left, and the other pair will turn to the right. "Who is lefty?" Balanchine asks. Only Ricky Weiss. The others try, but they are right-handed, or more exactly right-footed, turners, and tours to the left leave them off balance. Balanchine goes back to Plan One. The four, each in turn, rocket into the air, spin once to the right and, as they land, come down on one knee. Balanchine leans forward from the waist as he watches, following each bird with his hawk's eyes.

Once more the dancers, quite out of breath by now, soar through the entire pattern from their entrances, banking as they swoop in from the wings and winging on through to the final tours. It's a stunning variation, filling the air around it with vitality. Balanchine used the sequence when he made other ballets to this music. He did not invent it. The choreography is by Marius Petipa, the great ballet master of Imperial Russia, the original choreographer of Glazounov's full-length *Raymonda*, which had its premiere in 1898.

Fairly frequently, under the name of the choreographer in a

ballet program, you will find the phrase "(After Petipa)." Petipa was ballet master of the Imperial Theater in St. Petersburg from 1855 until well into this century. When you think of American ballet, you are thinking of Balanchine. When you think of Russian ballet, you are thinking of Petipa: *The Sleeping Beauty, Raymonda, La Bayadère*—that is Petipa. Like the "begats" of the Bible, there are generations in classical choreography, and Balanchine, the current patriarch, is descended in a true line. Although *Raymonda* was made a few years before he was born, Mr. B. casually remarks that he was at the Imperial Theater when Petipa still conducted rehearsals of his ballet, working with the same score Balanchine is using now. "At *Raymonda* rehearsals, Glazounov played the piano," Mr. B. remembers, "so I know all the tempi and all the music; I heard the composer play it. And I know the colors of the costumes. Other people talk about Petipa, but they don't know, they weren't there. I was there. I was born a long time ago." (Since Marius Petipa died in 1910, before Balanchine had ever taken class, Mr. B. seems to be confusing the spirit of those *Raymonda* rehearsals with the flesh of *Raymonda's* choreographer.)

Balanchine saw the variation for four men when it was young, and knew it, and kept it alive. He does not claim to have made it— although there is to be no "(After Petipa)" in the program. "Yes, that is pure Petipa," he says. "It is marvelous. So I used it. The rest of the ballet is me, but that is Petipa." Ballet is a transient art, even now that choreology, notation, and film are available to record it. There are no Oscars or Pulitzers for classical choreographers. But years from now, perhaps some dance master will be making still another ballet to the score of *Raymonda* and will say of one passage, "Yes, that is pure Balanchine; it is marvelous, so I used it." Perhaps he'll use Petipa, too. It seems a greater honor than anything you can stand on a mantlepiece.

The next day, April 12, the cast is called for a full run-through of *New Raymonda*. Ordinarily, a run-through of a new work would not be scheduled so early—it is only the first week of rehearsal period and nearly six weeks before the ballet's scheduled premiere. However, Balanchine accomplished a great deal during those ten rehearsals last winter. When you see him making a dance, moving people around the empty space of the floor with complete assurance and certainty, you imagine he must see the stage laid out in front of him like a chess board. The kids assure you that this kind of choreography is easy work for him: "You ought to watch him when he's making an abstract ballet with really complicated moves and counts—he seems to have a mind made out of graph paper." Mr. B. himself says of his new ballet, "I just threw it together— this was my childhood," and you remember the rehearsals when Glazounov played the piano and the great stars of the Imperial Ballet performed the leading roles.

Rosemary leads today's rehearsal, trying to maintain Balanchine's formulations, but the action becomes muddled. The basic structure is clear: the sections derived from character steps alternate with those in the classical style, variations are flanked by corps sequences, to carry out the tension of the theme, dignified processions prepare the entrance of the leading dancers. "It's like a goulash," Mr. B. has said, "I made a big goulash," but the line of development is logical. At this rehearsal, though, the mass of the ballet still is undefined, like a gooey pudding that won't settle into shape.

During her variation, Melissa has difficulty moving backwards as she drives her toe shoes down sharply into the floor. Those staccato steps are just slightly beyond the speed limit imposed by her fifty-year-old leg muscles. She stops the music, marks the steps out, tries them, marks again. "You know," she tells Jacques, "the original step (in *Raymonda Variations*) was this," and she whirls happily across the front of the room, spinning to the side instead of marching backwards. "I'll do it when he comes and maybe he'll leave it in." He doesn't.

Colleen Neary does her allegro solo, showing off her long legs and the high carriage of her head, moving with stern concentration at the start, and with joy near the finish. The four men sweep through the variation they rehearsed yesterday. Merrill Ashley's serious face floats over her solid body like a whipped cream topping as she accents the legato line of her variation, a soft contrast to the exhilarating spins Balanchine devised for Colleen. By now, Mr. B. is in the rehearsal hall, watching, but he does not interrupt as Milly and Jacques perform their pas de deux.

These two have danced together for so long that they know one another's bodies as comfortably as long-time lovers do. Both are a bit old for this, but Milly retains her style and command and Jacques his boyish ease of movement. You can see the way Melissa's leg reaches straight in front of her, then takes the most direct path to the rear. Suddenly, in the middle of doing his spins, while his flying dark hair flicks sweat onto the spectators, Jacques loses his footing and slips to the side. "Ah, shucks!" Nobody says, "Ah, shucks" any more, but for Jacques, it is in character. The sound of his harsh, throaty voice always comes as a shock after the casual charm of his dancing. He should have been a tenor.

Jacques wants to begin the pas de deux again, "because it's like running a race." This time, it is smooth. The couple counts through the ceremony of coming together and moving apart, of the lifts and turns and little movements of the feet. Jacques lifts his ballerina to his shoulder. Milly is breathing hard, and in her eyes you can see the counts being ticked off in her brain, but her torso is proud and her head high. She sits on Jacques' shoulder and dares you not to believe her beautiful, even in her worn rehearsal tutu, her heavy knit pink top and her ear-covering kerchief. At the end of the duet, the company applauds—something it does not often do for its own.

The next day's rehearsal is for the corps. Balanchine has made a grand adagio in which a pas de deux is danced, not by one couple, but by a stageful. He makes adjustments and answers questions. "Which arm, here? . . . Both arms here? . . . Which couple passes which way?" He makes quick, comfortable decisions, and goes on. "You are just showing me feet—no feet today, I want legs; show me all of you, not just part of you." They extend themselves, dancing with full style instead of marking it, stretching their arches and pointing their toes cleanly, filling the outlines of their tights with ripe rounded muscles.

Virginia Donaldson and the company's administrative personnel also are concerned with the new ballet: It needs to be named. Mr. Balanchine wants to call it *Cortège Hongrois*, the title of one section of Glazounov's score. The French "cortège" comes from the Italian corteggio, a derivative of corte, or court, and means a train of attendants, or a procession. Mr. B.'s ballet employs processions and contains Magyar character sections to justify the "Hongrois." However, there are some doubts in the office area about the ability of New York ticket buyers to pronounce the title comfortably. It is predicted that the box office will be asked for "Two seats for 'Short and Hungry'," or, at the best for "Cawtedge Hungwah," or that the title may discourage some people from seeing the work at all. In the end, though, Mr. B. wins. He usually does.

Balanchine prefers to have ballets called by the names of the scores to which they are danced. He even has changed some titles to suit this policy: *Tchaikovsky Concerto No. 2* originally was *Ballet Imperial.* The choreographer's purist approach to nomenclature creates a problem at the box office and the subscription department: Casual ballet-goers have a tendency to get confused when faced with *Suite No. 3, Concerto No. 2* and *Divertimento No. 15.* Just because Mr. B. knows the difference between Mozart and Tchaikovsky, and can immediately associate score and choreography, doesn't mean that the average customer can do it, too. However, Mr. B. names ballets to emphasize the importance of music, and NYCB names ballets the way Mr. B. wants to.

On Sunday, Balanchine schedules a rehearsal of the pas de deux. In the hallways, you can hear the opera's matinee performance coming through the theater's intercommunications system. In the main hall, Mr. B. has settled into his familiar stance—one foot in front of the other, leaning forward from the waist, eyes closed, mouth counting, hands weaving steps. Then he paces off the steps for Milly, partners her neatly as she tries the first section, pauses a moment and begins again. Jacques takes over the partnering. It is lovely to watch him catch Melissa; his big hands appear to go to the right place at her waist of their own volition. He holds Milly for a second, balances her and sets her on her way again. As they work, Jacques, Melissa and Mr. B. seem to fit together like pieces of a puzzle. Gordon, at the piano, is a fourth partner, stopping and starting the music without cues.

Milly objects to a one-footed step because she's "not a very good hopper." The step is discarded. She sings her way through a short passage, while Balanchine looks at the steps as if trying to decide whether they are edible. He shifts his weight slightly, making small, neat steps, considers them for a bit and asks Milly, "How about that? First you go ta-ta-ta, then you turn around." He floats through the ta-ta-ta and turns around. She follows as surely as a shadow. Then Gordon plays the melody and she does it alone. The new step looks very right on her body; it suits her high carriage and the line of her arms. That is the reason dancers like to work for Balanchine. "When he choreographs for you," Sara Leland says, "it's always right for you. He knows what your body will do. I was anxious to see what he'd give me the first time he made something especially for me—it lets you know how he sees you." He seems to see royalty in Melissa.

Balanchine works out Milly's final, showy variation. She is on full pointe, dancing the passage again and again, trying to find the most economical way to do it. John Clifford, who has come to rehearsal to watch, shakes his head in disbelief: "It's impossible, *nobody* can do it that fast." Mr. B. obviously thinks Melissa can. The biggest problem comes at the end of the solo; Milly insists the six counts set by Balanchine don't suit the music. He tells her to ignore the music and do the steps to the counts; he knows how it will look from out front. The passage is brutally fast, and no matter how often Milly tries it, she can't synchronize her steps with the counts. "*You* do it," she challenges Balanchine. "If you can do it, I'll do it." So he does it, and she does it, and the counts, the steps and the music end at the same time.

The low-heeled boots to be used in the Hungarian segments of *Cortège* are being made and by Wednesday, April 18, a few pairs are ready. One of the corps men has a pair, and Karin is rehearsing in hers. The new boots clatter crisply on the floor of the main hall during the czardas, out-snapping the street boots most of the corps wears for rehearsal. The boots are not finished yet—the wardrobe staff must spend about fifteen man-hours stitching gold trim onto white doeskin—but already they look good and sound marvelous. At $175 a pair, they ought to.

Karin stamps and stomps, relishing the sound. Karin takes things seriously—rehearsing, Sunday painting, breaking in boots— but she manages to enjoy them at the same time. Just now, she's smiling like a little girl with her first pair of ballet slippers and her eyes are just as serious.

The day's rehearsal is devoted to the procession that introduces the ballerina and her cavalier, and Balanchine seems dedicated to producing a C. B. DeMille entrance for Milly (and, therefore, for Jacques). The corps couples come on, led by Karin and Jean-Pierre. A second collection of couples, the classical corps, assumes a wedge-shaped formation, then the entire company draws into a long diagonal line. Balanchine walks the row, spacing the couples precisely, as if planting seeds and leaving so many feet between each. Then, as he reaches the back of the room, he takes Milly and Jacques by their hands and leads them center stage.

The dancers walk through the processional from the beginning, to music, and Balanchine decides he is not satisfied. He starts again. "We'll do this way, see . . ." and he splits the company into two lines, one on each side of the stage, erasing the diagonal he had drawn earlier. He motions the leading couples to come to center stage with the rest of the corps behind them, then brings them down into two files behind Milly and Jacques. The principals exit, and he lines the corps straight across the back of the stage, ready to move down and mass behind Karin and Jean-Pierre.

As they try the new version, Mr. B. goes to the piano to look over Gordon's shoulder at the score, strolls back to his observation post and then onto the floor, looking at his work from the inside. John Clifford says Balanchine is the only choreographer he knows "who can work from the middle of his own ballet," moving among the dancers rather than seeking a vantage point at the front of the room.

There is too much confusion as the dancers close ranks in the center of the floor while Karin and Jean-Pierre step toward the audience. Balanchine changes the pattern again. Now, the corps is aligned on one side of the stage. Karin and Jean-Pierre enter from up left, like officers reviewing troops, and each member of the side-line army raises an arm in salute. All march center and follow their officers upstage, forming a line at the back. Now, Mr. B. alters the formation of the classical part of the corps, the court attendant on Milly and Jacques. "Now it is more formal," he says, explaining that he could not align the classical dancers until he had changed the configuration of the character group.

While Balanchine works setting up their grand entrance, forming up the corps, Milly and Jacques waltz a few steps together; he hums a tune, clearly and on key, and they whirl gently and happily. Now, the choreographer is ready for them. He organizes a double line of march; one part of the corps is led by Karin and Jean-Pierre, the other follows Milly and Jacques. Four lines of performers are in motion, two in each direction, flowing through one another like a current in a stream. The dancers' arms hook intricate daisy chains in the air.

A few visitors—dancers, friends and critics—have been invited to a full rehearsal of *Cortège Hongrois* on April 27, the last Friday before the spring season opens. The stage still is filled with opera sets. A rehearsal of *Brahms-Schönberg Quartet* is going on in the practice room. In the main hall, gray metal chairs are unfolded and spread across the room in front of the mirror. The guests are settled when Balanchine enters and takes his seat in the center of the row. Almost as soon as rehearsal starts he is on his feet, walking through the maze of dancers to tell them, "Spread yourself a little," and pushing out with his arms. They move farther apart, giving the pattern on the floor a more elegant outline. "Too cluttered," he says, "open even more." The dignity of the classical steps, accented by the wider spacing and the greater expanse of air that outlines each couple, turns the rehearsal studio into a gracious ballroom.

Gordon's piano calls for the czardas. The dancers stamp, cross their arms and unfold them, flash their knees, toss their heads. Gloriann Hicks gallops by, her field of brown hair ripe in the light. Delia Peters bounces through the steps, but always seems to be standing aside and watching herself, a quality that gives her precise dancing an air of irony.

Jacques does his variation at full energy this time, displaying the long-legged self-assurance that makes him beloved of middle-aged ladies in the subscription audience. No matter how difficult the steps, Jacques glides through them as if to say, "This? It's nothing. I do a few dozen of these entrechats sixes before breakfast every morning." Even in the rehearsal studio, where strain is more apparent than it is on stage, Jacques' lean body seems to carry him almost effortlessly across the music. But when the variation is finished, Jacques, all six-foot-two, one-hundred-and-eighty curly-haired pounds of him, sits with his back against a wall, knees up, head back, mouth open, chest desperately pumping. It is several minutes before his breathing settles into an even rhythm again.

The entire ballet is performed, and after the first few minutes, Mr. B. does not interrupt. He lets the dance flow, and each variation and corps sequence becomes a tributary enlarging the swell of the choreography. Afterwards, with the dancers standing around him, he makes corrections and suggestions in his quiet, nasal voice, using no written notes, illustrating his comments with his hands.

At succeeding rehearsals, he behaves the same way. The ballet is made. He will alter the details, make corrections, hone the piece to performance edge, but the structure is settled. The ballet gets its first chance on the stage on May 8, just over a week before its first performance. Most of the dancers have their boots, and Richard Dryden has been issued spurs. Eddie Bigelow, the assistant manager, kneels to strap them to Richard's boots, then he and Balanchine listen as the dancer jogs through some steps and makes a few trial jumps. The spurs are not equipped with spikes as they are intended only to dress up the boots and to jingle. They certainly do that. Once the whole company is fitted with them, *Cortège* should sound like a tambourine band.

Robert Irving sets a chair next to the piano bench stage right and sits to follow the score. As Gordon plays, Robert conducts, getting the feel of the tempi into his hands and wrists. Robert doesn't beat time, he caresses it.

A few of the dancers are missing in action. Teena McConnell has conjunctivitis. Heather Watts also is afflicted with sore eyes— she thinks she is allergic to the adhesive that glues her false eyelashes in place—and has an injured thigh. Rehearsal goes on without them; someone nearly always is injured. It's expected.

Mr. B. interrupts the dancing. "It's too fast," and he strolls to the piano for a consultation with Robert. The choreographer and the conductor discuss the matter in "ta-ta-ta" talk and beat time at one another. A tempo is selected, and the ballet starts again. At the end of the first section, the dancers suffer from a shortage of music and have to scurry toward the wings to exit. Balanchine is displeased. "We'll never be able to get off," he tells Robert. The conductor suggests slowing the music at the end. Mr. B. turns to the dancers: "Don't run. It's terrible to run. We'll adjust the music. When we have the orchestra, we'll see how we can do it."

Balanchine will not moderate the tempo of a score to make life easier for a dancer, but he will insert a ritardando to provide enough time to end a balletic sequence with style and dignity. It will do no violence to the music: Even a concert conductor might call for such a ritardando.

Robert Irving is noting in his score the tempo for each segment of the ballet. Before a sequence begins, he learns from Gordon whether the orchestra or the dancers will enter first. Whichever group initiates the section, it will take its cue from his baton. Last week, during a final pre-performance rehearsal of "Divertimento" from *Le Baiser de la Fée*, Gordon reminded women in the corps, "Now, remember to watch Robert tonight for the cue to start." The conductor signals the dancers exactly as he calls in the orchestra, with a nod of his head or a stroke of the baton. Robert generally gives a large, clear downbeat with his stick; often, he will bob his big body, too, making a firm sign so the dancers need not be anxious about missing a cue.

During the rehearsal, and before and after, choreographer and conductor discuss the choice of tempi for a new ballet. During early rehearsals of *Cortège*, Mr. B. made his preferences known to Gordon, who now is passing them on to Robert. The final decision rests with the choreographer—especially if the choreographer is Balanchine—but it is arrived at during conferences with the company's music director. "We work it out together," Robert says. "With Balanchine, it's easy, because he knows music."

The question of tempo arises as Melissa does her concluding variation. She is rehearsing the section that troubled her last week, and still seems uncomfortable with the speed of it. Setting her jaw, she hammers down her pointes, forcing her way through the passage by sheer determination. She is certain Gordon is increasing the speed of his playing as he goes along, that the end of the variation is being taken more quickly than the beginning. Balanchine and Robert Irving assure her that the tempo is the same throughout, that Gordon is not rushing the finale. Milly is not satisfied.

"My bourrées have to articulate with the music," she tells the pianist. "Did you hear them last time?" Gordon did not. "You didn't hear me stamp the floor?" She executes the bourrées again, striking down hard so that her shoes rap the rhythm on the stage. Gordon listens, then plays at the speed she indicated. She tries it, and nods. The tempo has been negotiated.

Jacques is on a concert tour, so John Clifford steps in to partner Milly. They are not accustomed to one another, the way she and Jacques are, but they do quite well. Johnny displays an unaccustomed maturity and dignity, as if he is just a bit awed by Melissa. He keeps his eyes firmly on his ballerina, taking great care to place his hands just so, to steer her dextrously, to offer a secure point of balance.

Mr. B. still is concerned with that first exit of the corps. The company simply cannot be allowed to flutter into the wings like birds surprised by a cat. Instead of slowing the music as the section ends, Balanchine decides to reinstate sixteen bars of the original score at the opening of the sequence. This will give the corps time for a proper exit. *Cortège* does not use all the music of *Raymonda;* the score is picked up several pages after Glazounov's opening notes. There is no difficulty in beginning a bit earlier in the score than was intended, since the music that now opens the ballet has the same rhythmic pattern as the original selection, being a pre-statement of the theme. Once the steps are set, it is simpler to vary the music than to unravel the pattern of the choreography and knit it together again.

During the past two weeks, the schedule posted on the call board often has carried a special notation for the morning: a list of dancer's names and the cryptic direction, "To Karinska." Mme. Barbara Karinska directs the atelier in which the costumes for *Cortège* are being made. She has dressed Balanchine dancers since the company began, and although she is in her eighties and her eyesight is failing, she is not about to stop just because of that. She still vacations at her home in Domrémy ("It's where Jeanne d'Arc came from, you know. It is very beautiful there.") and travels to Paris to buy fabrics for the company's costumes. Eddie Bigelow, who acts as liaison between the company and Karinska, says, "She doesn't buy just what she needs now. She finds a wonderful fabric somewhere, and brings it back and tucks it away. Two years later, when we're looking for a certain material, she just happens to have it stored and ready."

Karinska's shop, on West 57th Street, is as well-ordered as a good recipe. Costumes hang neatly from every shelf and rack. Melissa's unfinished tutu and bodice for *Cortège* dress a mannequin. Before the entire costume is complete, it will have required seventy man-hours of work. Green-and-gold toy soldiers, the costumes for the men of the corps, are held at attention by hangers. Clothes from other ballets, in the shop for repair, hang in assigned places or are stretched on long tables being prepared for their operations. Elderly women sit on high wooden stools, making hats and stitching gold trim onto doublets. At the big cleaning-store steam irons, men press down seams.

The morning after the on-stage run-through, Karin and Jean-Pierre are being fitted for their Magyar outfits. ("Actually," Rouben Ter-Arutunian has confided, "they aren't Hungarian at all; they're sixteenth-century Polish.") Mme. Karinska, in a beautifully tailored blue suit and beautifully coiffed blue hair, sits in the small fitting room as one of her retinue tacks gold braid across the breast of Karin's green-and-white costume and pins it into place. Karinska leans over and fingers the trim, noting the way it is aligned and measuring the spacing between the gold ropes. Her eyes may be weak, but her hands see very well.

A bridal party of headdresses is arranged on a wooden work table. Most are white, but Karin chooses one in pink and gold. The fitter approves. "All the girls will have white," he tells her, "so you should be different." Karinska and Balanchine, who is standing near her chair, agree. Karin tries a few steps in front of the tall mirror, watching the costume as it moves with her. Her strong feet are bare, and they are covered in bumps, bruises and Band-Aids, a harsh contrast to the long elegance of her body in its green-and-gold gown. You remember suddenly that dancers are shy about their feet. On stage, under the boned or billowing finery enriching that eloquent body line, inside those arching boat-shaped shoes, there is a foundation of sore, swollen, sadly put-upon feet.

Karin works her arms and shoulders and the long tippets of the sleeves flutter like butterflies. She smiles, a little girl playing dress-up before the mirror, then gravely studies the length of her skirt, making quite sure she will be able to move freely when the time comes. "It's very light," she says, "and it moves well." A bit of pinning at the shoulders, and Karin is free to change back to street clothes.

Jean-Pierre's costume matches Karin's in color. He comes to the fitting room dressed in it, and stands in front of the mirror as Balanchine, Karinska and the fitter pat their hands over him as if searching for concealed weapons. Balanchine has a feeling for fabric and design. He moves frogs and buttons on Jean-Pierre's chest, giving the costume a more martial air. Rouben's original sketches are resting on a chair, and Balanchine compares the realization with the blueprint. He and the fitter decide to alter the original design of the trim to make Jean-Pierre's costume complement Karin's more closely.

Now the dancer tries his hat. It ends in a long stocking, like the hat Santa Claus wears, except that this one is green. Jean-Pierre shakes his head a few times and predicts trouble. The Santa stocking is going to swish across his face during the ballet's more exuberant moments. Mr. B. and the fitter make soothing sounds and reach for the pins. The fitter shortens the dangles, and everyone is happy. Karinska asks for the hat. She examines it and shifts a pin or two, somehow giving the stocking a smoother line, then hands it back to the fitter. Jean-Pierre goes to change into mufti while Balanchine and Karinska look at Rouben's designs and talk Russian. (With Jean-Pierre, Madame spoke French.)

After the fittings, Karinska returns to her office and Jean-Pierre hurries to the theater for rehearsal. Balanchine and Karin stroll back toward Lincoln Center, arm in arm, graceful and erect. Their trench coats fade away into the light rain as if the morning were an English movie.

The same afternoon, Mr. B. works on stage with Melissa and Jacques, polishing the pas de deux. He has a stop watch with which to time the duet, and he sets Gordon's tempo very precisely, saying it was too fast yesterday. Milly smiles—she told them it was too fast yesterday. Balanchine snaps his fingers, crackling out the tempo for Milly's variation. The same difficulty arises again—the backward bourrées are just too fast. Melissa keeps trying, until finally, looking straight at Balanchine, she says, "I can't do it." He reminds her that in the old *Raymonda Variations*, she used to do it even faster, and hums the old tempo. "We can't slow it down," he insists. "It will look terrible." Milly tries again, squeezing her eyes in concentration, forcing her feet to go a little bit faster than they want to. She does it.

Mr. B. makes a few small changes in the adagio section. He eliminates some arm movements and tones down others. As Melissa flashes across the stage he calls, "Not so hysterical; let's do more smoothly." Jacques lifts Milly, then sets her down and Balanchine tells her, "A little more forward, the foot should be a little more forward." The couple try it again, and again, and again until they feel the rhythm of the step and lift clearly, and Milly lands perfectly in balance and prepared for the next step.

The last part of the session is spent working on the climactic lift of the duet, in which Jacques sets Milly on his shoulder. A ballet lift is not a job of weight lifting; it is not a chance for the male to show his muscles. Properly done, it is an exercise in cooperation and the audience sees nothing but the effect—that of a man effortlessly lifting a woman, and a woman exulting in her ability to fly.

What actually happens is that both partners take demi-pliés. The man's hands rest on his partner's waist, steadying her, and she places her hands on his wrists. As they push up from the plié, she presses down and straightens her arms, levering herself up with her partner's wrists as fulcrums, like a gymnast raising herself onto the parallel bars. At the same time, she rolls onto pointe and pushes her toes down into the floor, which allows her to make a strong but inconspicuous jump into the air. The man moves up from plié at the same time as the woman, and continues the motion with his arms, balancing and lifting his lady. Jacques and Milly have done it a few million times over the years. They are not doing it well today. Balanchine says nothing; he knows that Jacques and Milly are accustomed to one another, and leaves them to work out the problem for themselves. He simply watches.

The difficulty, Jacques says, is that Milly is working too hard. She is jumping too strongly, anticipating the lift, and once up, she is anticipating the action of sitting on his shoulder. "Don't do so much," he tells her. "Just spring into attitude on pointe as I loft you, don't try to get yourself up or to sit." They try it again. Melissa still is trying to perch on his shoulder. "You don't have to sit," Jacques' harsh voice soothes, "just let me put you there. Just spring into attitude." As she does, he adjusts his hands at her waist, trying her for balance the way a pinch hitter might test a new bat. "That's fine," he croaks. "Let's do it again." She springs onto her pointes, nothing more, and as Jacques continues the lift, she flies to his shoulder like a pet bird.

The problem was one of balance—Milly was trying to set herself for the shoulder sit, not realizing she already was in position. That sort of thing is hard to judge while you are being carried through the air. If you think too much about it, dancers say, it won't work; if you let your body do the thinking, there will be no problem.

They do the lift a few more times, and with each repetition Milly becomes more sure of herself. She has found her old economy of movement again. Her spring uses exactly the amount of energy needed to initiate the lift, then she holds herself erect, keeping her muscles firm for Jacques' grip, and lets him finish the job she began.

Balanchine, standing with his hands in his pockets, echoes the exhilaration of the lift with an upward thrust of his own torso. "That's RIGHT," he crows. "That's RIGHT."

6

Melissa's Gala

Gala performances are presented to make money. Every spring the company stages a gala for the benefit of the New York City Ballet Production Fund. Tickets are sold at premium prices. (Orchestra, first and second ring seats range from $25 to $100; locations in the upper regions go for $2.75 to $11. The amount in excess of the normal cost of a seat is a contribution, tax-deductible.) This means that the program must include some special fillip to justify the expense, and to attract an audience that will pay the tariff. Gala audiences, like benefit audiences, do not come necessarily because they love ballet: They come because it is a gala or a benefit. Some of the patrons of the spring, 1973, gala have not seen the company dance since the spring, 1972, gala and won't show up again until the spring, 1974, gala. (If they came more frequently, and offered financial support, we might not need galas at all.)

The New York City Ballet Guild, since its inception in the spring of 1971, has taken on the task of sponsoring the annual affair. The Guild may arrange a dinner at a posh restaurant before the performance (this season, it is to be at Le Poulailler, across Broadway from Lincoln Center) and certainly will host a party in the theater afterwards, at which the buyers of high-priced tickets are invited to mingle with the dancers and drink domestic champagne. (As a rule, the dancers come to the party and mingle with one another. The guests manage to hide their disappointment, since most of them don't know what to say to dancers, anyway. Most of the dancers don't know what to say to the guests, either.) But between the dinner and the party, something has to happen on stage, and it must be something out of the ordinary. A one-time-only performance, such as the George Balanchine–Arthur Mitchell collaboration of 1971, is a good bet. So is a world premiere. This season, the announcement of the Tenth Annual Gala offers "Previews of New Works by George Balanchine and Jerome Robbins." The word "Previews" is important: It tells the gala-goers they will get to see something before anyone else, and it allows the company to hold press premieres of the pieces a bit later in the season, thus filling the house more than once with the same ballets.

One of the difficulties in arranging a special program for the gala is that Mr. B. does not care too much about galas. Ladies from the Guild often have suggested that if Mr. B. would agree to dance—perhaps to do Drosselmeyer in *The Nutcracker* or the title role in *Don Quixote*—the theater would be packed. It would, but Mr. B. usually does not want to be a gala attraction. He does not share this era's longing for personal publicity. At a time when anyone who possibly can find an excuse calls a press conference, Mr. B. hates press conferences. He has given a few, and if the subject is important to him, as it was when he announced the company's week-long celebration of Stravinsky in 1972, he is irresistibly sparkling. Put him on television and in three weeks, he'll have his own talk show and a fan club. But he dislikes exhibiting himself and takes a disinterested view of publicity in general. He expects people to come to see ballet because they enjoy it; the art should sell itself. Therefore, he does not involve himself in planning goodies for the gala.

He does involve himself in making ballets, and a new Balanchine ballet is an attraction and, therefore, suitable for a fund-raising performance. This season, since his new ballet is a tribute to Melissa Hayden on the occasion of her retirement, it is a double attraction. *Cortège Hongrois* will have its press premiere on Thursday, May 17; it will be previewed the previous evening at the gala. Now, the problem is, what will Jerry Robbins do? The season has begun, the gala is less than two weeks away, and nobody knows. Not even Jerry.

Certainly, the New York City Ballet Guild doesn't know. The Guild is installed in a small office on the third floor, just around the bend from Virginia Donaldson's press office. The office is staffed by volunteers, usually Susan (Mrs. Peter) Ralston, the Guild's volunteer administrator. Sue works surrounded by photographs, books, posters, playing cards and other ballet buffery sold by the Guild at its table on the theater's promenade during intermissions. (The Guild also sells autographed toe shoes. After a performance, one of the Guild members took a collection of well-worn shoes to the corps dressing room to be autographed. "It was astonishing," she said. "The girls stood there, stark naked, signing shoes." It makes you wonder what ball players wear when they sign baseballs.)

Getting shoes signed and selling them to raise money is part of the work of the Guild. Another part is represented by an office full of file cards and piles of addressed envelopes containing invitations to Guild functions, including the gala. Sue Ralston is processing the invitations, but she does not decide who is to be invited. Much of that work is done by "The Ladies." The Guild is divided into two groups: one includes people like Sue, who serve at the sales table and take care of the day-to-day work; the other is composed of rich, social people, known as The Ladies, who can get other rich, social people to contribute to the Guild and the Production Fund. The Ladies are led by Mrs. David O'D. Kennedy (of the Kentile Kennedys), the Guild Chairman, a small, charming woman who always seems on the point of remembering your name, and Countess Guy de Brantes, Membership Chairman, a tall, charming woman who always seems to be on her way to someplace else.

One of the Guild's problems, this spring, is that the two groups don't understand one another. The middle-class group is composed of people who have been following the ballet and working for the company in one way or another for years. They have personal friends among the dancers; they know all the backstage gossip; they are as much a part of the life of the theater as the performers. The Ladies are not as single-minded. They don't show up at several performances every week. They are involved with other cliques and other charities, and they see the Guild differently. "A few of them joined as a sort of society game," one of the old-timers says. "After all, you can't suddenly become a big shot in the Metropolitan Opera Guild any more, or in the big charity ball committees. And here it is—ballet, with all its pseudo-White Russian mystique. Instant social climbing."

The Ladies work hard, and they have friends who can help the company financially, but they are just learning to deal with ballet and ballet audiences. Before the season opened, the Guild scheduled a seminar and sent out a lot of invitations. They asked composer Nicholas Nabokov to lecture on Stravinsky. They asked the company to attend. They arranged for the promenade bar to be open and prepared to serve about three hundred people. Sixty showed up. As Sue Ralston pointed out, "For three hundred a bar is fine, but for sixty you have to have a reception. Nabokov didn't give the second half of his lecture—there wasn't that much interest—so they stood at the bar and guzzled champagne. Only four people from the company were there—and that includes Mr. B. and Karin."

The Ladies had not taken into consideration that the dancers were rehearsing that afternoon, and that dancers don't much like being party prizes anyway. Neither had they remembered that a lot of ballet fans work, and can't get away for three-hour lunches at Lutèce, or even for lectures. As the Guild prepares for the gala, there is resentment of The Ladies by some of the old-timers and a lack of understanding on the part of some of the social types that the workings of the Guild, like those of the company, depend as much on the daily grind as on the more enjoyable preparations for major events. The factions work together, but there is as much tension in the little third-floor office as in the dressing rooms or on stage.

The press office also is involved with the work of the gala. On the day of the lecture debacle, Virginia Donaldson is in Chicago; Marie Gutscher, her chief assistant, is minding the store. Early in the day, *The New Yorker* magazine calls: "Is the program listing for May 12 correct?" There is a rumor that a "tentative change" is planned in that program involving the new Jerry Robbins ballet, whatever it may turn out to be. Marie makes several calls to the administrative wing—nobody knows. She tells *The New Yorker* to print the original listing, and trusts to luck.

In the afternoon, Marie takes another tumble into the company communications canyon (it's too wide to be called a gap). She is preparing a press release containing the official announcement of Melissa Hayden's intention to retire, when she learns that Milly already has given the news to Clive Barnes; it will appear in his column in this Sunday's *Times* (April 29). What should be the official date of Marie's release? It had been set for Monday, which would give Clive a beat on all the other dance writers. Marie does not want to offend Clive. (Actually, people don't mind offending Clive; it's *The New York Times* they worry about. Clive is a very pleasant fellow, but the *Times* is—well, put it this way: New York press agents believe that if God issued the Ten Commandments today, he'd give them to the *Times* before telling Moses.)

Marie does not want to offend other critics, either. She wishes fervently that Milly had abided by regulations and checked with the press office before talking to the papers. She wishes Virginia were not in Chicago. Eventually, she makes a logical decision: The release is dated to give other journalists a chance to at least tie with Clive. But none do. His story already is in print.

By the time all the stories have been printed, the season has begun. Milly is rehearsing *Cortège*, *Agon* and the role of Eurydice in *Orpheus*—the role in which she is sketched on the cover of the season's program. She leads some of the *Agon* rehearsals. Although Mr. B. is present, he acts more or less as a consultant, allowing Milly to instruct the younger dancers. Whether dancing or teaching, Melissa works at full throttle. During one sequence of *Agon*, she leans over to ask Mr. B., "Why did you make it so hard?"— then stands up and dances the passage cleanly, singing as she goes. Later, she remarks that she used to do a certain step differently, "before we speeded it up." Balanchine assures her "it always is the same tempo." Perhaps Milly herself was a bit faster in 1957, when *Agon* was made. And if Milly Hayden—who can take two classes a day, care for a family and dance Balanchine ballets at tempo—is slowing down, what hope is there for the rest of us?

Her dramatic power certainly has not diminished. Eurydice is acted and danced with concentrated feeling and clarity. Melissa is a strong woman, in spirit as well as in body; she is at her best in roles like this and that of the leading predator in Jerry Robbins' *The Cage*, parts in which the emotional impact of the dancing is as important as the execution of steps.

The season's first *Orpheus* comes on May 4, a Friday. Victor Castelli is listed in the program as Apollo, but at the afternoon dress rehearsal Balanchine was displeased with his performance. At 4:30, Michael Steele was told he is to dance the role tonight. Just before curtain time, Roland Vazquez asks Mr. B. if he should announce the change of cast to the audience. The choreographer says, "No. They will just think Castelli suddenly got good." Generally, cast changes for larger roles are made public.

Steele asserts that he doesn't care: "If I get the chance to do the role—and the compliment of Mr. B. asking me to do it—what do I care about the announcement? The important thing is that he thinks I'm good enough to dance it." Balanchine remarks to Rosemary that "Castelli is a nice boy, a pretty boy, but—nothing up here. He'll never learn because he's not smart enough." He replaces Victor with Francis Sackett in *Cortège* because of Castelli's inability to land properly after the tours en l'aire. And yet, by mid-season, when Victor really has settled down to work, Mr. B. will put him into leading roles in *Symphony in C* and other ballets—and his name will be announced to the audience. By the beginning of the next season, Jerry will be using Victor in a new ballet, and Michael Steele will no longer be with the company. Balanchine, like everyone else, can hold a grudge, but his chief concern is for the moment. It is what a dancer is doing now that counts, not what he did last week. If it will benefit the company for a dancer to appear in a role, he appears; if it will be detrimental, he will not, and if a dancer is "not smart enough" today, it is not impossible that he will wise up somewhat by next week.

Orpheus goes on before a fairly large audience. The Bacchantes count carefully as they rend Jean-Pierre Bonnefous, and Melissa gets a huge ovation at her curtain call. Eurydice is one of the roles in which her admirers want to see her before she leaves the company, and they are here in force. She does not disappoint them.

After *Orpheus* she dances *Agon*, singing along with the score as she always does when she knows she's really dancing well. As Bruce Wells and Tracy Bennett lift her high at the end of a variation, she tosses her head back with a soft, triumphant, "Pah!" and lands happily. As they lead her forward to bow, Milly whispers to her escorts, "Bravo." After the performance, she tells a young dancer who is worried about taking over a role, "Do the beginning and the end big, and think of everything in the middle, but as movements, not as steps. When I work, I see the beginning and I see the end. In the middle, I just think about *dancing*."

By the end of the first performance week, Milly has danced *Scotch Symphony*, *Orpheus* and *Agon*. Her final season with the company is becoming a triumphal procession, and during rehearsals of *Cortège*, Mr. B. is building her arch. Sometimes, she tells stories about her Toronto childhood, her days with Ballet Theater, the beginning of her career. "I started late, you know. I didn't begin taking class until I was fifteen-and-a-half." Milly's official biography says she began at twelve. "Oh, that was vanity. When that was written I had just had a child; I hadn't danced for a little while; I didn't want to show my age—none of that matters any more.

"When I had Jennifer, I was worried about how Mr. B. would react—it was unexpected and you know how he can be about pregnancies—and whether I could keep on dancing, but he kept me with the company; he made sure I had a job teaching at The School. I was teaching when I was seven-and-a-half months pregnant, and I told Mr. B. that maybe I wasn't able to give the students as much as I should. He said, 'Is all right. They should know what a pregnant lady looks like, anyway. You teach as long as you can.' "

She talks about her plans for building a dance program at Skidmore College in Saratoga Springs, about bringing some of the older dancers of the company to work with her when it is their turn to retire, about expanding the program and finding funds for it, and her face takes on the same expression it had when she sang her way through *Agon*—eager and exultant.

She turns to the kids—usually, she talks at length only with the older members of the company—"Determination is your frame," she insists. "You have to have it. It's the frame on which to hang an expressive career. If you don't have it, you can't survive."

Throughout the rehearsal period and the first week of performance, Sue Ralston, in her office, and Virginia Donaldson, in hers, have been wondering about Jerry's contribution to the gala. Both have other things to worry about and Virginia really is not supposed to be working for the Guild but she winds up helping out, as usual. The Ladies hired a public relations woman to do "social p.r. for the gala," Virginia says, "and the first thing she did was to call Anna Kisselgoff at the *Times* with a lot of wrong information."

In the Guild office, Sue Ralston's dark hair just about shows over the pile of cream-colored envelopes, stuffed with invitations. And in the rehearsal studios, Jerry is working on three new ballets. Virginia, who is setting up press and television interviews for Milly Hayden, now that opening night is past, keeps asking the people in authority, "What's Jerry going to do?" Nobody knows. Jerry keeps changing his mind. Finally, on Sunday, May 6, ten days before the gala, it is decided: Jerome Robbins' contribution to the performance will be his pas de deux to four Beethoven bagatelles, danced by Violette Verdy and Jean-Pierre Bonnefous. At this point, the betting in the company is that Jerry's *Tchaikovsky Waltzes* will be presented at the Festival of Two Worlds in Spoleto this summer—he is committed to show something there—and that his *Prokofieff Waltzes* will be offered here later in the season. Meanwhile, the gala gets Beethoven. The only part of the program still unsettled is in the first ballet, the curtain-raiser.

On Tuesday morning, everyone comes to work to learn that the curtain-raiser will be Jerry's *Dumbarton Oaks*. It was made for the Stravinsky Festival and so is fairly new; it is in this week's repertory and won't need rehearsal; the leads are Anthony Blum and Allegra Kent, popular artists—it's a good choice. Then early in the afternoon, Eddie Bigelow calls to tell Sue Ralston that the curtain-raiser will be Mr. B.'s *Donizetti Variations*, led by Kay Mazzo and Eddie Villella. There are a number of possible reasons for the switch, although none are given to Sue. One is to toss Eddie to the gala crowd. Another is that *Dumbarton* is technically complicated; it requires a big set and a lot of props. If it should take too much time to clear the stage, a long intermission could bore the audience and put the stagehands into overtime. Then again, Jerry may want to use the *Dumbarton* hangings (which originally were the *Divertimento No. 15* hangings) for the new pas de deux. It hardly would do to have a gala audience see the same scenery twice in a night. Furthermore, Tony Blum has been looking tired lately; he almost fell last week during *Dances at a Gathering;* maybe he needs a rest. *Donizetti* is a lively, popular ballet; the dancers know it well; it needs to be rehearsed and the drops hung for the week after the gala anyway. Selecting one ballet from fifty for an occasion is not as simple a process as you might think.

Shortly after Eddie calls with the news about *Donizetti,* Sue is on the phone arranging a small buffet for gala night, while addressing invitations to the dancers. "Invitations for the dancers are ridiculous," she snorts. True. She also is less than happy with The Ladies, who asked her to locate a "high-class female to chair a committee, then went out and found their own. Of course, I had to call my woman and tell her, 'The whole thing's off.' It's a typical communications failure—we get them all the time around here."

Next door, Virginia is noting the name Jerry has chosen for his new Prokofieff ballet, *An Evening's Waltzes.* It will have its premiere May 24, the week after the gala. "I'm glad Jerry is settled and secure, now," she observes, "but we don't have much time to get publicity. OH, well." "OH, well," with the "OH" taken a fourth higher than the "well," is Virginia's customary answer to the uncertainties of NYCB. After sighing it, she reaches for the phone, ready to cope.

NBC-TV plans to show a bit of *Cortège* on a Sunday program along with interviews with Mr. B. and Milly. The camera crew packs in on Friday, and Balanchine rehearses on stage while cameramen and commentators literally follow in his footsteps. He is building up the first entrance for Jacques and Milly, and tells them to come on stage, "then stop, because there will be lots of applause and you won't be able to hear the music anyhow. Then, when they stop clapping, the music starts and we go on." Balanchine didn't spend those years on Broadway without learning how to present a star.

Martha Swope, the company's official photographer, sits in the first row of the orchestra, punctuating the music with shy clicks of her Leicas and Pentax. Virginia Donaldson is guiding the bwana of the TV crew around the theater, but bearers of cameras and microphones keep following Mr. B. every time he leaves his seat in the house to work with the dancers on stage. Halfway back in the orchestra, Lincoln Kirstein is sliding into sleep. The corps men try their new spurs, which Robert Irving approves because they only ring like sleigh bells, not like tambourines.

On stage, Mr. B. works with the corps. "Faster. Now we must have it faster. THAT's right. Now we have it. Now we are right. We . . ." he breaks off and spins around to stare at a TV cameraman who, for several minutes, has been puffing smoke from a cigar into his face. "Can't we ban cigars from United States?" Balanchine snaps. "It's killing me." The cameraman offers a patronizing smile: "Sorry about that," and stomps the cigar. The corps kids are nearly in shock: It is the first time some of them have seen Mr. B. lose his temper. It takes a great breach of manners to provoke him that far. For several minutes he is peevish; the cameraman's lack of consideration obviously appalls him.

The company has requested that NBC show only two minutes of rehearsal film—there are union reasons for the limitation. The television director is upset. "We should be encouraging people to come. Do they think four or five minutes of rehearsal instead of two will keep them out?" he asks his producer. The producer acquires the same sort of patronizing smile the cameraman wore when challenged about his cigar. "They don't understand," he says. The director is not so kind: "They understand; they're stupid, that's all." Fortunately, Mr. B. does not overhear.

At any press conference, you will find the television boys hustling their way to the front, pushing microphones and questions at the participants, trying to show the pad-and-pencil journalists how it ought to be done. Their bustle seems to say: "WE are the TODAY medium. WE are the ones that COUNT. WE have to hurry this up and get it in the can—then YOU can waste time with your silly long-winded questions." As Kevin Tyler snorts: "TV people; they all think they're God."

On Friday, Robert Irving leads an orchestra rehearsal for *Cor-*

tège. Musicians wander into the pit, filling it with tuning noises, scrapes of chairs and belches of brass. Hugo Fiorato, the associate conductor, sits in the second row of the audience, studying his score. Robert arrives on the podium, greets the musicians, sets his watch on the score table and begins the morning's work.

Robert's rehearsals are businesslike affairs. He gives precise instructions—"horns and tuba, first two notes fairly long"—and listens as they are carried out and acknowledges the fact—"That was good; rhythmical, but not too heavy"—and goes on. The orchestra follows his baton and their music, and he interrupts only when he needs to give direction—"Brass, please play diminunendo in the last two bars"—or answer a question—"Yes, you're quite right; that's a mistake in the copying. It should be a B flat, not B natural."

As the orchestra begins to play her variation, Colleen Neary comes onto the dark stage and marks the steps, then listens for a few more minutes and wanders off again. Robert instructs the cymbal player to accent a specific spot in the bar, then goes on. It's all very brisk and efficient; he tells the musicians what he wants; they give it to him; and everybody goes home. *Cortège* needs only two orchestra rehearsals. "Of course," Robert says, "it's easier than some other things we have to play, it isn't that complex a score. Besides, we used a lot of the same music when we did *Pas de Dix* and fifty percent of the orchestra remembered it."

Monday, while the dancers are doing their weekly laundry-chiropractor-masseur-movie routine, the stagehands hang the set for *Cortège*. The drops are the ones used in *Ballet Imperial*, but Rouben Ter-Arutunian has added a few touches and a new white back scrim. NYCB often reuses drops, to save a bit of money. Costumes are quite expensive enough. Tuesday morning, Suki Schorer teaches class while Balanchine, Rouben and Ronnie Bates light the new ballet. Gold-geled spotlights on stanchions behind the scrim are focused to project a diffused pattern on the white background. The Independents are focused; colors, with a heavy accent on gold, are selected. Everything must be ready by three in the afternoon, when an open rehearsal is scheduled for The Friends of City Center. The Friends, in return for their membership fees, are invited to a number of open rehearsals each season. The Friends, like the gala, are there because they bring in money, and if they like to see rehearsals in exchange for it, they are welcome.

By one o'clock, Jerry Robbins is on stage, lighting his Beethoven pas de deux. Two students from the School of American Ballet dress in Florence Klotz's peasant costumes and stand in for Violette and Jean-Pierre. Once he has them neatly posed, like knick-knacks in a breakfront, Jerry goes out front with Ronnie Bates to arrange the focusing of the Independent instruments. The two young dancers get fidgety; they are asked to pose for a long time, then move to another part of the stage and hold still for another eon as Jerry and Ronnie confer out front, and Ronnie passes instructions to the electricians. They still are working when the first wave of Friends starts to arrive and has to be herded out of the area of the orchestra reserved for the company, the press and special guests.

Sue Ralston comes downstairs from the Guild office to dole out tickets to the members of the company. She is allowed to give them only one apiece, "because The Ladies still don't know how many they can sell." The dancers are not pleased with this arrangement. "Well, maybe I can give you another one tomorrow. If not, you're certainly allowed to buy them. The Ladies wouldn't mind that at all." The dancers are not about to pay to get into their own theater. Most of the company is backstage by now, getting ready to work or to watch.

By 1:30, the costumes for *Cortège* have arrived from Karinska's shop. Three were here yesterday, four are still to come. Ducky Copeland, supervisor of men's wardrobe, knows they will be in the theater in time for tomorrow's performance—they always make it: "The pins still will be in them, but they'll arrive." While Ducky works on costumes in the corridor, Jerry Robbins has the flymen lower the *Dumbarton Oaks* set for use in the Beethoven duet. Then he has them take it up again and send down black drapes instead. By 2:51—remember, the Friends' rehearsal is set for 3:00—Jerry is finished with the stage, and the crew starts to prepare it for *Cortège*. The men manage to avoid tripping over the TV gear in the wings—a team from ABC has arrived to do what NBC did last week. Fortunately, there are no cigar-smokers.

Ducky is helping the men get ready for *Cortège;* Mme. Pourmel works with the women. Bobby Maiorano learns that his boots still are too loose. When he tried them on at the shop, he mentioned it and wrote a note on the left sole, "Loose and will get looser." He had hoped elastic might be installed to hold the boot closer to his foot. Nothing can be done about it now. The least you can expect of $175 boots is that they will fit.

Ronnie Bates is calling light cues over the bitch box from the front of the house. A wooden board has been hooked over the tops of a couple of seats, dead center, to support a small light, an intercom unit and pads and charts. This is Ronnie's command post for a dress rehearsal; the choreographer takes the seat next to him and tells Ronnie what he wants; and Ronnie tells the crew. While Mr. B. and the stage manager light *Cortège,* the men from ABC get ready to film the rehearsal. About half the orchestra and most of the first ring are filled with Friends, and above their chatter, you can hear Robert saying to the orchestra, at the end of each section, "Can we go on, please?".

At a few minutes after three, the conductor taps his baton and the dress rehearsal begins—a false start, as it turns out. The orchestra fails to come in together; Robert stops them, calls for attention and begins again. The stage fills with stamping dancers. The corps, in its green-and-gold uniforms, looks a bit like a high school marching band from California. The czardas gives way to the women's pas de quatre—Deborah Flomine, Susan Hendl, Susan Pilarre and Carol Sumner. The Friends applaud. They applaud at every appropriate interval, and at a few inappropriate ones. Dancers in costume slip into orchestra seats, watch for a few minutes, then hurry back to be ready for their cues. Mr. B., sitting near Ronnie at the board, times each section of the dance with his stop watch.

The dancers treat this almost as a performance, working through the ballet with few pauses, but during her variation, Melissa stops and asks Robert to take a few bars of music over again—she wasn't satisfied with her execution. Friends or no Friends, Milly takes a rehearsal as a rehearsal, not as a performance. She works to please Mr. B. and to gratify her audience, but, even more, she works to maintain her own standards, and she sets them high.

When rehearsal is over, Balanchine goes on stage to direct the finale. He has the lines of dancers fold back to leave Melissa standing center stage facing the house, the lights gilding her face as if she were staring into an autumn sun. She can't hear Mr. B.'s directions over the sound of the orchestra; Robert stops the musicians and the dancers walk through the passage in silence. Balanchine waves his arms, directing traffic. Then, as the company tries the finale with music, he conducts the dancers with the same gestures Robert uses to lead the orchestra, in perfect synchronization.

Teena McConnell comes over to tell Mr. B. that the long sleeves of the women's costumes are not practical. "When you give your hand to the boy, they get all wound around your arm, especially if you're doing a turn." The tassle-balls at the ends of the men's stocking-cap tails are a nuisance, too. When the men turn, their neighbors get batted in the face. Richard Dryden demonstrates, spinning around to catch Steve Caras neatly in the eye. Balanchine, Rouben and one of Karinska's deputies discuss the matter, while the television crew pushes the snouts of cameras over their shoulders. Although Mr. B. looks annoyed, he says nothing. It is decided to pin the sleeves, shorten the hat tails, and shorten the skirts a bit, too. Karin von Aroldingen is to get a more stylish headdress, with gold ribbons instead of green ones.

The dancers go off to change, and Violette and Jean-Pierre come on to model their *Beethoven* costumes for Jerry. The costumes are charming, frilly things—very eighteenth-century peasant— reminiscent of the character dress used in many classical ballets. ("They're really very simple," the designer remarks, "I just like things on top of things.") Violette, who is known as an interpreter of some famous classical roles when appearing as guest artist with other companies, enjoys flirting with her embroidered skirt: "It's my only chance to do *Giselle* in this house and I'm going to make the most of it"—and she dresses her hair to suit the style of the costume. Jerry Robbins gives a few last-minute instructions, Jerry Zimmerman sits at the piano, and the Friends see *A Beethoven Pas de Deux*.

Instead of ending his first variation in style, Jean-Pierre trails off—the audience applauds anyway—and calls Jerry to the stage. He tells the choreographer he is ending up too far from his exit; Jerry orders the houselights turned up and works with him. Jean-Pierre marks the sequence lightly and finds the problem—the passage is short on transitional steps—and finishes where he wants to go, giving him an easy exit into the wings. Jerry approves, has the houselights dimmed again, and Jean-Pierre picks up where he left off. As soon as the curtain falls, Robbins comes on stage to take the dancers through a turn that was not smooth enough. The Friends, their view cut off by the gold curtain, head for home. So does the orchestra, which has been working since morning. Betty Cage, the general manager, who has been sitting in the audience, no doubt figuring up rehearsal costs, sighs: "Thank goodness the musicians' union gives us a waiver whenever it's a Friends rehearsal—or anything to do with raising money."

Violette and Jean-Pierre finish their work and start for their dressing rooms. As they leave, Violette turns to her partner: "Jean-Pierre, veux-tu du No-Cal?" Diet soda is the same in any language. The stage crew, which, like the orchestra and dancers, has been here since early morning, is waiting to prepare the stage for the evening performance. Virginia is shepherding ABC reporters to Milly's dressing room for an interview. Sue Ralston is on the phone again, spending ten minutes listening to a young Park Avenue woman explain why she can't come to the gala. "Even if you live on Park Avenue, it shouldn't take ten minutes to say, 'I'm sorry.' "

At 8:30, while the company is dancing *Watermill* for a relatively small audience, Virginia is in her office assigning press seats for tomorrow night's gala. It should have been done last week, but "The Ladies don't want to do anything until they sell as many as they can, and they still don't know how many they're going to sell. OH, well—." By the time performance is over, everybody in the house is exhausted.

Wednesday, gala day, is busy. The dancers stretch through a John Taras class, the office staffs are bustling with last-minute preparations. Mr. B. rehearses *Donizetti Variations* with the full cast, including Eddie and Kay. "When you turn—Fast! Bang!

Head!—Snap your head. Is better for the public, better for you, too. If you snap, you will turn faster, easier." Rosemary drills the corps of *Cortège*, demanding precision: "Stay right behind the boy in front of you . . . Back people, don't get so close to the front people; we miss all the formation and it's just a mob . . . That's a STRAIGHT LINE back there." Everyone is on edge. The dancers have been given their second tickets for the performance, but they are even more pleased that the gala, which starts at nine, will be short, so they all can get some sleep.

At least, the late curtain gives them a chance to get some food. Allegra goes to the pre-gala dinner, gathers all the bouquets from the tables and goes home. Then, she comes to the theater to applaud Melissa. The gala performance, months in the making, is ready.

Aside from the late opening curtain, it's a normal night backstage. Dancers dress, glue their shoes, do their barres. Kevin calls for "Independent 1." Out front, Virginia is greeting the press; The Ladies are greeting their friends; tables are being arranged on the promenade. Dancers appear in the house, dressed as they seldom get a chance to dress these days. The house is very nearly full when the lights go down.

Backstage dancers say "Merde"; Hank pushes his button and the performance begins. *Donizetti* is applauded. *A Beethoven Pas de Deux* is applauded. Then, as the house lights dim for the third time, Robert Irving raises his wand and signals the beginning of *Cortège Hongrois*. The costumes have been altered and the dancers display them, flashing green and gold across the floor, stomping out the czardas, preening through the promenades. At their entrance, Milly and Jacques get the applause promised by Mr. B. Karin and Jean-Pierre dance freely, folding and opening their arms, slapping the floor with their heels, keeping their knees free and their upper bodies high. The four women and the four men perform their quartettes, showing no sign of the week's strains and struggles. Colleen and Merrill win applause for their variations, Colleen, tall and ripe, spinning and dazzling; Merrill, smooth and powerful, riding the music.

And then, the pas de deux. All the problems of rehearsal seem

never to have existed—besides, even if a step is not perfectly executed, tonight nobody will notice. The dancers are sure, serene in the
power of the stage, confident of one another. Jacques' legs flit comfortably from side to side; Milly's little backwards bourrées are fast
enough, her variation is breathtaking in its sweep and pride. At the
end of the coda, she soars to Jacques' shoulder as if she had never
had to rehearse it even once.

As the corps, the soloists, and finally, Jacques step back to leave
Milly glowing in the lights, huge stands of flowers are carried on
stage and set around her. The audience stands to applaud, just as
Balanchine knew it would. The company applauds. And the ballerina stands firm, downstage center, at the navel of the world.
She raises her head and looks straight into the golden lights until
the curtain falls.

During the curtain calls, there are more flowers for Milly. The
audience continues to applaud, not only for the ballerina, but hoping to bring Balanchine out from the wings. The curtain rises again
on Milly, and a boy comes across the stage with still another
bouquet. The curtain falls, the audience keeps clapping, wanting to
see more of Milly, to see something of Mr. B. For a benefit audience, they are responding very nicely. Hank's finger must be sore
from button-pushing. The curtain goes up again, Milly bows, and
a smallish, gray-haired man walks briskly from the wings, just as
the flower boy did at the last call. He presents a bouquet, makes a
small, neat bow to Milly and leaves as quickly as he came, grinning
like a schoolboy. For Melissa's gala, the man who made her ballet
also made himself her flower boy.

The Tenth Annual Spring Gala brought the New York City
Ballet Production Fund $41,000.

7

Soloists, Principals, and Stars

Promotion from the corps to soloist rank is a rite of passage, like getting your drivers' license or being bar mitzvah. Afterwards, you have delusions of maturity. Real, working-world, compromising, voting adults may somehow fail to notice the change, but *you* know something has happened. You feel wisdom and certainty setting in your features like cement. It takes a while to realize that people are not according you any increased deference, and that the universe has been unaffected by your metamorphosis. That understanding, which can be as great a shock to the system as ritual circumcision, may be the beginning of a true initiation into adulthood. From then on, there is a tendency to see things differently.

The company's fourteen soloists are more highly paid than the uninitiated caste of the corps. They have a bit more time to themselves and are more likely to have gained some degree of public recognition with the help of those small capital letters in the program. Some appear as guests artists, and even choreograph, with lesser companies. Not only are they older than the corps dancers, they also have seen a bit more of the world. Soloists are less likely to be content with a circumscribed existence than the teenagers still enthralled by the magic of being paid to do something they enjoy. In April, 1972, four young dancers—Susan Hendl, Susan Pilarre, Bruce Wells and Robert Weiss—were raised from the corps and dubbed soloists. The most junior of them, Bruce Wells, had been with the company for five and one-half years. Susie Pilarre had been in the corps for nine, Susie Hendl for seven, Ricky Weiss for six. Both Susies appeared with NYCB several years before they were old enough to join; blond Susie Hendl as a Candy Cane in *The Nutcracker*, dark Susie Pil as one of Medea's children, mothered by Melissa Hayden, in Birgit Cullberg's version of the legend. If you consider that performance as her starting-place, it took dark-eyed Susan fourteen years of dancing to achieve soloist status.

"Susie Hendl and I have danced together in the corps all the way," she said. "We share a dressing room, now, but all the others are gone. We're almost the only ones left from the time we started." Her voice is as earnest as that of a little girl promising to be good and never do it again. "There's a whole new corps out there—all the people we danced with stopped—but we lasted."

The soloists on the spring, 1973, roster spent an average of five years in the corps waiting for the accolade. Five years is a long stretch of "One, two, three . . . one, two, three, four . . . keep those lines straight . . . how did we do this last year? . . ." The four dancers promoted in 1972 had different thoughts about their advancement, but all agreed on two points: "It means more money," and "It means Mr. Balanchine thinks highly of us." They had danced millions of miles of ballet to prove to Mr. B., and to themselves, that they were dancers—that they not only could do the steps and had the personal flair required for solo work, but that they could last the course. And, having proven it, they went back to "One, two, three . . . one, two, three, four . . ." Now, though, they are bellwethers, individual creatures rather than part of the wooly mass. They have been allowed to discard their profession of anonymity, and slightly richer costumes proclaim their status, differentiating them from the corps the way an officer's uniform marks him out from the troops. Still, they are not fully autonomous, either on stage or in the structure of the company. Those distinctions are reserved for the principal dancers.

Principals are to soloists as colonels are to sergeants—farther removed from the ranks. In some ballets, soloists may be relegated to demi-soloist or even ensemble work and corps dancers may be temporarily promoted to choreography beyond their nominal rank. Principals never perform as anything but principals. They are the ones the audience pays to see. Balanchine wants people to pay to see the ballet, and for years the company gave almost no advance notice of casting. The spectators came hoping for specific performers, anyway. This season, cast lists for each subsequent week are posted in the theater lobby, and ticket buyers study them like tax accountants looking for a new loophole. A balletomane may purchase a seat to watch soloist Bruce Wells or corps dancer Christine Redpath—or even to see *Symphony in Three Movements*—but the average customer wants Edward Villella and Patricia McBride, and doesn't much care what they dance.

Leading dancers, like opera stars and quarterbacks, have followings. Admirers of technical finesse come to see Helgi Tomasson, Peter Martins and Gelsey Kirkland. Old-time fans show up to reminisce with Jacques d'Amboise. Lyricists arrive to see Allegra Kent; delighters in delicacy applaud Kay Mazzo. Everyone comes to watch Villella and McBride. All these performers are stars, which is not quite the same thing as being principal dancers. It is possible to be a principal dancer without being a star, just as, in rare instances, it is possible to have a star who is not a principal. On the spring roster, John Clifford is listed as a soloist, but to Mr. and Mrs. Third Thursday of the subscription list, he is a star. He jumps high; he is exuberant; he is exciting; he sends them home feeling good; and that is what they pay for.

Conrad Ludlow is a principal dancer, but the spectators don't clap like performing seals for him. Conny is a superlative partner who catches ballerinas the way Willie Mays used to catch baseballs. Unfortunately, there is no great élan to his dancing. Leading male dancers who are excellent partners frequently are less impressive in their solo work, and it is the showy stuff that helps to make a star. Balanchine, as has been noted, believes in a starless company in which the music and choreography are the attractions. Despite his genius, he has been unable to create one. Stars don't depend on billing; sometimes, they don't even depend on ability, although that is far less true in dance than in the movies. Ballet stars happen through a combination of style, strength, technique and a high concentration of energy, and when people see one, they know he is there, no matter what company policy may be.

A company may promote a star, as the Royal Ballet does, or it may officially deny it has any, which is the way NYCB operates. One advantage of promotion is that the Royal can charge higher prices during its London season for performances at which Rudolf Nureyev and Dame Margot Fonteyn appear. At The New York State Theater, Eddie Villella and Conny Ludlow come at the same price. Whatever the company does, when the audience spots a dancer who adds his own luminescence to that of the stage lights, they want to see him again.

The effect a star has on an audience depends more on the personality he projects than on the role he plays, and the ways in which people react to a star often tell as much about them as about him. There are spectators who go to watch Nureyev simply to see him dance, but others, including a special coterie of women and homosexual men, are either attracted or repelled by him for reasons that have nothing to do with leaps and beats. Watch their faces sometime—they are anticipating rape. All star performances are inherently sexual.

The public watches Nureyev or Villella with the same sensations circus spectators experience when a snarling tiger flashes into the ring, and for the same reason—what would happen if he escaped? Whether he dances well or badly on a particular night, Nureyev shines with an aura of animal power, and, if you watch spectators as they watch him, you realize that they are frightened out of their minds—and they love it. The leaping tiger is what fills theaters. Lord Olivier, Maria Callas and Mick Jagger do not play to packed houses because of their technical virtuosity alone. Olivier probably is the greatest actor now working in English, but people who know nothing about the art of acting go to see him simply because he excites them. Callas is a technically brilliant actress in music, but when she sang "Vissi d'arte" after she hardly could hit the notes, it was not just technique that sent chills up your spine. The tiger without the technique produces demogoguery, not art, but the technique without the tiger will never make a star. Only when skill is illuminated by animal power does the stage begin to glow.

The animal power is high-octane emotion—life, trying to burst through the performer's body. That emotion, that life force is indivisible from the sex drive. It takes us very close to the ultimate, orgiastic release that is the closest we can get to the instincts of our own, private animals. And since the surrogate playing out of those instincts and a subsequent Dionysian cartharsis is one of the chief reasons human beings invented the performing arts, the performer most luminously successful in releasing our feelings becomes the star—the one we pay to see.

Different stars produce different reactions in the audience because the animals they unleash are not the same. The great Danish dancer Erik Bruhn was the cool romantic prince, a beautiful white charger; Nureyev is a high-strung blood stallion. Allegra Kent is flexible as a kitten and seductive as a shadow. Violette Verdy seems like an otter playing in her river; Melissa Hayden measures her steps like a lioness; Patricia McBride flashes over the stage like a school of bright fish. Watching any dancer, star or not, even within the strict confines of classical ballet, will give you some idea of his personality, but stars show more of themselves than most of us can, or care to. They are not afraid, at least while on stage, to unfold themselves. Ordinary dancers just show the steps. Stars show themselves within the steps. The ability to do this does not make them less vulnerable to mundane problems.

Principal dancers with NYCB have triumphed in their profession, but they have not escaped it. Grueling physical work is a daily necessity; stress is ubiquitous. Principals have more time away from the company than other dancers, more time in which to think, and to complicate their lives. They also have time in which to travel, to teach, to buy homes and land, to perform in houses other than the New York State Theater. Principals are not merely better known than soloists or corps dancers, they are richer. A superstar can earn $80,000 in a year, and a relatively small percentage of that comes from NYCB. In 1972, a ballerina collected $16,000 from the company and $39,000 outside it. Since the com-

pany works together at least thirty-two weeks a year, much of the
leading dancers' touring is done between New York appearances.
This makes them good customers of the airlines, and frequent victims of jet lag. The most prominent victim is Edward Villella,
probably the most celebrated male dancer in America, and possibly
the most exhausted.

EDWARD VILLELLA does so many concert performances that his appearances in New York seem as brief as a
road salesman's visits to the home office. The man originally
planned a career at sea (he earned a degree in maritime engineering from New York State Maritime College), and sometimes must feel as if he got one.

In the ballet bestiary, Eddie is an American mustang.
His presence is as virile as that of Nureyev or Bruhn, but he
is less brooding than the Russian, less remote than the
Dane. His first fame was based on athleticism. Even people
who think Martha Graham is a brand of women's shoes
know that Villella is "that dancer with muscles who used
to box and play ball." The bulging thighs and lifeguard
torso give Eddie extraordinary elevation and power, but
there is more to his dancing than being the patent-holding
he-man of ballet.

In a pas de deux, this small, dark man, born in unclassical Bayside, N.Y., pounces on his partner like an Ar-
cadian satyr, but when his hands touch her, they are gentle,
filled with delight and surprise. He seems to be holding her
waist to be certain she really is there. He looks at his partner, without glare or stare in his wide, dark eyes, exactly as
he looks at anyone with whom he is talking. At his best,
Villella is not merely the dancer-as-athlete, but the dancer-
as-actor. These days, he is not always at his best.

If the first part of his career was based on muscles, the
current episode is based on money. Villella is supporting
himself, an ex-wife, a son, his-and-hers town houses and a
German shepherd. The only way he can earn enough—one
of the great subjects of speculation around the company is

Signing in

Looking on

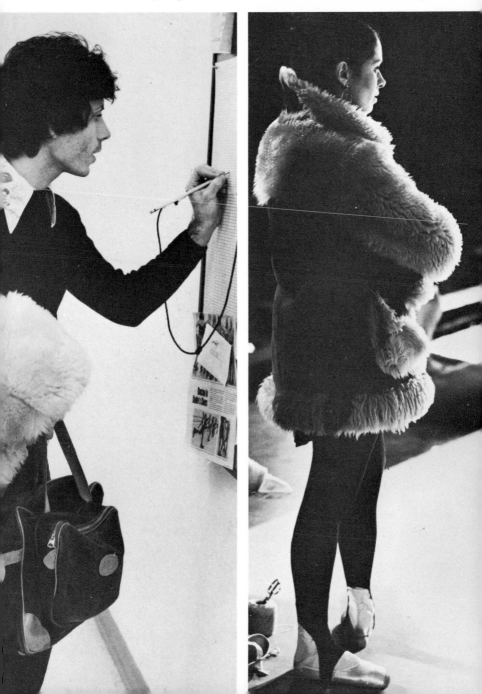

Changing shoes: Christine Redpath

Watching:
Mr. B.,
Rosemary Dunleavy,
and Victor Castelli

Sewing shoes: Ricky Weiss

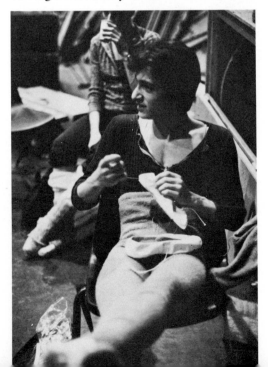

At tempo: Ricky Weiss

At ease:
Patricia McBride and Sara Leland

The Corps

Working

The choreographer works too

At the footlights:
Karin von Aroldingen,
Colleen Neary,
and Victor Castelli

Reaching out: Kay Mazzo

Supported: Kay Mazzo and Peter Martins

Halftime

Easing the legs: Jacques D'Amboise

Preparing the legs: Bobby Maiorano

Trying the air

Testing the ground

Balanchine

the size of Eddie's alimony payments—is by dancing. He
has an agent, an attorney, an accountant, a manager; he
dances with this company, with his own company, with
other companies. From dancer-as-athlete, he has become
dancer-as-businessman.

The constant work leaves him with constant injuries. He
admits there may have been "five or ten minutes in the last
three years" when he was not hurt in one way or another.
(If Villella had not been injured—by being mugged—back
in 1955, he might have gone to sea after all. He returned to
dancing after an absence as therapy for the injury and joined
the company two years later.) His current mugging is self-
inflicted; he dances injured, as all the performers do, and his
prowess suffers.

Villella is everything the magazine writers say he is—
candid, clever, driving, filled with an appetite for life and
good beer, a superb artist, a pleasant man to know. He's
also damnably tired.

For Villella, for many of the principals, stress is the result of
tensions between the life within the company and the one outside
it. Among the soloists, the same tensions exist, but often they pull
more lightly. Soloists must spend more time in residence than principals. They are called to rehearsal like corps dancers; principal
dancers ask for rehearsal time when they need it. Only when a
principal dancer is performing, learning or teaching a role is he
required to be in the theater. Soloists lack that kind of freedom.
Love affairs, family affairs, business affairs must be dealt with on
company time. Principals are with the group, soloists are of it.
Each situation has its disadvantages.

A soloist has three choices: to buck for principal, to settle for
non-commissioned status, to resign. Before resigning, he must find
another way to earn a living and decide to give up an occupation
which, separate from its side effects, is a source of elation and
pleasure. Even when a dancer does not like his life, he may like to
dance. Bruce Wells, the twenty-four-year-old soloist, has discovered things about his line of work that were unknown to Bruce

Wells, the eighteen-year-old corps dancer, but after listing all the drawbacks, he says, "But I like what I do—I enjoy dancing." If the corps members are the schoolchildren of the troupe—obedient, malleable, believers in good and evil—the soloists are its teenagers, subject to the discomforts adolescence brings us all.

ROBERT MAIORANO was born in Brooklyn, and looks it. At twelve, he shocked a Little League coach out of his sweatshirt by saying he couldn't come to practice on Saturday, he had to go to ballet class. Bobby is not the kind of guy Little League coaches figure for ballet class: he looks tough when he isn't looking Byronesque. Mariorano laughs when he calls the choice between baseball and ballet "one of the big decisions of my life," but it was. Three years after making it, he joined the company.

"I was losing interest and cutting classes at The School. They had a lot of money invested in training and they didn't want to lose me, I guess, so they asked me to join the company when I really was too young." Eight years later, he became a soloist.

He drives himself in class, in rehearsal, on his own; his dark skin takes on a glaze of sweat; his eyes harden in concentration. Like a true adept of karate, he is at least as interested in the technique and truth of his art as in the outcome of a battle.

Mariorano's injuries seem to happen just as he is reaching full form, or before he is scheduled to dance a major role. In 1972, his bare foot had an unpleasant encounter with a soccer ball. This season, he damaged a knee cartilege and has tried everything from exercise to acupuncture to heal it. He trains grimly. "At my age, you have to decide to work and become as good as you possibly can, or else to quit." At his age, which is twenty-six, he is articulate, open, a bit patronizing at times, a bit defensive at others. He talks as intensely as he dances, thinks as strongly as he moves, and writes poetry. It isn't bad poetry.

In Mr. Balanchine's army, mens sana and corpore sano often are at odds. Playing soccer barefoot is only one way of convincing yourself you really are alive when not dancing. Besides, for a dancer with a major company, an injury may give the only opportunity to catch up on one's reading.

Contrary to rumor, dancers are not stupid by profession. Often, though, they are undereducated. Few are college graduates (Villella is an exception) because an aspiring dancer rarely can afford to expend four years of his youth at any institution except a company. Those who begin to study for the profession at college generally are too late. Balanchine, asked to give advice about the founding of a university department of dance, said, "Don't. They [the students] are too old."

The lack of conventional higher education, combined with a stringent discipline followed since childhood, deprives dancers of more than the chance to ponder the mysteries of *Beowolf* and the differential calculus. It excludes them from the moratorium period described by psychiatrist Erik H. Erikson, ". . . a span of time after they [young people] have ceased being children but before their deeds and works count toward a future identity . . . [a way of] postponing the decision as to what one is and is going to be." That intermission which most middle-class youngsters may devote to studies, sex, stimulants, self-examination and idealism—whether or not those continue to exert much influence later in life—is not available to dancers. It is possible to regard an entire performing career as a moratorium—there's always some aunt to ask, "When is Johnny going to find a REAL profession?"—but the training is too arduous, the full term of dancing too long, to allow service with NYCB to be considered a pause in which a young person can "find himself." Any finding that is going to be done has to happen while sewing shoes or gasping for breath.

One result of the lack of moratorium is the astounding naiveté of many dancers. They are not a great deal less mature than the rest of society; they simply have not had time to learn all the little tricks most of us use to hint at our maturity. Soloist Carol Sumner was horrified by a college student's questionnaire which jokingly referred to critics as "parasites." She didn't know it was a joke. Things tend to happen later to dancers than to accountants, stockbrokers and lingerie buyers, and company rank often is more indicative of a dancer's stage of life than is chronological age. Two-thirds of the principals on the spring roster are, have been, or soon-are-to-be married. Only one of the soloists, and a very small percentage of the corps, live in wedlock. Marriage is hardly a cachet of maturity—maybe it's a stage you go through, like bubble gum and measles—but dancers seem to reach the stage later than their non-performing coevals. Soloists and corps dancers have their liaisons, but it almost appears as if marriage, like stage-level dressing sooms, is reserved for principals.

Some principals are chronologically as young as corps members, some of the corps kids are as old, and as mature, as principals; soloists balance between them. Still, about one-third of the principal dancers are thirty-five or better, and even the younger ones tend to act more "adult"—perhaps restrained would be a better word—than dancers in other ranks. Somehow, soloists tend to act twenty-five, principals thirty-five and corps dancers nineteen. The veteran corps dancers are honorary twenty-fives. John Clifford reacts to his promotion from soloist to principal by saying, "Now I've really got to grow up."

Once a dancer does grow up, life becomes even more difficult. The distance between the monastic existence within the company and worldly ways is more evident. When Lincoln Kirstein mocks dancers who say, "Don't I have a right to have a life, too?" and answers, "No, you don't," Allegra Kent agrees, at least in theory: "If you don't have a life you'll be a much better dancer—but I'm glad I have a life."

ALLEGRA KENT, once upon a time, was ranked as one of the world's best ballerinas and most beautiful women. Her elfin beauty has stayed with her; her technique has not. When she dances now, her line still is as clear and her style as elegant as those of Botticelli's *Venus*, and she remains superbly supple—"The second half of my career is built on flexibility"—but pristine purity of placement no longer is hers. "With each child, my technique slipped a little more."

To Allegra, the three children are more important than the five positions. She has been known to leave a picture session just as the photographer was about to click the button—"My children need me." She is as sweetly logical with her small son as she is with older friends. Allegra is slightly fey, and her logic has been known to confuse people. "Allegra," they tell you, "is a kook." Not really. She's simply so direct and honest that it takes time to adjust to her.

The children are the product of her marriage to photographer Burt Stern, from whom she is separated. Now, the children depend on their mother, a situation which solved one of Allegra's problems: "I used to wonder if I wanted to dance any more; now I don't have any choice. I have to support myself and my children." She's thinking about what to do when she retires: "Not teaching. I've taught class and I think I hate to teach. I can't tell the kids, 'Go out and work hard, really dance,' because I know what it is to be a dancer. Once a kid told me, 'I'm going to be a doctor,' and I said, 'Good.' "

Lincoln Kirstein regards Allegra's own children as a personal affront: "Her sister had three children, so she had to. Why did she need children?" From his vantage point, the question makes perfect sense. Allegra was a great dancer, a great Balanchine dancer, and each child whittled a bit from her technique and took time away from the company. A great dancer, especially a great Balanchine dancer, should do, indeed, need do, nothing to detract from her art or her worth to the company. Any woman can have children—it takes only nine months to make one, and it takes years to make a ballerina. Dancing should be more than enough.

But for Allegra, with her intelligence (she took her high school diploma at fifteen), her feline curiosity, her delight in the world, it could not be enough. So she raises her children and her roses, and after twenty years with NYCB, and five leaves of absence, remains one of the glories of the company while no longer quite a part of it. Jerry Robbins still sometimes makes roles on her; Balanchine does not. Allegra bit into the apple and found that Eden was not all it had been cracked up to be. But she was not trained to earn a living outside the garden.

Many of the principals and soloists separate themselves from the company as much as they can; for others, it is the major influence on their lives. As a rule, those who take Balanchine's class regularly are more involved in the group life than dancers who study elsewhere. Any profession demands commitment; any work shapes the lives of those involved in it, but few require the dedication of dancing or are able so completely to sequester their practitioners. Within the company, dancers know their place and precedence, their duties and privileges; they are secure.

The security is created, in part, by the final years of a dancer's training and his induction into the company. Any form of indoctrination removes an individual from his environment and attempts to redefine his existence, to convince him of the magnitude of what he is about to do, to alter his values and convictions and convince him of the genius of his leaders. If the indoctrination takes, you get a successful collegian or cell member, monk or dancer. If it is less than completely persuasive, you get a revisionist, exemplified by those who left the Communist Party revolted by Stalinist excesses or those who dropped out of college revolted by "the system." Sometimes, you get a rebel.

ROBERT WEISS is the company's union deputy for soloists, and takes the job seriously. He is a Christian Scientist and devout. He is married to corps dancer Kathy Haigney and most of their friends are outside NYCB: "We know several musicians and a few dancers from other companies; we don't really have time to make friends. You know what the schedule is like." Ricky dresses flamboyantly, almost foppishly, in contrast to the conservative cuts of most of the other dancers. He takes class with Stanley Williams at The

School of American Ballet, not with Mr. B. He was a leading member of the anti-Berlin faction. Weiss resents having
his life set out for him like a prix fixe dinner, and he senses
the manipulation of dancers in which Balanchine, Kirstein
and Robbins indulge. (They do not see it as manipulation,
but they are of another generation.) Therefore, Ricky Weiss
has a problem.

He likes to dance, is good at it, and works incessantly to
improve. He enjoys performing the Balanchine repertory
and admires Balanchine's choreography. He cannot admire
the structure of Balanchine's company, nor that of any ballet company he knows. Like John Osborne's Jimmy Porter,
Ricky despises an outdated class system which nevertheless
molds him, and for which no adequate substitute has yet
been developed. Arrogant and angry, tense and intense,
dedicated, intelligent and aware, he would rebel against imposed authority in any environment, but loves a profession
founded on an authoritarian structure. Bound by his art to a
system which has no place for impatient men, Ricky Weiss
cannot even find a church door on which to nail his theses.

There are others who find this company, if not the best of all
possible worlds, at least as good as any they are likely to encounter.
They are work-ethic Americans who find support in the structure
of the company, who are proud of what they have accomplished
and see no reason to rebel, to nibble at apples or look out windows.
They build their lives around the demands of the company, finding
the existence satisfies their needs, and enjoy the benefits that ac-
crue. Even a soloist who knows there is little chance he ever will be
promoted to principal can partake of the prestige of NYCB, and
will be invited to perform leading roles with smaller, local companies. An NYCB dancer, after all, has made it; dancing here is like
playing for the New York Yankees back when the Yankees were
the best, most-hated team in baseball. Being even a utility infielder
for the Yankees could make a young man the darling of a small
home town. Whatever is wrong with the organization—and the satisfied team player sees very little wrong with it—there's nothing

wrong with HIM. He's had to work like hell, but he's made it, and made it big. The work brings satisfaction, the structure is no more rigid than that of an office job and, as Teena McConnell says, "It's a good life."

TEENA McCONNELL, at twenty-seven, has a family life, a social life and a ballet life. They don't conflict. She started going to dance class because her older sister was studying, "and I had to do everything my sister did. After a while, I found out that in ballet class, I could do things my sister couldn't." Her sister went on to a Ph.D. in Romance Languages and work as a teacher. Teena joined the company at sixteen and became a soloist three years later. She learned about her promotion almost by accident, from another dancer—"I had to go to Betty Cage to check on it and she said, 'Oh, yes. I tried to call you about it but you were out.' " It must have been a bit like learning from a distant cousin that you've just become engaged.

Tall, snake-slender Teena would seem to be a perfect vehicle for Balanchine's choreography, but he doesn't create much for her. She doesn't worry about it. She attends class regularly, in full street make-up, rehearses, performs, and goes home to New Jersey. After nine years, she still gets a feeling of exultation while dancing: "After a good performance, you have the same sense of satisfaction you get after a good meal."

She can't understand why people complain about conditions in the company. "When I first joined, there were fewer dancers in the company and we had to do even more than we do now. These kids complain about little things, but Carol Sumner and I remember how it used to be. I was thrilled to get any part; I was terribly disappointed to be left out of the corps, in any ballet. Now, kids say, 'Oh, this part isn't good enough. . . .' " It's almost as if Teena were saying, "When I was a girl we walked twenty miles through the snow to get to school and were glad of the chance." Friendly, chatty, confident Teena is the sort of young woman you might meet during coffee break at a good ad agency. She likes her job.

After all, dancing is a job. Some people can treat it that way, as something important, but not all-consuming. They rarely become stars, because they rarely are the kind of people who can let their inner animals pounce in public, but if they are not inspired, neither are they driven; and if they are not great, neither are they sloppy or inspid. They are the solid citizens of the company who can go home to enjoy their families, their friends, their hobbies. It really is no more unusual to find a comfortable dancer than a comfortable stockbroker; it just seems as if it is because dancing is a less ordinary profession and requires greater adjustments. If you can go home to New Jersey, as Teena does, it helps. If you can accept your limitations, that helps, too. But equally important is the acceptance of your powers.

In ballet, it is impossible to reach perfection, and constant striving for the impossible induces restlessness. At a certain point, a dancer may decide that reaching for the unattainable is a waste of effort, especially if he already is very good at something within the realm of possibility. The knowledge that you are good at something is soothing, especially in a profession which seems devoted to proving that neither you nor anybody else ever can be good enough, because the only "good enough" exists in the petrified perfection of idealized sketches. To achieve peace in ballet, it is not enough to be good; you must admit you are. Then, unless you have decided to be great, you can relax.

CONRAD LUDLOW is the man all the girls want to dance with; he is conceded to be the best partner in the company. Ludlow is the person you hope will be passing in the street should you ever fall out of a window, because the odds are that he will catch you before the bounce. During his San Francisco boyhood, Conny discovered that his hands knew the trick of catching and his body the feel of balance—not in ballet class, but in ball games. The transference was easy; his wide, strong hands seem to know exactly how to steady a partner; his stance is solid; he seems as calm as a pond. An immense ribcage, as solid as the belly of a cast-iron stove, bulges under the light blue of his one-piece practice suit. As a result, Conrad is not very flexible, but he is immensely strong. He dances the way he talks, open-eyed and directly—great thrilling leaps never have been his specialty; support and solidity are. His mind knows exactly what his body is doing. Conny can break a passage down into its component moves, examine it, repair it, reassemble it so that others can use it. Analytical, gentle, precise, he is a superb teacher—"I lift her with my hands, then bring her *here* with my forearms . . . Think of your leg, not your back. If you pick up that leg you'll go back anyway." And he rehearses the dancers he is teaching with the patience of a nest-building bird.

He doesn't take class any more: "At these kids' age, taking class every day is important. As you get older, you know you can't do one of those classes every day and dance, too. You know what your body needs, and you do that on your own." At his age, Conrad knows what he needs, what he can do, what makes him happy. He works, enjoys it and goes home to his family. Now, nearing the end of his performing career, he is preparing to choreograph and teach. The dance historians won't write Conny Ludlow down as a great performer, but he holds a place in his colleagues' minds as a masterful partner, a gifted teacher, a professional and a gentleman. He's the kind of man you miss when he isn't there.

Most of the company's dancers were made in America—born here, raised here, trained here. The American pace and American training has prepared them, at least to some extent, for the Balanchine style. The foreigners have adjustments to make. Their classes had another emphasis, their cities different architecture, the traffic in their childhood streets traveled in other rhythms. Jean-Pierre Bonnefous still dances with the forward-thrust head and shoulders of Parisian boulevards. In class, you notice that he wears different, softer shoes than the native dancers. He also concentrates more than they do on placement; he thinks less of speed and more of steps. The men who show the purest classroom technique in the company are the three who were trained in Europe: Jean-Pierre, Helgi Tomasson and Peter Martins.

PETER MARTINS is dream casting for *Apollo*. Big, blond, beautifully muscled, with strong Scandinavian features that show well from the stage, he is the life's ambition of every female American teenager. His Danish training and his talent combined to make him a brilliant technician. Only recently, though, has he begun to move his big body with the speed beloved of Mr. B., and until this season he projected little personality from the stage. Scandinavians are not the planet's most boisterous people, and Martins' blond calm, his brood-before-you-speak manner, were not, at first, suited to the Broadway brashness of Balanchine classicism.

Peter came to NYCB because every Apollo in Europe was injured or engaged, and John Taras needed one to dance with the company at the Edinburgh Festival. Peter, who had done the role once, was in Denmark, dining with Stanley Williams, when a call came from Taras asking him to audition. "I was eighteen and arrogant," Martins remembers. "I was getting known in Denmark and I wasn't about to audition like an unknown for anybody. Stanley convinced me to go. He said, 'Taras means Balanchine, too. Go.' I went." He did Apollo at Edinburgh. In 1967, he was called to New York to appear as a guest artist in *The Nutcracker*, and in 1970, already a principal dancer with The Royal Danish Ballet, he achieved equivalent status at NYCB.

Peter seems older than his twenty-five years, especially in the adolescent atmosphere of the company, He speaks quietly, defining his words by leaving little spaces between them for the thoughts to play in. When he gets angry, the spaces become wider. When he becomes jocular, the spaces close up. Martins can tell you everything that, from a European viewpoint, is wrong with the company—the frenetic pace of performance, the meddling in dancers' lives, the high injury rate that results from the first two. And yet, "You have to be here if you can. Balanchine is a genius, the greatest choreographer of our times. He won't last forever. You simply have to work with him while you can."

Beneath the reserve there is pent-up anger, dedication and ambition. It bursts out in high-speed driving, an antidote to the measured steps of beautifully studied technique, in raucous laughter and precise thinking. After a week of aloof silence, he will come up, quite unexpectedly, to say, "I'm sorry I haven't been able to talk much with you recently. Dancers have problems, too." And some of them, like Martins, are sensible enough to admit it, especially to themselves.

There is enough suppressed anger around the company to fuel several years of disarmament conferences. You can see it in the tense shoulders, and the pulled brows, set mouths and chins. You hear it in the small, timid voices. At times, it seems as if everyone in the theater is holding back an urge to murder everyone else. A Freudian might decide that all those years of strict classes were the equivalent of rigid toilet training, producing a company full of compulsives. The principals, of whom the most is expected, often show the most severe symptoms. Even on stage, many dancers seem to be operating under a compulsion not to let go. Even the happiest of them behave as if under orders never to relax or to show too much emotion. In a sense they are, since Mr. B. prefers his dancers to underplay feeling and allow the emotion to be conveyed by the choreography and the score. Violette Verdy says Balanchine has told her, on occasion, "to tone it down," and Kay Mazzo, after a moving *Swan Lake*, remarks, "But Mr. Balanchine doesn't like us to get too emotional or go too deep." Balanchine is right in seeking to avoid the heart-throbbing sentimentality of ballet blanc and not to drown the music in schmaltz, but if the company-as-superego restrains the dancers on stage as well as off it, when are they to let go? Hysterical excess certainly is to be avoided, but such a bursting is the result, not of freedom, but of repression until emotions force their way out whistling like a tea kettle. (It's the "nice, quiet man" who ends up an axe murderer.) There have been no axe murders at NYCB, but there is a good deal of holding in.

KAY MAZZO, of the long neck and bright eyes, the dark hair and delicate ears, would grace a cameo brooch. But sometimes, during class, you see her shaking her head with impatience, and the corners of her mouth pull down. On stage, her line is delicate and lovely, her head erect, her body neat and clear, and yet often she refuses to let herself be swept up by the music; somehow, she always needs to be in control. Kay has a voice that laughs sweetly, but when she gets angry, it refuses the challenge. Her lovely throat won't let the rage through—the vocal cords act as a check valve. It is as if she fears that if her temper ever broke through, all the surrounding land would be flooded.

Kay is from Chicago, the daughter of a paper company sales representative and a piano teacher. She started dance lessons at six because a doctor thought she needed the exercise. Her Yugoslav-Italian heritage blended into a beauty which has led her into the sidelines of modeling and TV commercials. This season, she did a one-minute spot for perfume—"I don't really dance or act in it; I just sort of float around."

You have to like Kay. A man would need to be cast in cement not to relish the smile, the toss of the head, the teasing of her jokes. But you keep wishing the safety-valve would stick, just once—that she'd start swearing and throwing things. You also wish she wouldn't drink *quite* so much Coca-Cola. She has a freezer-chest for it in her dressing room, and she only survived the tour of Eastern Europe because corps dancer Richard Dryden, another addict, carried a bottle of coke syrup in his luggage.

Kay is determined without being stony, but she has fought too many rounds with the windmills of perfection.

She still gets nervous when taking on a new role; she still drives herself to the point of injury. Every so often, when she trusts herself, she gives a performance that goes far beyond the steps and glows with feeling. Two days later, she is sweet, contained Kay again, but always, she wears delicacy and vulnerability like her little pink sweater, and always, she is someone you are happy to know.

There are rare people for whom the company is neither cloister, cage nor simple place of business, but the world as it should be. They are, in the old and lovely sense of the word, "innocent." They have never needed a moratorium, never been called beyond the garden. Whatever fears or hatred they have repressed never push as much as an inquiring snout out of the carrying case. Of all the people in the company, they are the ones who most belong here. They have no need to mentally measure out their existences—so many drops for class, so many for performance, so many for the world outside. The supreme example is Patricia Mc-Bride. Most performers come off stage after a variation straining for breath, muscles tensed to trembling, looking like the Indians after John Wayne has finished with them. Not Patty. She lets go her breath with a soft, happy "whoosh," like a disconnected vacuum cleaner, and is ready to start again.

PATRICIA McBRIDE is slender and angular, with sharp elbows and protruding knees, but her eyes are clear and soft. She is the delight of the audience, the darling of the company. Patty was outfitted with the small, high voice so popular among dancers, and never, never raises it. John Clifford assures you that Patty Pureheart has, indeed, lost her temper—"Three times in the past eight years, and we were so surprised we were frightened out of our minds." It's almost impossible to imagine: Patty doesn't get angry, any more than she gets tired.

She will come off stage, after a performance she didn't like, shaking her head in disappointment and saying, "Darn." She was working with an injured foot and, "All I

could think about was doing the steps. I don't like to dance
like that; it takes a long time, sometimes years, to really
learn a role and settle into it. I like to dance the music, the
meaning, the emotion—not just the steps."

On stage, she trusts the music; off, she trusts herself.
One of her friends says, "Patty knows about people. Somehow, she knows to whom she can talk, and whom she
should avoid." Perhaps her own candor serves her as a pocket
mirror; she can hold it up, glance in it and see what others
are doing.

Patty was born in Teaneck, N.J., which probably is the
best thing that ever happened to the place. Karinska often
dresses her in a soft shade that has become known to af-
ficionados as "Patty McBride pink," and the ballerina
frequently wears pink to rehearsal, too; she knows what
suits her. Her fiancé, Jean-Pierre Bonnefous, suits her very
well. They both seem beautifully uncomplicated people
who can enjoy whatever they happen to be doing. Watching
them on stage together, sparkling like butterflies, one of the
corps girls remarks, "I'll bet they're like that at home,
too—I can just imagine them skipping across the living
room and dancing as they go to the laundromat." You almost can believe it.

At thirteen, Patty won a scholarship to The School of
American Ballet. By a delightful irony, she was seen in class
by Tamara Geva, who spent five years as Mrs. George
Balanchine long before Patty was born, and was invited by
her to dance in an off-Broadway play. Before the show
could open, she was invited to dance as an apprentice in
Symphony in C by Mr. George Balanchine. She became an
NYCB soloist at seventeen; at eighteen, she was a principal.

A friend remarked that "Patty and Jean-Pierre's children
won't win any Nobel Prizes for physics—they're not exactly
intellectuals." They aren't, but they're not stupid, either.
Patty doesn't have the probing intelligence of Allegra Kent
or Violette Verdy, nor the guts drive of Melissa Hayden.
Instead, she has an intelligence that refuses to be confined in

her head but flows through her body as well, combined with that peculiar sensitivity the French call "l'intelligence du coeur." If there are snakes in the garden, Patty simply will refuse to talk with them. Her mind works very nicely, thank you, but it works in concert with the rest of her. She thinks what she does what she feels, all-at-once. It is the secret of her dancing.

Whenever she is on stage, the wings of the theater are crowded, and the other performers are not there only to be dazzled by her technique. They are there to see Patty, being whatever the music asks her to be at the moment. They are there to see Patty being herself, because, on stage or off, she is gifted with the peculiar ability to make other people happy.

8

Jerry

It is rightly maintained, among New York's theater-and-dance-watching contingent, that Jerome Robbins is a genius. It is maintained wrongly, among members of NYCB, that Jerome Robbins is a son-of-a-bitch. A few souls in the company like Jerry, or admire him, or at least claim to understand him, but as a general rule the best way to start an argument at the New York State Theater is to say something nice about Robbins.

Management personnel remark that "Jerry is difficult." The dancers are less inhibited; some simply call him a bastard. The upstairs crowd, trotting out charts to prove it, complain that Jerry costs the company money: He calls the dancers for hour after hour of overtime; he calls the crew for technical rehearsals; he postpones openings; he changes his plans frequently; he is secretive when he is not being uncertain. The dancers' indictment charges the choreographer with screaming and sarcasm; with limiting their artistic freedom, and, worse, with being insufficiently like Balanchine. Ask any dancer whether he would rather work for Balanchine or for Jerry—it's Mr. B. every time. "He gives us a chance to work some things out for ourselves, to decide how we want to do it," they say. "With Jerry, everything is set up beforehand."

The joke of it is that audiences who dislike Balanchine's ballets because they are "too cold and calculated, too inhuman," love Rob-

bins' because "they have real emotion, they have more freedom."
Critics have been known to write that Jerry's ballets always are better danced than Mr. B's, that the dancers obviously love to work
for him. Su-u-ure they do. Even performers who say their lives are
being manipulated by Mr. B. prefer that to being manipulated by
Jerry—the older man does it with more finesse.

Jerry's ballets take so much of the company's time, work and
money and receive so much publicity that a dancers' joke—"So old
Clive Barnes repeated it back to me," purrs Delia Peters—insists
that if Jerry ever retires from the company, Mr. Balanchine will
take over. A lot of outsiders are convinced that if Balanchine
should die (he never will retire), Jerry would be his most appropriate successor. And dancers swear that if Jerry takes over the company, they'll leave: "I would never work for him . . . I'd quit the
next day . . . If Jerry took over the company, he'd have to hire a
new company." I doubt that.

Robbins can give parties after his premieres; he can offer medical advice and dancing advice; he even can give the shirt off his
back. (Richard Dryden once admired one of Robbins' purple shirts;
a few days later he was summoned to Jerry's office. "I didn't know
what he wanted," the dancer says. "I figured he was ready to
scream or to fire me or something. He just chatted for a while, then
reached into his desk and said, 'You liked this, so you may as well
have it,' and gave me the shirt.") He can give young dancers their
first big roles; he can help older ones get back into shape. None of
it helps. Jerry is the resident monster.

Even his smile doesn't help. Jerry has quite a good smile. It
flashes on like a neon tavern sign, showing clean white teeth above
his clean white beard. (That beard is so dazzling you get the feeling
he washes it nightly in one of those miracle washday products.)
He stands downstage, in his purple shirt and white tennis shoes,
his gleaming beard and ripe tan (even the top of his balding head is
the color of morning toast), in an erect, square stance, looking like a
successful high school athletic coach. He's developing a slight
belly, but the body still is in damn good shape, especially for someone who began his dancing career back in 1937. He's still strong,
still taut, still ready to move with the ball.

Balanchine claps his hands to stop a rehearsal. Jerry claps his hands and whistles. As he issues directions, a tanned forefinger flicks out like a switchblade. "Now, dancers, let's take it from the entrance. . . . Dancers, I'm going to separate you more . . . Dancers, do you have enough time or do you want me to move you in?" He calls them "dancers" the way the coach calls his group "men" or "team." He says, "Do you want me to move you in?" not, "Do you want to move in?" It's quite certain who calls the signals around here. He stands on the balls of his feet, ordaining with his finger, precisely enunciating instructions in his slightly-tense-at-the-throat voice. All he needs to complete the image is a whistle worn around his neck on a lanyard.

You have to admit, the coach brings in winners. The first ballet he choreographed, *Fancy Free*, was made in 1944 and still is a send-'em-home happy number for American Ballet Theater. Since then, he's compiled quite a record—*Les Noces, Moves, The Cage, Afternoon of a Faun*, lots of them. He's not as prolific a choreographer as Balanchine, nor as innovative. Jerry's genius consists less in stating an idea for the first time than in making a definitive refinement of that statement. Balanchine transplanted the tradition of Russian classical ballet to the American theater and trained it into new shapes. Robbins grafted to it the tradition of Broadway. Without Balanchine, there would have been no Robbins; without Robbins, there would have been no *West Side Story*, as we knew it, no *Dances at a Gathering*, no long list of works that other artists derived from his, and we all would be the poorer.

West Side Story, as produced on Broadway, was the textbook example of how dance and dramatic direction should be integrated, and blended with the other elements of a play, in a musical. When that mambo scene blew across the stage like a hurricane, the audience knew that something major was happening up there and that the American musical would have to be a little different from then on. It was right for the characters, right for the music, right for the era. Everything was right about *West Side Story*—score, book, lyrics, design, performances—but it was Jerry Robbins who "put the pieces together," and he put every one in the right place.

Dances at a Gathering was made in 1969, and by now the dancers are sick of it. They'd love to have it taken out of the repertory for a while. But *Dances* stays in the subscription brochures because it keeps bringing people into the theater. It was Robbins' first ballet for NYCB after ten years away; it may have been his most important ballet ever. In *Dances*, Jerry had no lyrics, no book, no dialogue—all he needed was Chopin, dancers and his imagination. Spectators left the theater in tears after the first performance, critics left in wonder. Something major had happened up there, and American ballet would have to be a little different from now on. *Dances* is pure ballet, but it also is theater of a kind recognizable to people who don't expect to find theater in a ballet house.

There are story ballets, such as *Sleeping Beauty*, *Petrouchka* and *A Midsummer Night's Dream*. There are "pure" ballets, such as *Agon*, *Symphony in C* and Ashton's *Symphonic Variations*. *Dances at a Gathering* is a plotless ballet which delineates too many emotional events to be termed "pure" or "abstract." You watch the people on stage walking, flirting, quarreling; although you do not know who they are, you know what they are feeling. The stage is bare, but you know the dance is set outdoors—the lighting and choreography tell you that—and it is all you need to know. A pianist on a platform stage right sends Chopin floating over your head and you become enveloped by the music, by the beauty of the steps and by a rich aroma of emotion.

At the beginning of the ballet, a young man in brown enters from stage left and wanders slowly onto the stage, sensing the country weather with his body. He arrives upstage and raises his arm, sweeping it through air that somehow begins to seem autumnal. With that armsweep, he transforms the stage into an open place. Near the end of the ballet, the same man touches his palm to the ground and it is earth, not stage, that meets his hand. Joe Eula's delicate costumes and Jerry's choreography are somehow closer to our time than to Chopin's, yet the longing romanticism of the music dominates the mood of the ballet.

There are no complete characterizations and no classical plot in *Dances*, but the essence of the work is theatrical. All the sentimental boy-girl bilge of Broadway, all the hopes and aches and yearning of Hollywood are present, but they have been distilled and refined, made what they always should have been and almost never are. The theatrical techniques make *Dances* léss remote than ballets such as *Liebeslieder Walzer*, which evoke less tangible emotions. *Dances* is important, not because it shows the emotional interplay between people, but because of the theatrical, American way in which the interplay is defined.

The music may be Polish, but the sentiment was made in the U.S.A. Only Americans have that particular longing for the love-but-light-on-the-sex-please romanticism of the fête champêtre. (When Britain's Royal Ballet does the work, it looks as if it should be called, *Dances at a Garden Party*.) *Dances at a Gathering* is the unacknowledged American Dream, created with techniques of the American theater, and it is a tribute to Jerry's genius that the ballet never lapses from American sentiment into American sentimentality.

NYCB dancers point out that *Dances at a Gathering* is not a seminal work: "Mr. B. used the same idea in *Liebeslieder*." They tell you it is not real; it is dishonest or "contrived . . . You feel something because Jerry planned it out. Every one of those gestures, every heart-breaking exit, the end of every section, is calculated." Sure it's calculated. And it works. The first time I saw *Dances*, I cried. I knew just what the choreographer was doing, what theatrical devices, what movement signals—just like the mime signals in the old *Swan Lake* but more subtle—he was using to make me cry, but the tears came anyway. It is generally maintained that *Dances at a Gathering* is a masterpiece. Nearly everyone says so, except the dancers who gather to do it.

The performers dislike the ballet because they've done it for too many years. Perhaps they've worried through too many tough rehearsals with Jerry. (Dancers who were in the original cast have never quite gotten over those rehearsals, and replacements still find the process difficult.) Perhaps they cannot be moved by it because they've seen the moves being drawn for them, like pass patterns on a blackboard. But to a great extent, they don't like *Dances* because they don't like Jerry.

The Goldberg Variations is another justly lauded example of Jerry's recent style, but one of the soloists shrugs and says, "It really isn't that good. It's not honest enough. Bach is deeper than Robbins, and that's all there is to it." The company rehearsed *Goldberg* for nearly two years before its New York debut. Robbins generally works slowly and a case of hepatitis delayed him further—and the ballet is ninety minutes long and difficult. It is easy to grow tired of a work you are performing. Gordon Boelzner, who was the original rehearsal and performance pianist, claims to have played *The Goldberg Variations* more frequently than anybody since Goldberg. No matter how beautiful the music or how satisfying the steps, there comes a time when dancers lose interest.

During this spring, 1973, season, Robbins has rehearsed three new ballets, allowing three times as many people to dislike him. By now, the *Beethoven pas de deux* has been shown at the gala and spirited off to Spoleto and the Tchaikowsky waltzes have been abandoned. The Prokofieff ballet, *An Evening's Waltzes,* is being polished for performance. It is nearly impossible for an outsider to watch Jerry rehearse in the studio. Like many theatrical directors, he finds he cannot work well with visitors present, but, occasionally, an observer can slip in to see his sessions on stage.

The choreographer stands front stage in his coach posture, studying his cast. He seems more detached than Balanchine, more distant from his work. The gray expanse of stage floor adds to the sensation of being in a gymnasium. Outside, it is gray, too, and the dancers look tired. The season is only a third over; they feel it has been going on forever. Their bodies are trim, now, the layers of fat they brought to the early classes and rehearsals have been boiled off, but skin is pulling tight over the bones of their faces and injuries happen more frequently than they should.

Jerry stops the dance (clap hands, whistle) to talk with Robert Irving, who is in his place near the pianist, beating time with cat-stroking gestures. Most of the discussion is based on Robbins' desire to slow the music for this segment—"I want to get more difference between the waltzes." The score is made of five, Prokofieff's "Suite of Waltzes," Opus 110. For each, Jerry has choreographed a different mood and texture. The First Waltz is danced by a corps; the Second and Fourth (the former more romantic, the latter more dramatic) are led by principals backed by an ensemble, the Third Waltz is a pas de deux and the final dance involves the entire cast. Obviously, differentiation of tempi is important, especially since to many who will be in the audience, a waltz is a waltz is a waltz.

Jerry turns to the dancers again, positioning them exactly on the gray of the daytime stage. "Dancers, I want to separate you more," the finger knifes out, "move further right. Further. Good." Balanchine might have said, "Move that way a little," but Jerry aligns the dancers as he might focus a camera, moving them until two spots, the one in his mind and the one on the stage floor, overlap. He doesn't walk through the maze of his own ballet as Balanchine does, but stands in front, not changing his viewpoint until he has seen a section through. Then, after breaking in (clap, whistle, "Dancers"), he strides upstage to demonstrate a step. The demonstration is thorough; he knows exactly what he wants. "Don't twiddle," he tells the corps. "Step into the ground so we get long, deep steps, not twiddling around." He shows what he means by "long, deep steps," and the knees of his white trousers bend to creases and he leans his weight into the floor.

Then he walks briskly back to front-and-center to watch. They're still not bending their knees enough. Clap, whistle, stride in, show it, stride back, watch again. He can rehearse the same short sequence for fifteen minutes, demonstrating, explaining, snapping, soothing, until it is right. Watching Balanchine, you get accustomed to spur-of-the-minute changes in the ballet. Robbins' work appears more pre-planned. From time to time, you catch him off in a corner before rehearsal, trying steps on himself. Once in rehearsal, though, he does not seem to be using an analytical, graph paper mind. He dislikes talking about theory: "You do what you have to do, and that's it." He has an image in his head and in his body and he works the dancers until the picture on stage duplicates it.

A few days later, there is a dress rehearsal of *Pulcinella*, which Balanchine and Robbins co-choreographed for last year's Stravinsky Festival. As a rule, except for new ballets, there are no dress rehearsals at NYCB. They take too much time and cost too much money. *Pulcinella*, though, is complicated, requiring sets and props and at least a million children dressed as commedia dell'arte figures. The dancers are certain the dress rehearsal is Jerry's idea: "He tries to hold one whenever he can."

Jerry sits with Ronnie Bates in the center of the orchestra behind the communications board. He holds a small microphone through which he instructs the dancers. "Hold it, hold it!"—the amplification accentuates the bark in his voice. Somebody has missed an entrance. Then, more calmly, "Where are the other Pulcinellas, please?" David Richardson rounds up the children and gets them into place. David is a corps dancer who serves as ballet master in charge of children. "All right," says Jerry. "Now stay awake, stay awake."

Balanchine comes in and takes the seat next to Robbins, folds his hands, tilts his chin up and leans back to watch. Jerry bends toward the stage manager to whisper, "When it gets this dark on stage, Eddie's light should be down a little, too," Edward Villella, dancing the title role, is picked out by a follow-spot. Ronny relays the instruction to the operator in the booth—"A little less on Eddie"—and the circle around the bobbing dancer dims, a halo with its battery running down. Robbins is as intensely concerned with the lighting and production of his ballets as he is with the execution of the steps. It seems to be a heritage from his Broadway work, similar to his insistence that dancers do not depart even fractionally from his choreography in any performance of his ballets. Actors' Equity Association requires that artists "maintain the directed performance"; Jerry expects every finger flick to be exactly the same every night.

The morning after a performance of *Dances at a Gathering*, he accosted Ricky Weiss and held up three fingers, "You made three mistakes," and unfolded them in order. Unfortunately, Weiss remarked, Robbins has changed passages of *Dances* several times. Ricky was using the most recent incarnation, having forgotten that the choreographer had discarded it and returned to an earlier version. This constant alteration of steps is one of the things that makes Jerry the local bad guy. He will redesign a sequence several times in one season. ("You have to come to *Watermill* tonight," one of the corps men says. "You'll want to see what he cuts this time.

Last night he took out the potato pickers.") Balanchine changes ballets, too, "but not at every performance," the dancers tell you. "You get a chance to remember things once you learn them. Jerry changes from one performance to the next and it's confusing. You don't remember which is the right way."

Jerry does not change ballets to confuse dancers. He changes them because he is not satisfied with his own work, and because he needs every moment of every dance to be perfect. Even more than the dancers, he is driven in pursuit of the ideal; consequently, he is even more insecure. ("You have to work harder than that," says Mr. B. in class. "Otherwise, how can you dance in Jerry's ballets? You know he's such a perfectionist. My ballets don't matter—mine are a mess.") When Balanchine is dissatisfied with one of his ballets, he rechoreographs at leisure. If a dancer departs slightly from pattern, he accepts it as part of the nature of the art. Jerry must make it right this minute, so it will be ready for tonight's audience. During a *Watermill* rehearsal he warns Jean-Pierre Frohlich, "Don't raise the kite so high—otherwise, we'll have another rehearsal for it."

"He thinks he's still on Broadway," one of the technicians whispers. "Balanchine has confidence, so he doesn't care. Jerry is insecure, so he keeps changing ballets and calling dress rehearsals."

In many ways, Jerry does work as if he were on Broadway, which is part of the problem. The dancers aren't used to it. He dictates notes to an assistant as a theatrical director does; he insists that performers hold tightly to the "script" of a ballet; he "blocks" his dances the way a director sets the movement for a stage play. He even suggests motivation to the dancers as if they were actors. The dancers respond as people usually do when asked to do something in an unaccustomed manner; they resent it.

If Balanchine needs to direct a dancer, he will say something quite simple, "You chase her because you think she is the other girl." Robbins, rehearsing *The Concert*, a very funny ballet about listeners fantasizing their way through a Chopin recital, is explicit. One sequence demonstrates that people with umbrellas tend to look, not at the weather, but at other people with umbrellas.

Dancers with open umbrellas meet dancers with umbrellas closed, and lower theirs. They meet other dancers with open umbrellas, and unfurl again. By the end of the sequence, all are huddled under one bumbershoot and discover that it isn't raining. Before the season's first performance of *The Concert*, Jerry rehearses the scene again and again. "I hate rehearsing this scene at least as much as you do," he tells the cast. "I've done it hundreds of times and I'm bored with it. But we'll have to keep rehearsing until we get it right."

Robbins admits that he hates reviving his old ballets, because he finds himself making the same corrections, in the same places that he did ten years ago. "Different dancers," he says, "the same mistakes."

He turns to a girl new to *The Concert*. "Don't walk out there like a dancer. *Look* at the other girl. *See* her. Is her umbrella up or down? Is it raining? Right. That's all the decision I need. The only thing you have to do in this ballet is to look and react like normal people." They try again, and she looks at the other girl. Jerry's methods may not be culled from a course in personnel management, but they work. He picks up the "don't walk out there like a dancer," theme again. "Give yourself someplace to go. It's a rainy day, like yesterday, and you've been shopping at Saks and you're going home." Any first-year acting student knows enough to give himself a sense of direction. Most NYCB dancers don't. It is hardly their fault; they are not trained to be actors. Unfortunately, Jerry needs them to be actors. Even more unfortunately, his aggressive insistence frightens younger dancers and antagonizes older ones.

He can be harsh and crude. At another *Concert* rehearsal, he snapped at doll-neat Elise Flagg, "You look like a housewife. You think you're cute, but you're not. You think you're a dancer, but you're not." Quite probably, Jerry wanted an emotional reaction from Elise and was using a directorial approach to get it. There are plenty of stories about Broadway and Hollywood directors who get wonderful performances from actors by screaming at them, and even slapping them. Some of the actors don't object because they need the work, they're masochists, or they think it's all part of the game. Dancers, not having been raised to this particular form of theatrical psychology, assume it's all part of Jerry.

The joke of it is, Jerry cares. He wants very much to be liked, and is afraid somebody might notice, so his subconscious or whatever bristles out his quills. (Porcupines, by the way, also are shy.) But he does care. Dancers remember that a few years ago, Sally Leland was letting herself get badly out of shape. Everyone noticed; nobody did much about it—except Jerry. "Every time he saw Sally," the kids recall, "he would poke at her and say, 'You're fat! Do something about yourself. You're fat, you're fat.'" Hardly the most tactful way to deal with the problem, but Jerry cared, and Sally lost weight.

But he cares about his ballets too, and that can be hard on dancers. During the original rehearsals of *Dances*, the performers say he drove many of them nearly to tears, having all the performers learn all the roles and then indulging in unflattering comparisons: "Patty, why can't you do that like Allegra? . . . . Allegra, why don't you do that like Violette?" and so on. Part of the problem was that he didn't make up his mind—at least he didn't let the dancers know— who was going to dance which part until a few days before performance.

Delia Peters, who has worked with Robbins and is perceptive enough to have survived, is convinced that many of his gaucheries are intentional. "He wants you to do something a certain way, and you can't do it. So he yells and screams and gets sarcastic until he beats you down and breaks you open. Then, when he's emptied you out, you can do what he wanted you to do in the first place. When I did The Wife in *The Concert*, I couldn't get angry enough. So Jerry worked on me until I got angry at him. The next day, he was charming."

The usual advice given to anyone about to deal with Jerry is, "Don't fight back. He may attack you, but he has to know you won't attack him. In his own way, he's very shy. He's insecure." Jerry is a private person. He hedges himself in with curtness and precision as Mr. B. does with *politesse*. His control over his dancers is more overt than Balanchine's and therefore seems less remote and more available for resentment. Yet people never complain about Robbins, as they do about Balanchine, that he is trying to run their lives. It is the means, not the ends, that rankles.

The two ballet masters did not conspire to create a God-Satan, buddy-cop-touch-cop dialectic. It just worked out that way, and the tension between their methods adds to the curious feeling of isolation, of a world-within-a-world, that pervades the theater. The two men have been cast in the roles of Good and Evil: If you are a young corps dancer, you worship Balanchine and refute Robbins, and it never occurs to you that both of them are human.

In some ways, Jerry is more human than George. Both appear to work by the dancers-are-difficult-children system and neither is a permissive parent, but in a strange way, Robbins gives his charges more credit for potential than does Balanchine. Mr. B. apparently decided long ago that nothing in this world is perfect and that his ballets probably never will be performed exactly as he would have them—dancers have limitations and there is nothing to be done about it. On the other hand, Jerry seems to have decided that, limited or not, his pupils can and will do his ballets perfectly, even if he has to beat them black and blue. His defense against insecurity is a belief in perfectibility, a search like Faust's for the moment to which he can say, "Stay, thou art fair." It seems that unlike most of us, he cannot bring himself to say, "Thou mightst as well stay, thou art fair as thou art going to get."

Rouben Ter-Arutunian, who was given several months to design *Cortège*, had about two weeks in which to do the costumes for *An Evening's Waltzes*. Part of the difficulty was Jerry's propensity for working on several projects at once. Nobody, including Jerry, was certain which ballet would be offered as the company's scheduled "New Jerome Robbins Ballet." It was very close to gala night before the decision was made, and Rouben could not submit sketches for the Prokofieff work without knowing for certain which ballet he was dressing. This gave Matera's costume shop about two weeks in which to construct the clothes.

It would have been less costly to have the costumes made at Karinska's, since that establishment is owned by NYCB, but Karinska was occupied with the costumes for *Cortège*. "Besides," it was explained, "Karinska is a very old woman—over eighty. You

can't subject her to working with Jerry and his constant changes."
The costumes for *An Evening's Waltzes* are long, floating Empire
gowns for the women and fitted jackets and tights for the men.
Originally, Rouben prepared three basic designs with color repeats, and Jerry approved. Then, the choreographer decided on
different colors for each pair of dancers, an idea which helped double the costume bill for the ballet.

On the afternoon of the gala, while Jerry is rehearsing *Waltzes*
on stage, Rouben brings the men's jackets to the theater. The stage
lights are turned up full as the men return from the corridor where
Mme. Matera and her assistants have been helping them into the
sleek, shiny tops. Over their shoulders, duller material is draped
like scraggly capes, to show how the tights, when made, will complement the jackets. The dancers move carefully; the costumes are
merely basted, not fully constructed. Jerry looks them over from
the audience, then from the stage, then from a few feet away.
Tracy Bennett has been outfitted in a gray-blue fabric, highly satu-
rated in color. "It stands out more than all the others," Jerry decides. "It will have to be changed." The men peel off their costumes, the jackets go back to the shop.

They return to the theater less than a week later, on Tuesday,
May 22, two days before the premier of *Waltzes*. This time, the
women's costumes also are ready. Again there is a halt in rehearsal,
everybody changes, and as the dancers come back to the stage,
Jerry hands around black domino masks to those in the Fourth
Waltz. Colleen Neary comes on in her Fourth Waltz gown and
Jerry snatches at the material. "No net," he raps at Mme. Matera.
"I told you no net. I was there, and I said no net." Colleen acts as a
mannequin as Jerry, Rouben and Matera inspect her costume like
hypochondriacs with a new symptom. They decide to eliminate a
front panel from the gown as well as the overlay of net, to make it
more simple. Well, the girls do look as if they'd just stepped out of
Bloomingdale's lingerie department. The costumes go back to the
shop again.

During the course of the season, the costumes for *Waltzes* will
undergo several alterations. The ballet will open, in two days, with
the men dressed in tights that match their tops. During the season,

they will wear black tights, gray tights, and end up again in matching ones. All the changes, of course, will be called for by Jerry, who is searching for the closest possible approach to the moment which is fair.

At this moment, though, the costumes are not his most serious concern. During the Sunday matinee, Helgi Tomasson danced *Tarantella* and wrenched his back during the spins. The Third Waltz of *An Evening's Waltzes,* the virtuoso display, the most showy, dashing, dynamic section of the ballet, filled with spins and abrupt lifts, was made on Helgi and Gelsey Kirkland. A choreographer doesn't expect to keep the same cast for the life of his ballet, but he hopes the opening-night audience will see the work with the dancers on whom he made it. The audience is supposed to see *Waltzes* two days from now, on May 24.

Jerry conducts his rehearsal, passing over the Third Waltz. He has been trying to be nice during recent rehearsals. Now, he's tense and playing coach again, calling the performers "Dancers" at every opportunity, flicking his pointing finger even more sharply than usual. "Dancers, can we do that again—so you don't bump into one another." The corps kids say, "Jerry is so subtle." He works the ballet through, scratching at mistakes like a dog trying to rid himself of fleas. "Is it just because we haven't rehearsed this for a while" (they did it Friday) "or are you confused? Do you want me to straighten it out for you?" (They don't.) "O.K. It's the first time on stage with lights."

The whirling ballroom scenes, the crosses and chance meetings, begin to sort themselves out. Jerry whispers about the lighting with Ronnie Bates, then climbs to the stage for work with the corps. The stage is sown with waltzing couples when Robbins does his clap, whistle routine. "It's not that you're wrong," he tells a pair of dancers. "You're different. You're not doing it with the others." There is no sarcasm in his voice; he is trying to be gentle. He simply has an instinct for picking words that sandpaper people. Somewhere, walled up inside that fortress of a superego, under the armor and the insecurities, is a thoughtful, tender man. But every time he shows his face, the rest of Jerry stomps on it. And it is very hard for the dancers to react to the thoughtful, tender man when all they get to see is the stomping perfectionist.

Stagehands set electric fans in the wings to direct air currents through the upstage drapes and the women's gowns. "This is going to be another *Watermill*," the dancers grumble. "We'll all end up catching colds." Jerry used off-stage fans in *Watermill* to provide atmospheric breezes. It looks fine from the audience, but everyone in the cast is certain he will end up with pneumonia—sweat and atmospheric breezes don't mix.

While the fans and lights are being arranged, the dancers get a short break. Jerry recalls them from the wings; "Would you come on stage and do it from the à la secondes? It's a light cue, so I have to ask you to do that." His voice is nakedly apologetic; he knows they are tired. He's leaning into his orchestra seat as if he is more than a bit worn out himself. After the light cue, and another break, they rehearse the Second Waltz, which is led by Patricia McBride and Jean-Pierre Bonnefous and ends in a spectacular lift-and-carry. Jerry, watching from the center of the theater, dictates a note to Carole Deschamps, an administrative assistant who has been detached for special duty as Jerry's aide-de-camp: "Check with Patty—I think her arms are wrong." Afterwards, he gives the whole Second Waltz team an arms drill, counting cadence for them. His voice has the fuzziness that comes with overwork. Dancers suffer most of the physical exertion of a rehearsal, but they get breaks during which they can sit off stage and relax. The choreographer pins his attention to every moment of dancing, and when not working with the performers, he is discussing costumes or setting lights. It gets to you. Besides, Jerry has had to conduct this rehearsal while considering a successor to Helgi for the Third Waltz. He must choose a dancer, teach him the steps and give him enough rehearsal to find his way into the music and form a compatible partnership with Gelsey Kirkland. He has about fifty-four hours in which to do it—less, actually, since even dancers and Jerry have to sleep.

Wednesday morning, while Mr. B. teaches class, John Clifford and Ricky Weiss work in the practice room with Helgi and choreologist Jurg Lanzrein, learning the Third Waltz. Helgi, in street clothes, is well enough to mark the steps for Ricky and John, but it's obvious that he won't be able to dance tomorrow night. A wrenched back needs time to heal.

Helgi isn't the only one missing from the lineup. If NYCB combined with the New York Mets, who also have been posting long injury lists this season, according to the newspapers, the two clubs might be able to field one healthy team. Last week, Gelsey Kirkland hurt her foot, leaving Elise Flagg to do her role in *Brahms-Schönberg Quartet* and Susan Hendl—who is working with a pulled tendon—to substitute in *Scherzo Fantastique*. Luckily, Gelsey was well enough to at least walk through some *Waltzes* rehearsals and by last night, she was back dancing *Scherzo Fantastique* to bravos. But Peter Martins, who had been dancing despite a pinched nerve, has had to give in for a while; he can't move his left arm. Edward Villella pulled a leg muscle. Silk-blond Deborah Flomine is out. Marilee Stiles is out. Debbie Koolish still is out. Karin von Aroldingen slipped and fell during a performance of *Cortège*, and Kay Mazzo slipped and fell during *Serenade*. Neither was hurt, but falls are symptoms of the tension that leads to injuries. Saturday, one day before Helgi wrenched his back, Jacques d'Amboise wrecked a knee cartilege and won't be able to dance for quite some time. John Clifford learned *Cortège* in time to do it at the Sunday matinee.

Now John and Ricky Weiss are learning Helgi's role in *Waltzes*. Jerry spoke to both dancers last night, but gave no indication as to which of them would perform. Most of the company is betting on Ricky, who has done more work with Jerry than John has. Besides, Johnny has had to stand in for Eddie Villella and for Jacques. He and Ricky, though, are convinced that, on the basis of the choreographer's past record, "Jerry won't decide until five minutes before the performance."

By the time class is over, both men are on their way down to the stage, where Jerry is rehearsing. He looks as tense as the dancers; even his beard seems less soft than usual. This is an orchestra rehearsal, and Robert Irving calls instructions to the musicians while Jerry talks to the dancers. They are trying to coordinate their tempi, and Jerry insists the conductor is taking it too slowly. They try again, and this time it is Robert who interrupts. "Not so rough, smooooth it," he instructs the orchestra. "I don't want those notes detached at all. Slur it. Let's slur it, shall we? Both bars." His beautifully buttered British speech makes a properly musical con-

trast with Jerry's stacatto style. The choreographer also is giving
notes, reading from a pad in true theater-director fashion. "The
three couples in the back who are walking. Don't. Just stand still."
He has allowed the company an uninterrupted run-through of the
First Waltz, noting errors on his pad instead of stopping the rehearsal to correct them. Now, while Robert drills the orchestra, he
makes his comments. He looks down at the pad, then up at the
dancers. "Teena and Danny, you get separated from the group
here. You know where I mean? Right." He doesn't take time now
to have the dancers repeat troublesome passages; he must assume
they will remember his notes at the next rehearsal.

The dancers still are complaining that the music is too slow. An
overly quick pace makes dancers scurry and causes them to lose
their line, but a too slow tempo can cause even more serious difficulties. The women have to balance too long on pointe and take a
chance of slipping; the men must jump higher and further so as to
land on the proper beat; stretches turn into sessions on the rack.

During the Second Waltz, Jerry stands in the first row, directly
behind the podium, so he can watch the dancers while murmuring
instructions into the conductor's ear. Then he runs around the
orchestra pit and climbs up to the stage with his pad, slipping on
his glasses to read. "Jean-Pierre, on that step," (he does it quickly
but very beautifully—what a dancer he must have been) "you have
to keep looking at Patty; you seem to forget her." He asks the principal couple if they were comfortable with the tempo for their
duet. Patty and Jean-Pierre think it was a touch too fast. So does
Jerry. So does Robert. No problem.

Now to the Third Waltz. It is going to be John Clifford after
all. Johnny certainly is a quick study; it has made him the company
workhorse this season. If we do merge with the Mets, he'll be utility infielder. Recently, he told Helgi, "I hate substituting for you. I
don't mind doing it for the others so much, but you're so damned
good." It's true, Helgi is damned good, and this pas de deux was
made for his neat body, impeccable technique and cool style. John
already has learned the steps, now he has to take on the manner.
He and Gelsey try the whirling athletics of the waltz, getting accustomed to one another's bodies. You can see that John is going to

be more exuberant but less polished than Helgi would have been, but that the waltz will look good. Gelsey is small enough for him to balance comfortably and he is, as Violette pointed out, an intelligent partner. Even on this short acquaintance with the steps, he catches his slim ballerina neatly and guides her with assurance. He is putting more effort into the steps than he should, though, and it distorts his line. A good dancer does not make steps look either difficult or easy; he makes them look as if there were nothing else he logically could be doing at that moment. Right now, John's dancing allows you to notice that the steps are hard.

He and Gelsey stop and breathe deeply for a few seconds—the duet is very fast—then begin again. This time, they move together more comfortably, and the lines in Jerry's forehead begin to smooth out. As the dance goes on, his eyes start to relax, too. The second time through, John and Gelsey do very well indeed. Despite the concentration that narrows her face, Gelsey is almost as lovely to watch in rehearsal as in performance. Her slim legs taper down from narrow hips to fully stretched feet; they beat like twin metronomes. Her spine is arrogant as an exclamation point, her neck is ungiving, her head high, but the hazy tumble of red hair softens the image. She rehearses with conviction, attacking each step and showing it who's boss, controlling her muscles so that they know, too. She is so young and light-boned that her determination is attractive—like that of a young animal insistent on learning to forage for itself.

Jerry is on stage, talking to John. "The second time you danced, it was lovely, because it was light and relaxed. The first time, it was a bit too heavy." John keeps his face blank. Jerry has just given him a compliment (and Jerry, they tell you, almost never gives compliments) as well as an astute observation, but the tension in the choreographer's voice and his habitual precision of speech made the words cut like a judicial reprimand. Everybody up here is too tense; even "good morning" would be interpreted as a threat.

Now they begin to take the waltz apart, like a soldier cleaning his rifle, to oil and polish each piece. The rest of the cast watches from the wings, quietly. Even at an ordinary rehearsal, Jerry does not permit casual conversation, and we are too close to opening night for this to be an ordinary rehearsal. John and Gelsey repeat steps and sequences, learning to sense one another's bodies. Jerry's comments, despite that precise, dry tone, are gentle and encouraging. John lifts Gelsey and sets her down on half-toe, then half-carries her across the stage as her foot skitters over the floor like a flat stone skipping a pond, to end in a glide. They start to repeat the step, but Gelsey's foot, instead of sliding over the stage, crashes into it like a kamikaze pilot into an aircraft carrier. A second later she is hunched on the floor holding her foot against her breasts. The red hair flows over shoulders curled forward in pain. For a moment, it seems as if she has merely stubbed a toe and will recover as soon as she's had a breather, but her face is much too pale for that, her eyes far too frightened. She is not crying, not making any sound at all, just sitting on the floor, staring at her foot and soothing it, but she suddenly seems incredibly small and fragile, much too fine-boned to support such a weight of pain. Her face is thinner than ever.

Some of the women help her off stage, half-carrying her. She is limping now, not gliding and skipping. Her foot drags behind her like a disobedient puppy as they take her to the elevator and upstairs, where someone will call an ambulance.

In the executive offices, some quick rescheduling is accomplished, and *Song of the Nightingale* is replaced on this evening's program by *Movements for Piano and Orchestra*. Gelsey was scheduled to do the title role in *Nightingale*, and she has no understudy. Elise Flagg will have to learn the role in time to dance it Friday night. Meanwhile, Jerry pulls Christine Redpath out of the corps of *Waltzes* and starts to teach her Gelsey's role. There still is a possibility that Gelsey will be able to dance, but nobody is making book on it, and there is an open dress rehearsal for The Friends of City Center scheduled for this afternoon.

Jerry, as has been noted, dislikes open rehearsals, and nobody could blame him if he wanted to cancel this one, but open rehearsals are bait for attracting more Friends, who mean more money. The invitations were mailed long ago, the recipients already are on their way to the theater, and nothing can be done about it. All Jerry can do is to rehearse with Christine who, luck-ily, was tapped as a stand-in for Gelsey when the red-haired bal-lerina hurt her other foot last week.

Stagehands fly in the drops and the bending drapery that hangs across the back of the stage to be breezed about by Jerry's electric fans. The curtain is down; the dancers are pretty down, too, but dressed and ready to go on. The audience, which nearly fills the orchestra, is composed largely of middle-aged ladies wearing but-tons which read "I am a Friend of City Center." On days like this, City Center needs all the friends it can get.

Eddie Bigelow stands with his hands in his pockets at a micro-phone that has been dragged before the curtain. Eddie gets all the neat jobs around here—like explaining to the Friends why they are not going to see Helgi and Gelsey. While he's at it, he may as well explain why they often have not seen, during the past week or so, the dancers they thought they would, and why there may be even more disappointments during the next week or so. "Programs are something on paper, planned months in advance, but things happen—people get hurt. What we try to do is to give you the best dancing we possibly can." Eddie smiles his little-boy smile at the middle-aged ladies, and informs them that both Gelsey and Helgi are injured. The ladies ooh and ahh in a mixture of sympathy and disappointment. The auditorium sounds like the observation room of an infants' ward on the day the grandmas come to wave.

We feel sorry for injured dancers in the way we sympathize with the anonymous widows of commuters killed in six-car crack-ups. The victims never are quite real. The Friends of City Center like ballet, some of them love ballet, but most never understand that the elevated platform they watch is a battle zone and a sacrifi-cial altar. The performers may have led peculiar, sheltered lives, but they know what can happen to them up there and choose to ac-cept the jeopardy. In some cultures, dancers are masked, and while performing give themselves up to the gods. The bullfight may have begun as dance, but in ballet, the ordained victims are human. Circus spectators hope in secret (secret even from themselves) for a fall from the trapeze. Surrogate sacrifice always is preferable to the do-it-yourself variety. Dancers on stage are a little more than human, and it is hard to remember that what goes on up there today is a contact sport, a sort of Super Bowl set to music, played by overworked, overtired, overstressed youngsters, some of whom have tiny bones and big eyes, and can sit hunched over on a cold gray floor, hurting very badly.

After Eddie has read the injury list and announced who is dancing for whom, the Friends settle down. Robert Irving raises his baton and the ballet begins. Backstage, during the Third Waltz, you can hear Jerry's voice, amplified by his hand mike, soothing "Take it easy, Chris, just take it easy."

Chris and John take it as easy as they can, and get through it. Bart Cook and Sara Leland play their dramatic hide-and-seek in the Fourth Waltz, the company dances the Fifth and the curtain is dropped. The Friends would like to watch Jerry working with the dancers, to see, as they are accustomed to seeing, a "real rehearsal." Under the circumstances, Jerry has too much need of a real rehearsal to give the Friends a "real rehearsal." As soon as the curtain is down, he is backstage, talking with John, Christine, Patty, Jean-Pierre and the others, and telling Eddie Bigelow that he needs time to work. Eddie gets to go out in front of the curtain and be charming again, and he does very well. The Friends are sent home early and disappointed, but they seem to understand.

The curtain is raised. Jerry starts training a new girl to succeed Chris Redpath in the corps. Robbins' movements are sharper than usual, his shoulders are tense, his eyes bright. He takes to repeating his instructions and speaking in capital letters: "Keep your arms even, EVEN," or "Don't bounce, DON'T BOUNCE!"

He begins a session with John and Christine, rehearsing the passage with the skipping-stone step over and over again, having the dancers do it, showing them how to do it, talking it through with them as they do it. It won't work. John is on edge—this is the step that wounded Gelsey, and he feels responsible. Everybody, including Jerry, assures him the accident wasn't his fault, it was one of those slips that happen to dancers, nothing more, but a vague guilt keeps chomping at him like a vulture snacking on Prometheus. He and Chris cannot coordinate the sequence of moves that will result in her foot caroming from the floor and sliding in the almost reflexive bounces the choreography requires.

Over at the piano, Jerry Zimmerman shakes his head, making his bushy hair do a little dance of its own. "Mr. B. would have changed the step fifteen minutes ago," he murmurs. Everyone agrees. Perhaps Mr. B. would have decided that what was right for Gelsey and Helgi is not necessarily a good step for Chris and John. Jerry, though, works through his belief in the perfectibility of dancers. If it is a good step, and it is, if it can be done, and it can, then John and Chris can do it—and he keeps on with his teaching. Finally, he does alter the sequence slightly, substituting a slide for the skip, and goes on with the rehearsal. (By the end of the season, though, John and Christine perform the step as originally designed, which should prove something about Jerry's theory.)

The next problem comes as a present from the costume shop. As John lifts his partner, the slippery fabric of her gown slides through his hands; she nearly falls. John might as well be trying to lift a handful of chicken soup. Jerry has Chris hold her gown at her sides, pulling it tight so that Clifford can grab flesh instead of orange fabric. It works.

Jerry Zimmerman begins the next sequence, and stops. Gelsey is coming onstage, leaning on crutches. Her foot is wrapped in a soft cast. She still looks kitten-fragile, but the pain is gone from her eyes and her voice is steady. She broke a small bone in her foot. "Dr. Engle at New York Surgical"—who once treated Jerry Robbins—set it. The choreographer, who has had experience in these matters, warns her to be careful, very careful. A soft cast is more comfortable to carry than plaster, but affords far less protection. Just be careful. Jerry was a dancer, and has been a choreographer, too long not to know something about injuries. His advice is more than expert, it is given with solicitude that would have done credit to Florence Nightingale. He knows how it feels to be an injured dancer—he's been there. His sympathy is as restrained as Gelsey's explanation of her injury, but it is genuine. The dancers are gentle, too. Gelsey Kirkland is unlikely to be voted Most Popular Girl at NYCB, but everyone is doing his damnedest to make this easier for her—they've been there, too. She goes off on her crutches, planting them as delicately as she places her pointes during a difficult passage, moving with as much dignity and grace as she wears on stage. A friend of mine once managed to save a wounded nightingale by setting its broken leg in a soda straw. I know how he felt.

Experienced dancers insist Gelsey is likely to suffer from foot injuries throughout her career. She is narrow in the hips, which makes it impossible for her to achieve a big turnout and take the strain of dancing in her legs. A good deal of her lovely technique is based in her feet, and the strain on the muscles makes them vulnerable. Two weeks after the accident, despite the punishment of not being able to dance, Gelsey will be more relaxed than she has been since the season started. She even will take a vacation—her first in quite a time. What's that old insurance company joke?—"Death is Nature's way of telling us to slow down." Injuries sometimes are Nature's way of telling dancers.

The Wednesday performance turns out to be pinch-hitters' night. Ricky Weiss dances *Valse Fantasie* for John Clifford who dances *Tarantella* for Edward Villella who performs *La Source* for Helgi Tomasson. Ricky, who has not done *Valse Fantasie* in eight months, has no chance to rehearse because his partner, Sally Leland, spent the day doing *Waltzes* and is exhausted. Ricky has done *Tarantella* recently, and done it with Patty McBride, who is tonight's ballerina. At curtain time he's still trying to figure out why he and John should not have had their assignments reversed (probably because Mr. B. wanted John's showy style for *Tarantella*). Everyone else is a bit nervous, too. Delia Peters reads in the *New York Post* that President Nixon now has "a clearer recollection" of some of the facts about Watergate. "Good," she says. "If he has a clear recollection, let HIM dance this ballet. I can't remember a damn thing about it." But she does, and Ricky remembers *Valse Fantasie*, and Eddie Villella gets through *La Source* without doing any more damage to his leg. As Eddie Bigelow said, "We try to give you the best dancing we possibly can."

Thursday morning, the morning of the premiere, Jerry works with Chris and John. In the afternoon, he holds a darking rehearsal. Most choreographers hold lighting rehearsals, but Jerry keeps telling Ronnie Bates to "take it down a little more," so this is a darking rehearsal. Robbins likes atmospheric lighting, but the dancers think he carries the idea a bit too far. His ballet, *In the Night*, is referred to backstage as "In the Dark," and *Watermill* is even dimmer. The lights for the dramatic encounter of the Fourth Waltz are going to be very low indeed.

From three to five in the afternoon, there is a final dress rehearsal. There also is a final question about costumes: to glove or not to glove. Jerry considers the problem with the same concentration he gives to every detail, and decides to keep the gloves. In the dim light of the Fourth Waltz, the girls' long white evening gloves will accent their arms and fill out the line of movement. Finally, Robbins rehearses the fall of the curtain three times, and goes home to change clothes.

The first performance of *An Evening's Waltzes* is offered to a well-filled house. A Jerome Robbins premiere is one of the most eagerly anticipated events in the dance or the theater. Among American choreographers, only Twyla Tharp can cause as much anticipation, and only Martha Graham can excite more. Balanchine's premieres have become too much a fixture of the New York dance scene to start nervous twitching and, besides, people think they know pretty much what Mr. B. is going to do. Balanchine's premieres can be exciting in retrospect if he has made another masterpiece (he turned out several for the Stravinsky Festival), but the house is seldom all a-twitter before the curtain. Jerry's new works, though, are Big News—he just might be showing another *Dances*, or another *Goldberg Variations*, or he may have changed his style again and be doing something as unexpected as the time-stretching *Watermill*. As a matter of fact, this time he just shows a new ballet. The critics and ballet fans will report tomorrow that *An Evening's Waltzes* is pretty but hardly profound, and that it contains no stylistic advances. Right now, though, the audience is hoping for another miracle.

During the first intermission, the one before the premiere, Lincoln Kirstein is backstage giving presents to everyone in sight: to the dancers, the designer, to his secretary. Lincoln takes it as part of his duties to purchase the official bouquets for opening night

curtain calls and the "good work, good luck" gifts for the participants. His selections prove again that he has the two qualities
needed to make an impresario—money and excellent taste.
The premiere goes well. The corps sets the mood in the First
Waltz; Patty McBride and Jean-Pierre sweep through the romanticism of the Second, and are rewarded with applause and bravos;
John and Chris, turning nervousness into exuberance, flash acro-
batically through the Third Waltz (more applause and bravos);
Sally Leland and Bart Cook meet in the dark encounter of their
dramatic dialogue—the corps behind them sets the scene and comments—(loudest bravos yet); the Fifth Waltz, with the entire cast,
finishes the ballet and the curtain falls exactly as Jerry had insisted
it should. The curtain calls are properly loud and long. The ballerinas collect their bouquets and bravos (and a few, correct, bra-
vas). Jerry is called for a solo bow before the curtain and his smile
is at least as white as his beard in the exulting lights, while the
dancers race for elevators, dressing rooms and their *Cortège* costumes.

Friday morning, Jerry looks more relaxed than he has since the
season began. His smile flashes easily, without the tension in the
cheeks and corners of the mouth that held it back during the last
few weeks. Is he pleased? Is he happy? "I'm tired," and he
chuckles his way down the corridor to his office.

In the main hall, warming up for class, Chris Redpath is giving
her chic body a working-over. She does not look at all pleased with
herself—that long, lovely face is pulled into a self-accusing frown.
Last night, she and John drew enough applause to nearly knock
them over with the wind of it, and she's almost certain to be given
more chances to show what she can do with major roles. She
danced with a long-limbed elegance and a sophisticated style of flir-
tation, and the audience knew she was up there. That isn't why
she's frowning. Jerry gave a party after the premiere, and it was a
good one. All the dancers are moaning, "I'll never do THAT
again." They will though. They have to let go somehow. Even
when there is a Balanchine class to sweat through the next morning.

The bulletin board carries a note from Eddie Bigelow, asking the dancers to sign up for charter buses to Saratoga and charter flights to Los Angeles and Washington, D.C., for the summer tour. It reminds them to be very careful in picking flights, because the company is in a financial bind and he will have to be stingy with refunds for cancellations.

Another note, on the off-stage call board, is from general manager Betty Cage. It says, in effect, that attendance has been lousy this season, and what do you think we can do about it? There's a suggestion box in the office; please, somebody, suggest something.

9

Money

Toward the end of the second week of rehearsal, on Friday, April 20, an unaccustomed notice is inserted in the day's schedule. Mr. Balanchine wishes to speak with all the women in the company immediately after class. Nobody knows why, and one of John Taras' precise, pulling classes—"Show the leg, please, show the step"—keeps everyone too stretched out for speculation.

A few minutes before noon, Balanchine marches into the rehearsal hall, his smallish feet punishing the ground more severely than usual. His mouth is pulled down, his eyes and forehead hard. When he begins to speak, his voice lacks the customary nasal purr. He sounds like a man who has decided in advance exactly what he will say, and is not pleased at having to say it. He wants, he says, to talk about shoes. The girls must use their toe shoes more thoroughly, and not throw them away after one performance. "We owe Capezio at least a quarter of a million dollars," (which turns out to be an exaggeration). "We can't throw away shoes." Also, he says, as he has said before, he hates the patter of new pointe shoes, especially in quiet ballets like *Serenade*. The girls should take old, soft shoes, clean them and reuse them. They should detach the ribbons, wash and iron and sew them back again, "not throw shoes away because ribbons are dirty." They should segregate shoes in their dressing rooms—these for rehearsal, these for class, these for performance, this pair for *Serenade*, that pair for *Stars*. (Several of the women whisper that, so far as they are concerned, this is old news; they do it as a part of the routine.)

Balanchine goes on, with none of his usual joking. The girls should talk to the "real professionals," like Patty McBride and Violette Verdy, and learn to care for their shoes, "and if you can't do it, we'll cut down the size of the company; there are too many here already."

For Balanchine to threaten a cut in the size of the company is remarkable—not that anyone except a few very young corps girls believes him. The statement is comparable to his often iterated comment that if he cannot keep the company as he wants it in New York because of financial difficulties, "We'll go dance in a gym in Hoboken." The quality of his voice, the knife in his eyes, show that Mr. B. means these things when he says them—but it is doubtful he would seriously consider cutting the team or moving to New Jersey once the anger abated. Only two problems can send Balanchine's mind down the road to Hoboken: interference with his plans, and money.

Mr. B. came into the Main Hall thinking about the company's budget and looking like a man who has just quarreled with his mother-in-law and is seeking a reasonable excuse for kicking a dog. Toe shoes were kickable. They cost $10.50 a pair, plus $1.25 for the custom work needed to suit them to the dancers' individual requirements. The company receives a ten percent discount. According to Roland Vazquez, who places the orders, the shoe bill for a year has been as much as $250,000. Betty Cage, NYCB's general manager, says the company never actually owed Capezio a quarter of a million, but it once was in hock to LeRay Boot Shop for $36,000.

The girls average nine pairs of shoes a week.

Ballet slippers are not built like logging boots; they have a limited life expectancy. There are fifty women in the company, and simple multiplication shows that in this nine-week spring season, they will wear out 4,050 pairs of shoes. That makes the charge for women's shoes alone—not men's, not character shoes, not boots—$42,228.75 for the season, not including those worn during

the rehearsal period. Now you know why Balanchine worries
about shoes.

The use and care of toe shoes is something about which Mr. B.
can talk to the company, something he can try to improve, something that seems obvious—an eminently kickable dog. Unfortunately, it is a very small dog. The animals that take the biggest
bites of NYCB's budget are harder to intimidate.

One of the great problems for anyone involved in the arts in
America is trying to explain where the money goes. A Balanchine
ballet seems to be composed of fifteen to twenty people, dressed in
nothing in particular—tights, white tee shirts, leotards, miniscule
rehearsal skirts—jumping around on an empty stage. The company's annual budget, according to the general manager, is about
$5 million. The yearly payroll, $3,569,000, accounts for most of it.

Betty Cage sits in her comfortable fourth-floor office, where
every piece of furniture seems covered by pieces of paper, which in
turn are covered by figures. She is working on the budget for the
coming fiscal year, which begins July 1. The general manager, who
has been with NYCB since 1947, is a bulky woman with eyebrows
so heavy they seem ready to purr and a hesitant voice that apparently was unwilling to grow up when the rest of her did. The
voice says softly that the inflation in NYCB's annual budget is "less
than that of food." The contract the company signed with the
dancers in 1970 raised the performers' pay more than fifty percent,
but that was because the dancers were hideously underpaid. First-
year corps members now earn $150 a week, which means that
before the new contract was drawn up they could have done nearly
as well working behind a luncheonette counter for the minimum
wage. Material costs rise about ten percent a year, which Betty
considers a reasonable figure; the big worry is payroll. All unions
with which NYCB deals have been requested not to ask for pay
increases next year, 1974, because of City Center's budget deficit.
However, Betty fears a musicians' strike against the company next
fall, and the dancers' gossip also includes that possibility. It seems
likely that the cost of ballet, like the cost of steak and shoe leather,
is going up. Where, exactly, does the money go?

City Center of Music and Drama, Inc., rents the New York

State Theater from New York City for one dollar a year, and
NYCB, a component of City Center, uses the theater without paying rent. However, the company must pay the salaries of the theater
staff while it is in residence. (The New York City Opera takes on a
similar obligation during its season.) Costs involved in operating
the theater for the longer, winter season have been calculated at
over $650,000. The spring season, about one-third shorter, in-
volves a comparably smaller expenditure. The company also must
pay the people directly connected with performance,—stage managers, musicians, dancers and the young men who bring flowers to
the ballerinas during curtain calls.

The salaries of executives and non-union personnel are considered prepaid expenses. Although those expenses are charged to
NYCB, the checks are issued directly by City Center, and are not
part of the company's weekly payroll. People such as Balanchine,
his personal assistant, Barbara Horgan, Betty Cage, Robert Irving,
the theater's general manager and its executive secretary, are not
included in the weekly accounting of salaries which is deducted
from box-office receipts and reported to City Center. There are,
however, a very large number of people who appear on the weekly
payrolls of Zelda Dorfman, the company manager (dancers and
musicians) and Thomas F. Kelley, theater manager (everybody
else).

The staff of the front of the house—people who seldom go
backstage and are not involved with the production of ballet—consists of about 110 workers. Some of them almost never are seen by
the audience; others are so familiar that they have become invisible,
like the postman in the mystery story.

To deal with the routine matter—to the theater-goer—of selling
a ticket, the New York State Theater employs a box-office trea-
surer, his assistant, and four ticket-sellers. During a typical ballet
performance week, that of June 3, 1973, the population of the box
office cost NYCB $1,810 in salaries. When the dance fan arrives at
the theater on the night of performance, his ticket is torn in half by
one of four ticket-takers, and the stub is examined by one of forty-
one ushers. During the week of June 3, the company paid $3,532
to ushers. (The ushers and ticket-takers, by the way, belong to a

different union than do the box-office people, who belong to a different union than does the house manager. There are at least nine unions represented at every performance of NYCB.)

In command of the ticket-sellers, ticket-takers, ushers and other front-of-the-house personnel, is the house manager, Tom Kelley, who is to the front of the theater what production stage manager Ronny Bates is to the stage: he runs the show. Tom, a pleasant-faced, prematurely balding gentleman, takes a post near the box office as the audience starts in. If there is a ticket mix-up, an accident, a potential contributor who needs four seats in a hurry, Tom is expected to take care of it. His salary is $500 a week.

The only other front-house workers likely to be seen by visitors are the matrons of the women's rest rooms. Four of them cost the company $372 during the June 3 week. (They pay dues to still another union.)

The remaining half of the house staff is not familiar to the public. It consists of six mail room workers (paid monthly, not on Tom Kelley's weekly list); ten security guards; two full-time and three part-time switchboard operators; eight engineers who service the air conditioning and other comforts; one electrician; one seamstress (ushers' uniforms lose buttons, too), and a cleaning staff of approximately twenty. During the week of June 3, expenses for salaries included $400 for the switchboard; $1,456 for security guards; $3,219 for cleaners; $2,802, engineers, and $98, seamstress. A bit of short division will prove that most of these people are not overpaid by today's standards. Those who make good money have major skills, strong unions, or both.

The backstage crew has both. The theater supports twenty-two stagehands, and may hire extra men if needed. The carpenters, electricians and property men are paid according to a contract negotiated by City Center and the International Association of Theatrical Stagehands and Electricians (IATSE), Local One. The difficulty of joining IATSE, and the benefits thereof, are virtually legendary in theatrical circles.

In many countries, a stagehand is a respected professional. In America, actors and technicians sometimes feel about one another the way pitchers and outfielders do—"They should pay to get in."

To performers, stagehands are those overpaid people who hang around backstage all night. To technicians, performers are those klutzes who get in the way when you are trying to move scenery. NYCB enjoys a much warmer relationship, because the stage crew, like the company, is a resident group. The company knows the crew, the crew knows the company and they get along. Besides, the stagehands always are very happy to see the ballet move into the theater—the opera is much more work.

Technicians are paid by the hour, at a base rate of $9.10 for chiefs, $7.50 for assistant chiefs and $6.20 for Indians. At that rate, Hank, the curtain raiser, is quite substantially remunerated for pushing his button, and the men who sit playing cards behind the little house that dominates the set of *Harlequinade* do even better. Few of us get $6.20 an hour plus overtime to play five-card stud.

During the opera season, the men can bring in quite a bit of overtime. But, as Hank points out, "What good is the money if you're too damn worn out from working fourteen and sixteen hours a day to spend it?" Another technician, Jimmy, adds that he can come to the theater at 9 A.M., not leave it until after ten at night except for lunch and dinner breaks, and not earn any overtime at all. The stage crew, like the dancers, has an eight-shows-a-week contract, and can be required to work eight hours a day in addition to the show, before overtime rolls in. The ballet does not require a full crew call every day. Often, the men come in, work the show, and go home, well paid. During the opera season, though, and at times with the ballet, they go home well paid and dead tired.

Life backstage is not all card-games and buttons, it also involves pushing around some weighty scenery. The week of June 3 showed some fairly big production numbers, and the crew earned its pay. The carpenters earned $4,464, the electricians $5,364, the property men $3,232: a total of over $13,000 for the technical contingent. The company also pays weekly salaries to four stage maintenance men.

The third category of weekly wage-earners are the performers and their support teams. The cost of the company varies from week to week, as does the price of the stage crew, depending on overtime charges, the need for orchestra rehearsals, the use of singers and similar variables. Still the general scheme of expenses, and the ratio of one item to another, remains fairly constant. During one week, that of June 3, as during every other week of the season, the biggest chomp of the apple was taken by the orchestra, which accounted for $26,039. The musicians (Local 802) have a contract which gives orchestra members a starting salary of $292 for seven performances a week. (Dancers and stagehands, remember, have contracts calling for eight shows weekly.) There are about sixty members of the NYCB orchestra, and not all are called to every performance. Obviously, you need more musicians to play a Tchaikovsky concerto than a Mozart divertimento, and you call the euphonium for Sousa and not for Bach. Since the musicians have signed for seven performances each week, and the company gives eight, you either have to finagle the schedule or pay overtime, or have spare musicians available.

Rehearsals are not included in the orchestra contract. Robert Irving, as music director, schedules rehearsal time as he needs it. "You call rehearsals and pay the people for them, and that's it." Betty Cage does her figuring on the basis of $20 per musician per two-hour call, which works out to $2,200 if fifty-five musicians are required for the work being rehearsed.

The $26,039 paid the orchestra was not the company's only musical salary expense for the week of June 3. Singers, used in *Pulcinella* and *Liebeslieder Walzer*, earned $1,095; rehearsal pianists got $1,043 and the conductor (associate conductor Hugo Fiorato; Robert's salary is a prepaid expense) received $675.

That week, music cost NYCB considerably more than dancing. Principal dancers earned $8,714, soloists $4,230 and the corps, $13,250. Apprentices—all those children from The School of American Ballet dashing about in *Pulcinella* and *Harlequinade*—cost the company $45. Never have so many run so fast for so little.

The support troops also have to eat. In salaries, the wardrobe department cost $2,191 for the week; make-up men, $475; ballet master (Rosemary Dunleavy), $295; stage managers, $1,018 and company manager, $333. The flower boy got $20.

Salaries of production and front-of-the-house personnel, exclusive of those prepaid, accounted for $87,372. Box-office receipts for the week were $88,900—the number of people who paid their way into the theater was 12,892. In other words, playing at about fifty-five percent of the theater's capacity, as it did during most of the season, NYCB ended up with only $1,528 left over after meeting the weekly production payroll. That sum obviously did not cover the costs of salaries for executive and administrative personnel, insurance, pensions, light bulbs, costume cleaning, royalties, resin, shoes or the telephone bill.

If the company filled the theater at every performance, it would take in $159,348.80 a week at the box office. Lincoln Kirstein, noting that somehow "we manage to meet every payday," adds, "and the total payday is about $150,000." Which means that prepaid and administrative class salaries cost the company nearly seventy-five percent as much as production salaries. Figuring on the basis of a fourteen-week fall-winter season and a nine-week spring season, and discounting rehearsal weeks and touring, Lincoln's estimate multiplies out to be a bit short of the $3,569,000 annual payroll of the company.

Betty Cage thinks that Lincoln overestimates some expenses and underguesses others. One of the problems is that it is nearly impossible to find out what anything costs. Lincoln says *Cortège Hongrois* cost about $50,000 to produce, a figure which includes $1,000 for each costume. Betty is not at all sure of that figure. In fact, she's not at all sure how anyone can be certain of any figure for production costs. "How are you working it?" she asks. "Out-of-pocket capital expenses? Rule-of-thumb? Operating expenses? If you're asking for production grants, you put in everything you can think of, and even then, it isn't always easy to think of everything." In 1965, when Balanchine made his three-act *Don Quixote*, which used a specially commissioned score, complex scenery and a huge complement of Karinska costumes, Betty kept a careful account and learned that the production had cost $250,000. "But you can't always do that kind of figuring. There are too many variables."

There is, for example, the question of Karinska's costume shop. Costs can be computed for individual pieces of work, but Betty finds it more practical to consider the total cost of running the shop for a year, which is about $300,000. Expenses would be lower, she says, if the costumers belonged to the Theatrical Wardrobe Union, instead of to the International Ladies' Garment Workers Union. But Karinska is a part of City Center. In 1963, when NYCB applied for its Ford Foundation grant, the Foundation asked what the company really needed, and Balanchine decided it really needed Karinska. He is convinced she is the only costumer who really understands ballet, and he wanted her to use all her time for his company, rather than squandering some of it on Broadway productions. He even hoped to develop the shop into a school for costume builders, but that project has not been successful.

NYCB acquired the shop, but there was no room in the theater in which to house it. Karinska kept her old business address on West 57th Street and her old union, and therefore, her old expenses.

Karinska makes costumes for new ballets and for people promoted into new roles, repairs torn clothes and replaces worn ones. In other words, it is not a question of $1,000 (or more) a costume for a new ballet, but $300,000 a year for a service, an expense paid by one component of City Center—NYCB—to another—Karinska. There is no question that costumes could be made more cheaply— couture sewing and $20-a-yard fabric are not really needed for the stage. The underskirts of *Liebeslieder Walzer* did not have to be made of the finest lace, but they were; the Tsaravitch's hat for *Firebird* need not have been trimmed in mink, as it was. Money could be saved on costumes, but it would be saved by sacrificing the durability of the clothes, and the art of them. Karinska constructions are works of art as surely as Balanchine's are, and they derive from the same tradition. There are few couture houses in the world, let alone costume shops, that do sewing of the quality that is commonplace chez Karinska. The original costumes for *The Nutcracker* did not need to be replaced for ten years, and *Nutcracker* has the longest annual run of any ballet in the NYCB repertory.

Still, it must be pointed out that ballet costumes often are worn only eight or nine times each year, that some ballets are taken out of repertory after a season or two, and that costumes can be made which look almost as good, from the audience, as those sewn by Karinska. Whether any American company can continue to afford her kind of art is a question that probably must be answered in the negative—but then, can we afford to be without that kind of art, either? It depends on what we mean by "afford."

Even considering their durability and their wonderful way of moving with dancers' bodies, haute couture costumes made from $20-a-yard fabric are not needed on stage. Certainly, real mink is not needed. But Karinska's work must be regarded as more than an appurtenance to another art form—it must be considered art, and craft—in its own right. When the costume curator of the Metropolitan Museum of Art finally gets around to organizing a show devoted to Karinska, the response and admiration will be as great as that accorded the exhibition of Balenciaga's work—and Balenciaga created only for the financial elite. You can see Karinska's couture for the price of an NYCB ticket. We must be able to continue to afford Karinska, but a slight limitation on expenses would be in order.

One question for a businessman surveying NYCB is, "Is Karinska's shop an operating expense, a production expense, or both?" Production costs, at Betty Cage's estimate, take only from one to five percent of the annual $5-million budget, which would set them at anywhere from $50,000 to $250,000 a year. Lincoln says *Cortège* alone cost $50,000. *Don Quixote* cost $250,000. Production costs for all performances of the 1972–73 winter season have been listed at $613,000. Betty and Lincoln seem to have different ways of computing expenses, and it is difficult to blame them. This place is a cost accountant's nightmare. If Jerry Robbins works the dancers overtime while rehearsing *An Evening's Waltzes*, the cost could be attributed to production expenses. However, if Jerry works the dancers overtime touching up *An Evening's Waltzes* after opening night, perhaps the money must be charged to operating expenses.

Betty Cage says, "Nominally, I'm responsible for fiscal planning. Actually, things just happen." At times, the company resembles a family-owned restaurant with an accounting system composed of two cigar boxes on the counter, one for incoming cash, one for bills payable. The Ballet Guild took 1,100 photos from the publicity department to sell at its booth on the promenade. The

Guild was told it did not have to pay for the photos since, according to Betty, "it all comes out of the same pot." This bit of largesse gave the Guild $1,100 clear profit, and cut into the publicity budget. One of the people in management, reportedly forgot that the top ticket price went up $1 in 1972, and had this year's non-subscription performance flyers printed listing a $7.95 top. Nobody noticed the error until the brochures had been printed. Of course they could not be used, and $8,000 was wasted. This sort of thing is not as unusual as it should be.

Another part of the problem is the strange corporate structure of which NYCB is a part, and the fact that for many years it was part of no structure but an independent firm. All bills are paid by City Center, from its central accounting office. However, Ballet Society, the predecessor of NYCB, still exists as a corporation with a bank account. Betty Cage can pay emergency bills with Ballet Society checks, for which the company is reimbursed by City Center. "Of course," Betty murmurs, "it may take them six months to get around to repaying us, but they do it. Being part of City Center gives us security in the midst of poverty."

City Center pays the bills for NYCB, but it has several other components to worry about—the Opera, the City Center Joffrey Ballet, Alvin Ailey City Center Dance Theater, City Center Acting Company and a few more. It also offers lecture-demonstrations of opera and ballet to schools, through the City Center Education Department. It also, this spring, 1973, season, is one-and-one-half-million dollars in the red. Facing the deficit is Norman Singer, executive director of the City Center of Music and Drama, Inc. "We are completely responsible for the New York City Ballet's operating costs," Singer says. "We keep the box-office receipts and pay the bills." Singer signs all contracts, and approves all budgets. He is the man in control—with the approval of his board of directors—but his control has limitations. After all, Balanchine and Lincoln Kirstein built NYCB; it would be a bit difficult to prevent them from running it. If one did, it would no longer be NYCB. Singer must govern, if he is to govern, by mediation. When Jerry Robbins wanted to order a completely new set of costumes for *An Evening's Waltzes*—an expenditure which would have twisted the budget into

a corkscrew—Singer did not say "Yes" to Jerry's artistic integrity
or "No" to his financial mayhem. He said, "Let's ask Balanchine."
Balanchine thought the company could live with the costumes as
planned, and live with them it did.

This season, City Center is preparing to change its accounting
system. Currently, everything goes into, and out of, one set of
cigar boxes. The corporation is switching to fund accounting, providing a different set of cigar boxes for each of its stores. The
Friends of City Center traditionally has given part of its general
fund to the opera, part to the ballet. Under the new system, the
Ballet Guild and the Opera Guild each will have a separate account. One of the first results of the change will be the loss, after
this spring season, of Susan Ralston, the Ballet Guild's volunteer
administrator. The Guild has been instructed to hire a full-time
professional administrator, preferably someone with good credentials who will work cheap.

City Center is planning a computerized accounting system
which, Norman Singer says, will work very well for the Opera, for
which it is easier to itemize expenses than it is for the Ballet. He
also thinks it will make it easier to evaluate each company's financial situation. Furthermore, Betty Cage has been instructed to submit a budget for the coming year. Betty always has submitted a
budget, you understand, but this one is supposed to work. "We are
completely autonomous," she says, "within certain fiscal limitations." Those limitations may become a bit more restrictive under
the new system. As Singer attempts to erode City Center's deficit,
he must have a clear idea of what each company will spend each
year.

Rummaging through her desk, Betty comes up with a copy of a
Ford Foundation survey which shows that NYCB pays more than
seventy percent of its expenses at the box office, while the New
York City Opera covers more than eighty percent from ticket sales.
"Those are the highest figures in the world," Betty says quietly.
"The Royal Ballet, The Vienna Opera, The Bolshoi—none of
them pay anywhere near seventy percent of their costs by selling
tickets. They're all far more heavily subsidized than we are." For
the remaining thirty percent of its expenses, the company depends

on contributions and donations. The Ballet Guild will bring in about $70,000 this fiscal year, of which $41,000 comes from the Spring Gala and will be turned over to the production fund. In 1963, the Ford Foundation gave the company a grant of $200,000 a year for ten years—a grant which is due to expire and which the company now is trying to have renewed. For the fiscal year ending this June, the company received $235,000 from the New York State Council on the Arts, and $113,000 from the National Endowment for the Arts.

The size of those sums alone shows how much the company has changed. Back in 1950, it could present five new ballets for $35,000. Operating procedures have changed, too.

There was a time, Betty Cage explains, when a spur-of-the-moment substitution of one ballet for another could be made without too much difficulty. If a dancer was injured, they just changed the program. Today, if a change is required, "You have to know if the sets are hung, if there are enough musicians in the pit that night—and what's on the subscriptions."

In 1963, when the company moved from City Center to the New York State Theater, a strong drive for a subscription audience was launched. It was believed that a guaranteed audience was needed to support the company in its new home, and since opera has always maintained a subscription audience, it should work for ballet. Subscriptions, although they guarantee ticket sales, limit company planning and programming. The subscription office has an amazing assortment of charts, showing the programs that have been allotted to each subscription series in the past. Subscribers are creatures of habit—if they are accustomed to coming on Thursdays, they like to keep coming on Thursdays. However, they do not want to see the same ballet every Thursday. They do not even want to see the same ballet every year. The prescription of the subscription department, according to Betty, is, "Try to give them nothing they've had for three seasons." In other words, if Mr. and Mrs. Third Thursday have seen *Firebird* every year for three years, you can't schedule *Firebird* on third Thursdays again next year. You also have to try to include a performance of a new ballet in each subscription series; otherwise, there will be complaints. If

Mr. B. or Jerry has created a work that wowed the critics, the subscribers want to see it—and they don't want to have to purchase extra tickets because it isn't on their subscription.

However, Mr. and Mrs. Third Thursday also like a certain amount of familiarity, and a certain type of ballet. They want to go home saying, "The costumes were beautiful . . . it was very colorful . . . the dancing was lovely." They don't want to talk about the architecture in the second movement or the marvelous use of inverted turn-out. Mr. and Mrs. Third Thursday still think ballet should be pretty—they are not really concerned with whether or not it is beautiful. This subscriber principle of aesthetics places a limitation on program-building and subscription-creating. A popular work—popular with the subscribers, not with the dance freaks—gets a lot of performances each season. This spring, *Firebird* had six; *Swan Lake* received four; *Watermill*, which is not popular with subscription audiences—the slow motion of the time-extending device can make it a difficult ballet to watch—still is sufficiently new to the repertory to have rated four performances. Ballets which command what Betty Cage calls "a limited audience" are scheduled for two or three performances. *Concerto Barocco*, one of Mr. B.'s masterpieces and a darling of the dancers, was offered three times during the spring, 1973, season—one of them was a Saturday matinee and one was on the last night of repertory. *Episodes* was scheduled twice. A lot of dance buffs would sooner miss a meal than an *Episodes* or a *Barocco*, but dance buffs are not the power at the box office.

Subscriptions are not the only limitation on programming. A glance at an NYCB schedule shows that performances of ballets come in bunches, like grapes. *Scotch Symphony* was danced three times the first week—on Tuesday, Wednesday and Friday, and again on the following Tuesday. That was it for *Scotch*. *Agon*, which is considered one of Balanchine's greatest contributions to the art, was performed on Thursday, May 3, Saturday, May 5 (matinee) and Wednesday, May 9. If you missed one of those three, you had to wait until next season.

The so-called "Greek Program"—*Apollo, Orpheus* and *Agon*—was given twice, at the Saturday matinee and on the following

Wednesday night. This is one of the company's best programs, but the matinee audience was nearly outnumbered by the dancers. "On a matinee, you have to give stuff to which people want to bring the kids," everyone said. "Who wants to bring the kids to this? This is for the real dance people." It was assumed, no doubt, that "the real dance people" would come on a Saturday afternoon, and they did, but there are not enough of them to fill the theater. (They would have come another time, too, leaving the matinee for the real matinee people.)

The grouping of performances irritates many audience members who would like to see the showings of, let us say *Agon*, spread over the length of the season. That way, if they had to be out of town for a week, they wouldn't have to miss the ballet. If the company tried that system, it would lose even more money than it does now. When a ballet is to be performed, the sets must be hung, the costumes taken from storage and prepared, the parts brought from the music library and distributed, and the dancers must rehearse. *Stars and Stripes*, which was used as the finale on opening night, May 1, did not appear in the repertory again until June 6. The dancers had to rehearse it twice—first for opening and again when it was placed in repertory. The scenery had to be hung, taken down and hung again. The costumes had be be taken from storage two weeks in advance of performance, prepared, cleaned, replaced after opening night, and then unpacked, prepared, used again, cleaned again and replaced again. That procedure takes time and costs money. When performances are grouped, the sets can be hung one week and taken down the next, making room on the pipes for the next assortment of drops. The number of crew hours is much smaller than it would be if the repertory were arranged the other way, and the minimum cost for one stagehand for one hour, remember, is $6.20.

Arranging a season, then, is a cross between a juggling act and a treaty negotiation, a compromise between what management would like to do and what it can do without breaking the bank or offending the audience. To make life more interesting, scheduling must be done far in advance. In the spring of 1973, Betty Cage knew the opening and closing dates for the company's seasons through 1976. City Center, which arranges these things, must work around the commitments of opera singers, who agree long in advance to perform with different companies in different cities. The New York City Opera season must be scheduled with this in mind, and the New York City Ballet season must mesh with that of the opera. Furthermore, there must be, eternally, five weeks of *The Nutcracker* during the Christmas season. *The Nutcracker* pays the bills; it is the biggest money-maker in the NYCB repertory, and it is a New York Christmas tradition. Scheduling at the New York State Theater starts with the charting of those five weeks of *The Nutcracker*—everything else is worked out from there.

The specific plan for each season also must be laid out in advance, so that subscription brochures can be printed and mailed. By May 15, 1973, one week after the season began, the winter season, opening November 13, 1973, had been set. "Often," according to Betty, "you have to change it later. You have to post 'New Ballet Number One' and 'New Ballet Number Two' and schedule around them—and often you know absolutely nothing about 'New Ballet Number One.' " *Jewels*, which is a suite of three ballets, started out to be a twenty-minute entertainment. *The Goldberg Variations* was not given at all during the season for which it originally had been scheduled.

However, the postulated existence of at least one new ballet allows the scheduling to begin. From the approximately sixty-five ballets in the repertory, forty or so are chosen to be shown during a given season. The choosing is done by Balanchine. "Ballets get to be badly done," Betty explains, "so you take them out for a while and rest them, then restage and really rehearse." Sometimes, a ballet that is being "badly done" from the viewpoint of the dancers—*Dances at a Gathering* is a case in point—is left in the repertory for economic reasons, or because Mr. B. does not think it needs a rest yet. New ballets and revivals from the previous season, even if the critics thought they were the biggest bombs since Hiroshima and Nagasaki, are given maximum exposure in the coming repertory. For one thing, there may be subscribers who want to see them—or who don't know how bad they are. For another, they may have received premieres after the ensuing season already had

been organized. Both *Cortège* and *Evening's Waltzes* went unper-
formed until after the May 15 deadline for winter scheduling.
There also is the fact that it hardly is worth spending the money to
do a new ballet if you are going to withdraw it from performance
after only one season, and choreographers generally are assured, either through contract or through courtesy, that a new ballet will be
offered a minimum number of times before being removed from
the charts. And now you know why that work you hate so much—
with the concurrence of the critical faculty—has been scheduled for
next season. Ballet isn't Broadway. The latter finds it economically
necessary to work on a hit-and-run or flop-and-fold basis. NYCB
finds it impossible to work that way—which may be just as well. A
ballet can be a bit more sophisticated than its audience; critics
sometimes judge wrongly, and a lot of touching-up can be done between one season and the next. A real stinker is not going to be
improved very much by time or work, but some pieces need a bit
of both before they can become at least acceptable, and the NYCB
system gives them a chance.

Despite the attempts of the schedule-planners and the subscription department to give the public what it wants; despite the great
increase in the audience for dance in recent years; despite the fact
that NYCB is acknowledged to be one of the world's great companies, attendance has been falling off since 1963. For much of the
spring season, the company played to half-filled houses. Spring
always brings a smaller audience than winter: There is too much
competition from other companies; too many people are away from
the area on early vacations or country weekends; spring lacks the
glamour of fall-winter threater-going. Balanchine, Betty Cage and
Lincoln were summoned to a meeting with executives of City
Center because "you're losing your audience." Betty's sign on the
call-board asked the dancers for suggestions, and an ad agency was
told to organize a new kind of campaign. The house remained half
full.

Part of the problem is competition. NYCB did not play opposite just the National Ballet of Canada and Martha Graham's
company. There is enough dance—ballet, modern dance, ethnic
dance, avant garde dance, deca-dance—in New York to keep a

critic, or a dance buff, busy every night of the week. There is dance at City Center, dance at Hunter College, dance at the Brooklyn Academy of Music, dance at the Metropolitan Opera House, the Kaufman Auditorium, The Space, the Cubiculo, the Felt Forum of Madison Square Garden. Some of it is good; some is gruesome; some creative, some dull as Philadelphia on Sunday; but it is there, and New York houses enough dance fans to offer it an audience. However, the city does not hold enough dance fans to make an audience for all of it at the same time.

"The trouble is," the dancers tell you, "we're always here. We're a resident company. People know that, so they go to see the others, figuring to catch us next year—but somehow, next year never comes." NYCB competes not only with companies playing opposite it, but with those preceding it or following it to New York. "Let's wait for American Ballet Theater . . . Hurok is bringing the Bolshoi . . . let's go to that instead . . . we can see the ballet when we go to England in the fall . . ."—you can almost hear the conversations. That's why subscription audiences, with all the problems they cause, are so important: You know SOMEBODY is going to be out there while you dance.

Bringing in those somebodies is the job of the subscription department, but, interestingly enough, NYCB's attendance began to fall at the same time as the subscription program was instituted. The company drew better houses in its old home at City Center than it does now. The first few seasons at Lincoln Center brought people who wanted to see the new theater; having seen it, they stopped coming. One thing about the subscription drive that seems to annoy people is that tickets are mailed out rather late. The drive peaks in the fifth week of the spring season, but subscribers do not receive their seats until the promotion is over and has been assessed.

It is quite possible that NYCB caters too much to the subcribers, in an attempt to retain their good will. Subscribers to the spring, 1972, season had tickets to Stravinsky Festival performances included in their packets. NYCB's Stravinsky Festival was a major event in American theatrical history. The theater was filled every night for a week. NYCB could easily have kept the festival

out of the subscription brochures and sold seats at prices slightly
higher than usual—and thus made that $1.5 million City Center
deficit a bit smaller this year. The inclusion of the festival on the
subs did not noticeably boost the number of subscribers to NYCB.

To complicate things still further, City Center competes with
itself, running dance programs at City Center while NYCB performs at the State Theater. It is quite common for the Alvin Ailey
American Dance Theater—a component of City Center—to open
at 55th Street the same night NYCB begins its season across town.
Norman Singer has decided that will not happen in spring, 1974.
Ailey is to open later than NYCB, and the self-competition is to be
limited as much as it possible.

Competition from other companies is not the only reason
NYCB has difficulty filling its theater. People simply do not come
to the ballet on impulse as much as they used to. "They're sitting
home in front of a little box," Betty Cage sighs. "It's a whole new
way of life. We have to figure out a way to get them away from
that box." Often, the little television box is not even in New York
any more. Attendance started to decline in 1963, and a lot of citizens have left town since then. Some retired to Miami or Phoenix,
some simply moved to the suburbs. Coming to Manhattan for a
performance involves more hassles, and more expense, than many
people are willing to face. By the time you find the baby-sitter,
drive in, park the car, get a meal, get to your seat, get the car,
drive home, take the baby-sitter home—well, who needs culture
anyway? And if you do need it, there's a real nice little theater
group right here in Hideola, Long Island. There was a time when
women would come to the city to meet their husbands after work,
have dinner and attend a performance. But now, when husband
(and frequently wife) works as well as lives in Hideola, they don't
bother.

Many of those who still live in the city, especially the middle-
aged and middle class, to whom New York's big-time culture industry is dedicated, are victims of urban nocturnal paranoia: They
won't go out at night. They see a mugger lurking behind every
parked car and it is not all in their imaginations. Some of those
people will come to a matinee; others won't come at all. People

who do go out for entertainment generally divide their loyalties. Unlike the few dance fanatics, they like a varied menu—this week the opera, next week a show, then the ballet, a few movies, a concert or two—it takes some time before the ballet gets its turn again.

NYCB tickets, at $8.95 top, are not brutally expensive by contemporary standards—the Met hits you for $20 top and some Broadway musicals come revoltingly close to that. Still, $8.95 times two is $17.90, and even if you eat at home and take the subway instead of a cab, an evening in orchestra seats will cost you close to $20. The cost of culture probably is not the chief factor in the decline of NYCB audiences, but when every other item in the family budget also is getting more expensive, it does have an impact.

In short, there are a lot of good reasons for not going to the ballet, unless you really like ballet. A great many people sort of like ballet, or think they should like ballet, or like friends to think they like ballet, but these are not sufficient reasons for risking time, trouble, travel and the chance of being mugged. Since NYCB does not constitute an "event," as a Hurok presentation of a European company does, there is no sense in going just to say you've been.

Another difficulty, tied to the movement from the city, is the alteration of the ethnic population of New York. The Cohens and the Santuccis, and the Germans and the Irish, went in for "culture"—either they truly liked it or it was expected of them and they went. They still do. The Rodriguez's don't, because they've seldom had a chance to find out whether or not they like it, and nobody expects to see them there anyway. Only recently has Broadway started to hunt for black audiences—another major segment of the population that has not been enticed into the theaters.

Very often, theater-goers are the children of theater-goers, and if your father is raising six kids on the salary from the only job he can get—working behind the counter at Nedick's—you are not likely to get to the theater very often. There are an increasing number of middle-class, middle-income blacks and Hispanics in New York who can afford the price of tickets, but they have not been indoctrinated—they don't have the habit. And those who do are just as afraid to go out at night as Cohen and Kelly. As the King of Siam remarked, "Is a puzzlement."

City Center and NYCB have tried, and are trying, to recruit a new group of dance watchers, by offering lecture-demonstrations in schools, by providing low-priced tickets to groups, by providing free tickets. To date, it hasn't worked. Most of the audience is still middle class, middle-aged, white and Anglo. That could change. Art is part of the universal experience, but specific arts, like ballet, are acquired tastes and few tastes are acquired after one or two bites. Theater-going is a habit and some habits can be as difficult to make as to break. For NYCB, or any other performing group, to build a new audience is going to take time. Affluence may help—there is no reason to suppose the rising middle class won't be just as snobbish as the one that is leaving the city. More black dancers might help, simply as an assurance to black audiences that they are welcome in the theater. Right now, many feel they aren't. Education of young people may help—not merely education of the "this is a fouette" type, but education that the question is not whether "art is relevant to your life-style," but whether or not your life-style is relevant to art.

For the more immediate future, several methods have been suggested for building an audience, some possible, some preposterous. The dancers and dance buffs suggest varying the program, reviving some works and dropping too-old favorites from the repertory. This probably would not bring a new audience to the theater, but there is a good chance it would capture some of the "wait until next year" crowd, and call a few old friends in from the suburbs. There are a number of problems inherent in the program: The cost of reviving several works in one season is the most obvious, but there are others too. A favorite story around the company tells of the time, a few years back, that Balanchine attempted to revive *Figure in the Carpet*. He couldn't remember the steps. Neither could members of the original cast, and there is no written record. Another candidate for revival is Frederick Ashton's *Picnic at Tintagel*. Barbara Horgan, Balanchine's assistant, points out the difficulty: "We'd have to get Freddy over from England to stage it—it's been so long since we've done it—and we've never been able to work out a schedule with him." NYCB has done revivals in recent years and more are contemplated, but there is no way the company can bring in a radically different repertory at the flick of a switch. Finances alone would make that impossible.

Another idea is to shorten the company's New York seasons. This would eliminate some of the "they're always here" thinking. The company could do a shorter season with a curtailed repertory—which the dancers would love—cram the same number of subscribers into fewer performances, lure the single-performance visitors, who no longer would be able to postpone their calls if they wanted to see the company, and pack the house. Limiting the number of ballets in each season would give the dancers more time to rehearse the performed pieces and would send some of the war-horses, of which the regulars in the audience are just as tired as the dancers, out to pasture for a season or two. It just might work—except for economic considerations.

City Center finds it financially difficult to have the New York State Theater closed for even one night between the opera and ballet seasons. Keeping it dark for several weeks at a stretch could be disastrous. Of course, the theater could be rented, but occupancy would have to be assured before the ballet season could be curtailed. Then there are all those people who have been guaranteed a certain number of weeks' work each year—what does City Center do with them? The company could tour, of course, but it does not take the orchestra on tour; the men have other commitments, and the cost of traveling with a sixty-piece orchestra is prohibitive. There also is the question of whether Balanchine, Lincoln and City Center want to limit the New York season of one of the city's major cultural assets. Furthermore, subscribers, as we have said, are creatures of habit. Would Mr. and Mrs. Third Thursday be willing to become Mr. and Mrs. Every Thursday, or would they say the hell with it?

The company could maintain the length of its season but limit the number of performances, dancing only a few nights each week, as some European companies do. Frequently, such troupes alternate performances with the opera company that shares their theater, a practice that would be difficult in New York. Consider the cost of crew calls to put down and take up the dance floor every night. Then again, a three-night-a-week company is not a Balanchine company. Mr. B. designed this troupe for a full season of every-night dancing, and he is unlikely to change now.

The limited New York season proposal, if the theater could be rented and contracts renegotiated, is a more likely solution to the cost problem. There are, of course, other plans and projects, perhaps the most interesting of which is Lincoln's reported scheme to have the New York City Ballet and The Royal Ballet trade places every so often. NYCB would do a London season while The Royal would dance in the State Theater. New Yorkers love The Royal; Londoners love NYCB; why not? Well, for one thing, London probably can't afford NYCB. It is a very expensive company to keep. But London can afford The Royal, so why not NYCB? Because, fellow capitalists, The Royal Ballet is Royal—i.e., subsidized by the state. It pays a lot less of its expenses from ticket sales than does our company. Would the British Government subsidize a season—or several seasons—for the New York City Ballet? Would the United States subsidize The Royal while it was here, or NYCB while it was there? Frankly, I doubt it.

The more interesting question is, would, could, should the United States Government help support NYCB while it is here? If not, who is going to do it?

A note on the program sheet for *An Evening's Waltzes* reminds the audience, "This production was made possible by a grant from the National Endowment for the Arts." Under the cast list of *Cortège Hongrois*, is the legend, "This production was made possible by a grant from the National Endowment for the Arts and a generous contribution from LuEsther T. Mertz." We all know about the National Endowment for the Arts, but what's a LuEsther T. Mertz? Ms. Mertz is a woman from Texas whose name sounds very funny when you say it, but looks absolutely wonderful when signed on a check. During the Stravinsky Festival of June, 1972, Ms. Mertz was so impressed that she offered the company a $50,000 contribution. Lincoln did a bit of fast work and managed to get her name on the *Pulcinella* program. The grant was not specifically designated for that ballet, but it was decided, very rightly, that Ms. Mertz deserved some recognition. Without people like Ms. Mertz, NYCB would be in worse shape than it is.

Every so often, during an intermission, you will see Lincoln giving a few people private backstage tours. Sometimes, they are artists from other cities or other countries; sometimes they are personal friends; sometimes they are money. The performing arts must rely more and more on personal and corporate contributions, and Lincoln's talents in helping to convince people to contribute are said to be considerable. People like LuEsther T. Mertz, who simply volunteer substantial gifts are, not surprisingly, rare. Many individuals and corporations who do support the arts seem to prefer making their donations to posher operations, such as the Metropolitan Opera. The Met's recently completed *Ring* was paid for by Eastern Airlines. On the other hand, when Mr. B. made a ballet called *PAMTGG*, because its musical theme came from a commercial that proclaimed "Pan Am makes the goin' great," Pan American Airlines did not underwrite the production. True, *PAMTGG* is a dreadful ballet—the completed score did not inspire Mr. B. as the theme apparently did—but how often does a company get Balanchine to choreograph a commercial? Pan Am might have made the going great for the Stravinsky Festival, and taken a nice tax deduction, too. This is not meant as a diatribe against a particular airline; simply as an illustration of an idea—that American corporations should take more responsibility for supporting the performing arts. Why couldn't General Electric, for example, back a Broadway show? (Considering the lifespans of most Broadway shows, G.E. would wind up with a neat tax loss.) Why wouldn't it be possible for IT&T to underwrite one season for The New York City Ballet, or for Du Pont to provide a few new productions for The San Francisco Opera? It means a tax deduction, the corporate name in the program, plenty of publicity if properly handled—why not? Xerox and other large corporations have sponsored quality television programs, and been neatly unassertive in their use of commercials. True, television commands a larger one-shot audience than NYCB, but a good public reations counsel could do quite a bit with a ballet season. Major corporations al-

ready control a lot of American life—perhaps it is time more began
supporting American art.

How would they explain it to the shareholders? The same way
they explain everything else. Considering the manner in which
some annual reports are written, the shareholders might never even
know.

Why should they bother? Public duty? Not necessarily—there
is such a word in public relations jargon as "image." Besides,
maybe there are some corporation directors who like ballet, or
at least would like their children to like it.

Some corporations have made a start. Eastern Airlines did buy
the Met its *Ring*, and McDonald Corporation (of the hamburger
McDonalds) has sponsored series of Christmastime concerts at the
Kennedy Center for the Performing Arts in Washington.

The other obvious source of funds is the Federal Government.
The United Sates, as is widely known, spends a far smaller percentage of its annual budget for support of the performing arts than
do other, smaller countries. The National Endowment is a start,
but it is horribly clear that performances are going to get more expensive, along with everything else, during the coming years. The
current grants of that institution will not be enough, nor can gifts
from individuals completely prevent art—at least, in some of its
manifestations—from pricing itself nearly out of existence.

Mr. Balanchine is not a devotee of government grants. He feels
that when people give you money, they want to start telling you
what to do with it. Mr. B. does not want anyone telling him what
ballets to produce or how to produce them, and he is perfectly
right. But federal funds, given in quantity with no directions on
the label, could help NYCB.

Raising ticket prices is not the answer. That system only helps
create a larger group of people who can't afford to go to the theater.
Several seasons after raising its prices, the Metropolitan Opera
found that being sold out no longer was a way of life. There are
other reasons for the decline in attendance at the Met—many of the
same reasons that keep people away from NYCB—but a $20 top
(and a $4 bottom, unless you want to stand) certainly doesn't help
pack the house.

NYCB must pay greater attention to financial matters—you can't run a supermarket chain like a neighborhood delicatessen—and City Center's revised procedures should help that. The company is trying to increase its audience—Eddie Villella's television appearances may help that. However, even if the company, or City Center, were to acquire the most imaginative, forward-thinking, ruthless financial management talent available, it would still lose money, unless it chose to stop being The New York City Ballet. It certainly would lose less, but it would lose money, because classical ballet, properly done, is expensive. Ballet began as an aristocratic art form, and never has forgotten it. Ballet in America is both an art form and a business, and it would be unwise to ever forget that—better economic planning is essential. However, art and business always seem to be playing tug-o-war in this country. When art wins, you get NYCB at its best. When business wins, you get Broadway at its worst. If the two cannot be disassociated then some sort of truce is needed, before they tear one another to bits like the Kilkenny cats, leaving us with high-priced, low-quality tatters, cheap art at high prices.

It has been said, rightly enough, that the country could survive without the New York City Ballet, or without any ballet at all. It also could survive without the New York Jets, or without any professional football at all. In what condition it would survive is another matter. Sports and art are not byproducts of civilization, but essentials—both provide the temporary Dionysian madness that prevents the public from succumbing too often to the greater, permanent madness that lies in wait for us all. It is not accidental that games and arts are as universal among human cultures as communal eating and sex—they just have to happen.

Even Puritan cultures have them, sometimes in rather twisted forms. Sermons such as "Sinners in the Hand of an Angry God," must have provided plenty of Aristotelian pity and terror, but I find *Hamlet*, and *Concerto Barocco*, bicycle-riding and the New York Mets a hell of a lot healthier brands of sublimation.

The Athenians knew all about it, of course. They made the theater a religious precinct. Admission was free, and the costs of each production were covered by a local capitalist, the choregus. It was a duty for the capitalist, of course, but those who put on a good show got quite a bit of image for their money. The system was not perfect—no system ever has been perfect—but the basic reasoning was sound: Art is a psychological necessity which costs money; somebody has to pay for it; let it be the state and the most prosperous citizens, and let them gain honor and advancement by doing so. Our most prosperous citizens are the foundations and mammoth corporations, and a few very rich people. The state takes in a few bucks in taxes, too. Let them support the arts—and the sports, too, should they ever need it—and gain honor and advancement thereby. Let them also have enough sense not to try to tamper with the product; the only people who are capable of controlling the content of art are artists. On the other hand, the financiers might make a few courses in basic accounting available to the theater folk; it wouldn't hurt the artists to learn to count.

In the long run, the future of NYCB will depend on sound—not restrictive, just sound—financial thinking, on the part of government, the foundations, the corporations, and on people like LuEsther T. Mertz. The choregus from Texas, God bless her.

10

Injuries

Warning: It Has Been Determined That Ballet Dancing Is Dangerous To Your Health. Dancers voluntarily have altered the course of evolution, and that practice invariably leads to trouble. Human beings are the dominant life form of the planet not merely because of the opposing thumb or the highly developed cerebral cortex, but because we are magnificently adaptable. Most organisms are, in varying degrees, specialists; humans are generalists, capable of survival in a remarkable range of environments. The sheep ked, a wingless fly, spends its entire life in the fleece of its host. If the sheep in a region go, so does the sheep ked. Certain frogs and toads have no teeth, which limits their diets. Human beings and cockroaches have been blessed with adaptability, and the cockroaches leave well enough alone. Humans, gifted with cerebral intelligence, don't. Humans always try to change themselves from generalists into specialists, and sometimes succeed too well.

Ballet dancers teach their bodies to do things that defy the principles of human design. Bumblebees, as every aeronautical engineer knows, can't fly: their wings are too short to carry their bodies. Fortunately, no bumblebee ever studied aeronautical engineering, and so they fly anyway. Human toes were not designed to stand on. Unfortunately, dancers know this very well, but they stand on them anyway. When an organism is as much modified in structure and purpose as a dancer's body, it becomes dangerously fragile. When breeders began trying to produce longer and longer dachshunds, the dachshunds started to die of broken backs—their spines were weakened by over-elongation. When dancers learn to turn out 180 degrees from the hips, to dance on pointe, to hold their torsos high off their waists, to arch and point their feet unnaturally, the muscles involved in these operations are strengthened in one way, but weakened in others. They become intensely vulnerable to injury. The pace of an NYCB season and the stresses of life within the New York State microcosm act on that vulnerability, and people get hurt.

Deborah Koolish's injury and opening-night replacement were not unusual, but they were prophetic. Spring, 1973, was the season everyone got hurt. The dancers had less rest than usual before the season began. They took on the immense task of preparing the Stravinsky Festival while dancing the spring, 1972, season, then made a tour of Eastern Europe from which they returned just in time to begin preparations for the winter season in New York. The lay-off between that season and this one was prolonged by the late start of rehearsals, but the extra three weeks rest only gave the dancers a chance to realize how tired they were. Every season brings injuries, but this spring, the accidents started to happen early.

THURSDAY, MAY 10: The company is in its second week of repertory, bustling with preparations for *Cortège Hongrois* and *An Evening's Waltzes*. Although Peter Martins danced *Apollo* last night, this afternoon he announces that the shoulder injury which has pained him for several days is worse. He can't do *Goldberg Variations* at the Saturday matinee. He can't do anything for a while. The pinched nerve in his right shoulder is sending terrible pains through his back and has nearly paralyzed his arm. Patty McBride suggests the name of a Japanese masseur who has helped her with the pressure technique of Shiatsu. Peter will try his own masseur first. Meanwhile, Jerry Robbins and Sally Leland snatch up all the unclaimed rehearsal time for tomorrow and Saturday morning, to work on *Goldberg*. Sally explains, "Bruce Wells will have to do Peter, so Bryan Pitts has to do Bruce and someone has to do Bryan."

FRIDAY, MAY 11: The *Goldberg* sessions start immediately after class. Sally directs the rehearsal, but most of the work devolves upon the dancers. Bryan, his shampoo-ad blond hair as unruffled as his disposition, follows Bruce along the paths of the dance. Bob Maiorano coaches Bryan in the passage in which they enter from opposite sides of the stage and mirror one another. Then Bryan takes back his usual role to help Sally teach it to Jean-Pierre Frohlich, a small, intense young dancer, quite new to the company. He learns the steps quickly.

Sections of the ballet are rehearsed so rapidly they overlap. Dancers scurry past one another on the floor like ants going about important business; they practice the essentials of one sequence, then hurry on to the next. There is little time for concern about finesse, but as Bryan and Jean-Pierre mime the steps, they also absorb the style of the dancers who are teaching them. After the session with Sally, Bruce Wells goes to the practice room to work with Peter Martins and Jerry Robbins and learn his new role. Robbins is rehearsing *Waltzes*, too; these injuries have made his schedule even more crowded than usual.

Just as problems appear to have been settled, Delia Peters sprains an ankle, stamping down too hard during the day's stint of the czardas in *Cortège*. She's in *Goldberg* too, and no replacement is available. Delia has no understudy for many of the ballets she dances (as a rule, there are general corps understudies who can step into any position after a quick emergency rehearsal) and in the ballets in which she does have a cover, the understudy is injured, too. Jerry decides that Suzanne Erlon will do some segments of Delia's part in *Goldberg* and Chris Redpath will cover the rest.

SATURDAY, MAY 12: *Goldberg* rehearsal continues on stage until Robert Irving starts for the orchestra pit to begin *Brahms-Schönberg Quartet*. Roland Vazquez broadcasts the lineup to the audience: Anthony Blum for Peter Martins in *Brahms*, everyone for everyone else in *Goldberg*. They get through it, somehow. As the dancers come down to the stage-right corner, you can hear Bruce Wells asking his partner, "Where now?".

"Stay here, I'll tell you when we go," and when the time comes, she tugs his hand, leading him in the right direction as if taking a young son for a walk. The process is called "Talk-me-through-it," and it is in constant use during the season. Standing in the wings, you can hear dancers whispering instructions to their partners, smiling more widely than ever so the audience won't see their lips moving. "Pilot-to-tower, pilot-to-tower, where do I go now?" The tower always answers. The dancers simply do not have the time to learn every sequence when they go on at short notice; they know the basic patterns, and rely on guidance for the rest. Since ballet has a standard nomenclature, the procedure is not as confusing as it sounds to an outsider. Tell a dancer "piqué," and he knows what to do. He can execute the step when it is named the way a practiced square-dancer can follow the caller.

There also is a certain amount of faking. "When in doubt," counsels Bruce, "smile, bow and sauté." Choreographers, like painters, select from their palettes for each canvas. They do not necessarily do it consciously, any more than Shakespeare needed to tell himself, "I think I'll use a lot of disease images in this 'Hamlet' thing." Some steps suit a piece of music and a theme and physical pattern more than others. Some steps follow others in a comfortable sequence, exactly as words do, while others would be awkward in context. Most ballets, therefore, have thematic steps which are repeated often in different forms. One dance bounces along with pas de chats, while another floats on arabesques penchées. A dancer quickly discovers which steps dominate a ballet, and when in doubt, he uses one of them. The audience assumes, since it has seen that movement several times during the past few minutes, that it must be right.

Audiences see and hear what they expect, anyway. The English actor Peter Bull once bet a fellow player that he could walk on during a Shakespearean scene and say "Haddock fish-and-chips" instead of his proper line, without the audience catching on. He won. "Talk me through it," and "Smile, bow and sauté," are dancers' versions of the ad lib. An actor stranded on stage makes up a speech, a dancer improvises a step. Neither invention, if skillfully done, is likely to be noticed by the spectators. If the performer just stood there, everyone would know something was wrong. As long as action appropriate to the situation is taking place on stage, everything is assumed to be going on as planned. The matinee audience thinks it is seeing *Goldberg* exactly as Jerry conceived it.

Having survived the afternoon, the company still has to compose itself for the evening performance. Kay Mazzo is suffering from an injured leg; Susie Hendl has a pulled tendon in her foot; Milly Hayden, who almost never misses a performance, is out with a badly pulled calf muscle; Karin von Aroldingen's foot is injured. The casting of the final ballet on the evening's program, *Symphony in C*, is a juggling act. The first movement is led by Marnee Morris and Jean-Pierre Bonnefous (Marnee for Milly Hayden); the second movement features Gelsey Kirkland and Conrad Ludlow (Gelsey for Kay Mazzo); the third movement brings John Clifford and Sally Leland (Sally for Gelsey); and the fourth presents Susan Hendl and Frank Ohman (Susie for Marnee Morris, see first movement).

This afternoon, while Bruce was being talked through *Goldberg*, Milly Hayden took her injured leg to a masseur, where she met Violette Verdy, also in for repairs. Milly asked if Violette could dance the first movement of Bizet—the company calls *Symphony in C* by the name of its composer. Violette said she was in no shape to dance, either, but she came to the theater and hunted up Marnee Morris, who agreed to move from fourth movement to first. The company finally knew who's on first, but the move left a position open. Everyone with access to a telephone started a search for Lynda Yourth, who knows the fourth movement of Bizet, but Lynda was unfindable, which is why Susie Hendl is dancing with a pulled tendon. She dances neatly, despite the pain. Delia Peters is in the corps, despite her ankle. It's a hospital ward out there. Dancers say that often, when you get on stage and start moving, you don't notice the pain of an injury. Of course, when you come off stage, it hurts more than it did before.

SUNDAY, MAY 13: In class, Kay says she used Eddie Villella's ultra-sound machine on her leg last night and slept with a heating pad covering the muscle. It still hurts. Mr. B. advises her against getting a massage, saying it might make the leg worse, but if the pain does not ease, she may go for one tomorrow. Monday is massage day, anyhow.

Nobody is injured during the matinee. Eddie Villella, Kay and

Karin are among the dancing wounded on stage. Rudolf Nureyev, who is appearing with the National Ballet of Canada at the Metropolitan Opera House, has taken the afternoon off and come to see NYCB as a guest of Jean-Pierre Bonnefous. There's a lot of excitement backstage when the word is passed.

Before the evening performance of *Jewels* there is an emergency rehearsal. Chris Redpath has to go on in *Emeralds* for Sheryl Ware, a pretty, usually healthy young woman who has contracted some sort of quick-acting intestinal flu. Peter Martins and Kay will lead the *Diamonds* section, he with a damaged right shoulder and she with an injured left leg. They decide to perform the difficult scherzo, despite their injuries. Rosie Dunleavy, having told the corps girls it was out, hurries back to inform them that it's in again.

Milly Hayden dances *Emeralds* and has trouble during her adagio; her determination and carriage are majestic as usual, but her balance is not—her leg still has not healed. Everyone is doing the "Damn-the-pain-the-show-must-go-on" routine, and they are unaware that it is corny because they mean it. The dancers are driving themselves, giving the audience its money's worth, and the theater is less than half full. This is closing night for Nureyev and the Canadians, and most New Yorkers who brave the night on Sunday to see dance are over at the Met.

The spectators in the orchestra of the New York State Theater tonight are mostly subscribers, who have their tickets and might as well show up. There are a few clusters of younger people dressed in slacks and sweaters, and the usual collection of NYCB fanatics who would be here if another theater were offering the Book of Genesis with the original cast. Edward Gorey, the author-illustrator, even sees every performance of *The Nutcracker* during its five-week winter run. Robert, Anne, Amy, Charles—the faithful camp followers who are as much a part of Mr. B.'s army as the dancers—are here as usual. Intensely involved with the company, superbly knowledgeable about dance, they are the closest thing New York has to the balletomanes of Imperial Russia, where constant ballet-watching was afforded virtually the status of a profession. Not being generals or Grand Duchesses, the members of Balanchine's Brigade will have to get up tomorrow morning and go to work, but

they keep the tradition growing. If anyone can appreciate the dedication of the dancers, it is they. Still, it would have been nice to
have a full house. I wonder what the injury list of the Canadian
company looks like.

MONDAY, MAY 14: Day off. Nobody possibly can get hurt.

TUESDAY, MAY 15: Wrong. In class, we get the news that Mme.
Karinska fell last night and broke her hip, her third such injury in
recent years. She's in the hospital. At least the costumes for *Cortège*
are almost finished. Eddie Bigelow says Karinska is resting easily
and, despite her eighty-three years, will be out of bed before the
season is over. He turns out to be right.

Injuries are like a plague; once they begin, they keep on happening. The dancers must do more work than usual to cover the
roles of those who are hurt, and the added strain makes them more
vulnerable to injury in their turn. The worries about Berlin, about
City Center's debts, about the probability of a musicians' strike in
the fall, don't make things any easier. Karin and Kay fall; Gelsey
incurs her first injury of the season and Elise Flagg goes in to dance
Brahms-Schönberg Quartet. Karin's foot still hasn't healed when *The
Firebird* comes into the repertory, but she dances the role anyway,
strapped into the huge air-catching wings that make it difficult for
her to run—and The Firebird does a fair amount of running.

May drives through the company like an ambulance: Jacques is
out; Helgi is hurt; Peter can't lift his arm; Eddie Villella is on the
sidelines with a badly pulled thigh muscle. The corps kids still
wonder how we would do if we merged with the Mets—with Peter
and Jacques injured, Gloria Govrin will have to play first base.
Susan Hendl keeps dancing with damaged tendons; Gelsey breaks
her foot; Bob Maiorano rips a knee cartilage. "It's going to get
worse," the dancers say. "We're all tired; we're over-dancing; there
are too many roles that have to be covered. It's going to get worse."

THURSDAY, MAY 24: The premiere of *An Evening's Waltzes*. The
wicked spirit who seems to have been haunting Jerry's ballet is not
exorcised yet. During the performance, Merrill Ashley damages
the tendons in her right ankle.

FRIDAY, MAY 25: After last night's triumphant curtain calls and
party, after saying he's tired but looking happy, Jerry is on stage

rehearsing for the evening's performance of *Dances at a Gathering*. He is replacing Peter Martins with Bruce Wells, Bob Maiorano with Bart Cook and Tony Blum with Jean-Pierre Bonnefous. Tony has not been in the theater for a week; Milly and Violette are concerned about him. Nothing physical is wrong, but he obviously has been deeply disturbed about something. He's not been taking class, either. Dancers say, "Tony abuses his body too much; he doesn't take care of himself." He's in no shape to dance. Just put him on the injured list, along with the others, and chalk it up to stress.

Jerry and Sally guide the revised cast on a quick tour of *Dances*, concentrating on the bits that most need to be studied. Jerry also has to begin training new recruits for *Waltzes*. He chooses Delia Peters (her ankle is a bit better) to replace Merrill, and Colleen Neary to take over Delia's role. In *Dances*, he teaches the role of The Boy in Brown, which Helgi had been scheduled to perform, to John Clifford. Upstairs, another rehearsal, necessitated by Helgi's injury, is going on: Victor Castelli, the young man with the ear-level extension, is being promoted into Helgi's role in *Symphony in Three Movemements*.

Everyone at the *Dances* rehearsal is overworked and tired; when not dancing, they sprawl around the periphery of the stage. While working, they use their hands to indicate steps whenever they can, and try to mark instead of dancing. Jerry is working with beautiful calm, assuring the dancers "It's going to be a good performance." He shows John Clifford the opening steps, starting his arm sweep from the middle of his back, so that his shirt ripples. The air opens before him. People who saw Jerry dance years ago still talk about those performances; it's easy to understand why. Like Balanchine, he finds the emotional core of a movement. Also, like Mr. B., he moves with minimal effort—his muscles do only as much as they must to accomplish their work. Most dancers seem to fight with gravity; Balanchine and Robbins have signed a mutual assistance pact with it.

Jerry is coaching as gently as he can. His insistence on perfection remains undiminished—he takes John Clifford through the opening walk-on several times—but he is keeping his voice even, trying his best to suppress mannerisms that might irritate the performers. He isn't even calling them "dancers." Even so, John stalks off stage in a fury, swearing because Jerry is being too damned precise for such short notice. Johnny, like everyone else, is being stretched to snapping tension. The only one in the theater who seems imperturbable is Mr. B.

Before being distributed to the customers, the evening's program is fitted with a yellow insert, which reads:

"Friday Evening, May 25, 1973, at 8:00 P.M.

"Because of injuries to Merrill Ashley, Gelsey Kirkland, Anthony Blum, Robert Maiorano and Helgi Tomasson, the following cast changes will take place in *Dances at a Gathering:*

"In mauve: Kay Mazzo; In pink: Susan Hendl.

"In mauve: Jean-Pierre Bonnefous; In brick: Robert Weiss; In blue: Bart Cook; In brown: John Clifford.

"In *The Song of the Nightingale*, the Nightingale will be danced by Elise Flagg; the Mechanical Nightingale: Meg Gordon."

At least nothing can go wrong in the curtain-raiser, *Donizetti Variations.* Pianist Gordon Boelzner is conducting, as he does several times each season. Standing in the corridor before performance, Gordon looks handsome, if a bit nervous, in his tail coat. He studies the score a bit, waves his white baton to get the feel of the tempo and chats with Renee Estopinal about the latest additions to the sick list. On stage, Kevin asks for "Independent 1, please," and trades jokes with the electricians. Dancers do their warm-up barres, some wearing bandages under their tights and around their feet. At Kevin's nod, Gordon leaves for the podium, and we begin.

Gordon is a good musician; he knows his score and his dancers, sets a proper tempo and keeps his beat regular and clear. The stage lights pick up Eddie Villella's anticipatory grin as he sees the semicircle of corps girls arranged for his delectation, the glow on Kay Mazzo's sweet, serious little face and reflect back from the shiny satin surfaces of toe shoes. The corps is prancing like circus ponies, stepping along at a good pace, showing their pretty tricks, when a stage light, hanging from a stage-right batan, bursts its lens with the kind of bang children produce by smashing an inflated paper bag. Fragments of glass spatter the stage; luckily, they land in an area free of dancers.

By the time the performers, on stage and in the wings, have figured out what has happened and let go their breaths, Kay is in the middle of a variation with Bruce Wells, James Bogan and Nolan T'Sani. Each man takes a turn partnering her while the other two leap in tandem behind them. They've done it so often not even an exploding light can break the pattern. The men kiss at Kay's hand; she flirts with each of them in turn. Bruce is her cavalier now, while Jim and Nolan leap like a team of acrobats, arching their chests against the air, opening their legs like compasses to measure space and time. They land, bending in plié, take off again, touch down, and suddenly Jim is doing an unexpected solo while Nolan limps to the wings on a badly twisted ankle. Kay turns to allow Nolan to kiss her hand, and finds herself extending her fingers to a vacancy. Jim takes his turn as partner, and Bruce takes his as half a duet. Nolan manages to get back on stage during the finale for long enough to support his partner in her pirouettes, but that's the last bit of dancing he's going to do for a while. Nobody quite believes any of it. Nobody knows what to say, either, except Chris Redpath, who shrugs and remarks, "Well, I know Ballet Theater wants to move in here, but they could be more subtle about it."

There is no time to say anything else. Jerry Robbins is on stage, conducting a last-touches *Dances* rehearsal with Sally Leland and Ricky Weiss. Sally is dancing with leg warmers around her thigh, hidden under her skirt—she's pulled a muscle, too. They don't stop work until Jerry Zimmerman is in his place at the piano and the stage lights are at opening intensity.

Susie Hendl, dancing for Gelsey, looks lovely with her blond hair shining over the pink of her costume, but is so nervous she scarcely breathes. Susie still is injured, and she's never done this role before. John Clifford makes his entrance, slowly, as Jerry taught him; he sweeps his arm high and wide. Playing down his own exuberance and subduing it to the role, he achieves more vulnerability and dignity than he has shown all season. He comes off stage screaming that Jerry Zimmerman played the variation much too fast. Johnny is no calmer than anyone else backstage, but he can't let his mood affect the ballet. He did the steps at the tempo set by the piano, then came off and erupted.

Tension hangs in the air like August humidity; you almost can taste it. Susie Hendl, waiting to make an entrance, tells Susie Pilarre, "I really can't do this—not with my foot. I'm just going to mark it." Her voice is flat with a "the-hell-with-what-Jerry-will-say" defensive quality that is a sure pressure gauge. "All right," soothes dark-haired Susie, "then I'll just mark it, too. We'll both mark it." Neither does. Blond Susie meant to walk through it, but that was in the wings. When she gets on stage, she dances.

We reach the tosses. Three men—in this performance Ricky Weiss, Jean-Pierre Bonnefous and Bart Cook—stand downstage left. Ricky picks up a girl and tosses her to Jean-Pierre, who passes her on to slender Bart, who sets her down. They play the game three times, with different women. Of course, they don't actually throw the girls at one another like medicine balls. As in a lift, the woman springs into the air, the man adds to her momentum, and she soars. Except that Jean-Pierre, although of medium height, is built like Don Giovanni's statue. When Jean-Pierre tosses girls, he is playing bean-bag with people. Bart Cook catches the ladies neatly, but he hasn't looked so surprised since he found out the truth about Santa Claus. The women need a moment to recover, too.

Susie Hendl, nerves and all, romances through the long, beautiful pas de deux with Jean-Pierre richly and sweetly, getting all the grace notes in the right places. The dancers in the wings are helping her along with little twists of their waists, sending telepathic messages of confidence. As the curtain falls, they applaud her. A few seconds later, the audience is applauding.

Song of the Nightingale is set up by the stagehands. Gelsey is backstage, leaning on her crutches, to wish "Merde" to Elise Flagg. She turns to Peter Naumann, who plays the young fisherman on whose shoulder the Nightingale rides: "Treat her gently," she says, and goes out to sit in the audience. It is so hard to have to watch, and not to do. Elise and Meg Gordon do a professional job, and everybody goes home. It's been the longest night of the season—everyone in the wings mentally danced every step of *Dances* and *Nightingale*. We need a stiff round of drinks, followed by warm baths.

SATURDAY, MAY 26: Milly Hayden brings the news that this morning, Jacques underwent an operation to repair his knee. She has no idea how long he'll be out. Kay is developing back spasms in addition to the pains in her leg. Returning to *Dances* after an absence, especially last night's *Dances*, was a strain. She's made an appointment with Milly's chiropractor.

During the matinee (*Swan Lake, Apollo, The Firebird*) Merrill Ashley comes backstage on crutches. Her right leg is in a cast and she's tied a big, red bow around her middle toe. "You want to spare people the sight of a dancer's bare feet." She hopes to be able to dance in two weeks. Conrad Ludlow partners Milly in *Swan Lake*, succeeding Jean-Pierre Bonnefous, who has to dance *Waltzes* and is too overworked to do both ballets. Conny eliminates the Prince's variation—he had no time to practice it.

At the evening performance, Eddie Villella cuts a variation from *La Source*. He's still in pain because of his thigh, and after dancing here, he has to run across to Philharmonic Hall to appear in a Promenade Concert. Victor Castelli does his first *Symphony in Three Movements*, subbing for Helgi. Victor was on stage rehearsing at 6:45. Lynda Yourth, his partner, joins him a bit later, and they work until curtain time.

Tonight, even more rumors than usual are flitting backstage about the company's financial discomfort. A few dancers, who are turning slightly paranoid, think City Center might cancel the company's fall season.

Violette has talked with Tony Blum, and says "he's going to take two weeks off and straighten himself out." She is concerned for Tony; she knows what this place does to people.

Mr. B. sums up the injury situation in one sentence: "If I were Hurok, we would have closed already."

SUNDAY, MAY 27: Peter Martins is back in class, using the piano for a barre as he always does. Maybe the jinx is wearing off. Maybe the chance to rest is healing some of the wounds.

At the matinee, *Donizetti Variations* gives off as much hum as a defective radio: Steve Caras had to go on for Nolan with almost no rehearsal, and the entire cast is talking him through it.

Divertimento No. 15 proves the jinx is still in residence. Susie Hendl hurts her injured foot; she's been dancing far more than she really should. Vickie Bromberg joins the infirmary, too—the bottom of her foot is severely swollen.

At 6:45, Rosie conducts an emergency *Swan Lake* rehearsal, to replace Vickie. It's hurried but efficient: "Lisa, which side do you come down on in the finale?—Right." Kay and Conrad are the principals. He still has not had enough time to work on his variation, and asks that it be cut. Kay trims a bit, too; she's still in pain. Hugo Fiorato, the associate conductor, who will be on the podium tonight, is informed of the cuts. Whatever happens in ballet, somebody must tell the conductor. If he does not know that a segment has been eliminated, he'll play it.

Kay dances a beautiful *Swan Lake*. It is one of those occasions on which she finally gives herself to the music and allows it to carry her. She floats like duck down in the lights; her dark eyes are sad and her arms as fragile as fledglings. She flutters through the pas de deux, balanced and carried by Conny's big hands. Then, as she revolves in a slow, supported turn, the forefinger of her free hand catches in the front of Conrad's tunic; the momentum of her spin bends it to the spraining point. Somehow, she finishes the ballet with the intensity she had at the beginning. She finishes the curtain call, too, then rushes to her dressing room with the funny, flat-footed little steps dancers make when they run, crying. Kay has danced with spasms in her back, an aching calf, too little sleep—and now, a sprained finger. Peter, her tall off-stage cavalier, taxis her the few blocks to Roosevelt Hospital for an X-ray examination.

By the time Kay has changed and gone, still trembling but dry of tears, intermission is over and the stage is filled with the green, white and gold costumes of *Cortège Hongrois*. Two dancers are substituting for Merrill: Kathleen Haigney (Weiss) in the corps and Marjorie Spohn in the variation. Some dancers fidget when they get stage nerves; Margie is tense to trembling. Her arms are rigid at her sides, her fingers hang as stiffly as winter twigs. By comparison, Kathy is calm, ready to trust herself. The music begins, courses through both of them, and they dance. Hugo Fiorato, conducting his first performance of *Cortège*, takes Colleen Neary's variation too quickly, Margie's not quickly enough. Mr. B. stands in the wings and twists his mouth as if tasting something unpleasant, as he always does when displeased with a tempo.

During the intermission, he stands near the stage-right property table and questions Hugo. The conductor says Margie told him to play her variation "slower." "Slower than what?" Balanchine demands. "They don't know about tempi. You have to take them as they are set. *They* don't know anything about it. They are a little nervous, so they say, 'Play slower.' "

We get through the last ballet of the week, *Pulcinella*, without anybody being injured. That is, nobody on stage is injured. During the intermission, one of the ushers hurts her foot.

The problem of choosing ballet tempi is complex. They must suit the composers' indications (providing he left any) and the mood of the dance. They also must suit the dancers. Mr. B. will not give houseroom to lackadaisical "ballet tempi"; everything is played at concert speed, and the dancers are trained to maintain the pace. However, the pace is not the same for every dancer. A good little man almost always moves more quickly than a good big man. Helgi Tomasson, for example, is faster than Peter Martins because he has less to move. If Peter and Helgi dance the same variation on successive evenings, the conductor should take the first performance a shade more slowly than the second. (Robert Irving can hum a piece at Peter-tempo, then at Helgi-tempo.) If the two performances are led by different conductors, the problems are compounded. Conductors are not metronomes beating time, they are humans playing music and they make subjective judgments. Hugo Fiorato may not make quite the same subjective judgment as Robert Irving, although he tries to take the piece at the same speed.

Hugo is a dapper gentleman whose white hair is so handsome you feel certain he must have grown it in that color on purpose. He dresses well, dines well, enjoys conversations and fashionable company. He began life as a violinist, playing under Stokowski and Bruno Walter, and therefore insists that "string players make the best conductors—they know articulation and bowing."

Hugo points out that his tempi sometimes differ from Irving's because he seldom gets to rehearse with the orchestra. The music director generally takes the season's first performance of a work, and the conductor doing that gets any rehearsal time allotted for the piece. Robert Irving agrees that he gets "three or four times" as much rehearsal as Hugo. During rehearsals, Hugo sits in the early rows of the orchestra, making notes in his score, knowing that he will probably be scheduled to lead the work later in the season, or that Robert may be taken ill. It seldom happens, but around here it is unwise not to be prepared for any contingency.

One of Hugo's problems is that, because much of the music used at NYCB was not written specifically for dancing, Balanchine and Robert do not always use the composer's metronome settings. Furthermore, he complains, they don't always mark the setting in the score and he is left to pick up the tempo by listening during rehearsal. Part of the reason for this is that tempi will vary slightly from performance to performance, as they must. Hugo also suffers from a surfeit of advice. "Dancers always want it slower—and tell you they want it slower than they really do. Mr. B. always wants it faster—and tells you to take it faster than he really wants it. The trick is to know how much faster than the dancers want it, and how much slower than Mr. B. wants it, is the right speed at which to take it."

Like a catcher in baseball, a conductor in ballet gives the signals and controls the game because he can see the entire playing area. Robert or Hugo, whichever is on the podium at a specific performance, is in charge. He must cue both dancers and orchestra with his baton; sometimes, when the dancers begin before the music, he needs to watch and take his cue from them. He must alter tempi during performance when necessary—maybe a dancer is recovering from an injury and is a bit slower than he was at rehearsal; perhaps a section of the ballet is not holding together and needs a bit more pace to weld it. He is, as Hugo says, "in charge of holding it all together, keeping the whole thing moving."

Robert Irving, who was music director of Sadler's Wells Ballet (now The Royal Ballet) before joining NYCB and is regarded as one of the world's finest conductors of ballet, makes the easily overlooked point that although the orchestra and the dancers must depend on one another, they cannot see one another. "It appears as if you're just conducting a concert, but actually, you're leading two groups, the orchestra and the dancers. It's much more complex than a symphony performance."

Because of Balanchine's musical tastes, NYCB's conductors lead a repertory that is diverse and contains scores that are rhythmically and texturally complex. Both the orchestra (which is superb) and the dancers must be lead through passages of extreme intricacy—the corps' first count may be a "silent #1," for example. A dance conductor also requires an absolutely firm, but flexible, beat. The pattern drawn by the baton is the foundation of the performance; if there is any uncertainty about it, the entire structure will topple. A good ballet conductor knows his dancers, he knows their strengths and weaknesses as well as their preferences in tempi. He is aware who needs a strong, visual cue and who is practiced enough to move at a casual nod. Also, he knows his music. The orchestra at NYCB is not there merely to accompany the dance; each performance is a concert to be played with as much attention to shading and detail as if it were being performed across the plaza in Philharmonic Hall. Balanchine will accept nothing less.

Ballet, especially Balanchine ballet, is built on music. The structure of the piece frequently orders the structure of the dance; the mood and rhythms of the music dictate the choreography. The style and spirit of the music's period are transmitted to everything that appears on stage—the steps, the costumes, the lighting, even the size of the cast. At times, the relationship is obvious. The orchestra plays a funny, lightsome little phrase and a couple flirts in its physical equivalent; Sousa's music marches four-square through the theater, and a regiment on stage forms ranks and files; Stravinsky inverts a classical phrase, Balanchine's ballerina inverts a classical foot position.

Rehearsing *Divertimento No. 15*, Mr. B. urges the corps, "No, RUN. It MUST be like that—quick and running. That's what

Mozart wrote, and what he wanted. It must be like that. And when you run, take short steps. Otherwise, it looks like soup, and Mozart didn't write soup."

In *Concerto Barocco*, made to Bach's Concerto for two violins, the counterpoint of movement is as clear and as complex as the interweaving voices of the music. How many ways can be found to arrange eight corps girls, two ballerinas and their cavalier, without disrupting the formal pattern? The mathematics of the ballet are as rich as those of the score because they proceed from it.

At other times, the relationship is less obvious. An audience may hear a strict waltz 1-2-3, and see the dancers moving in another pattern. They may dance slightly behind the beat, or slightly ahead of it, or even across it. The piccolo can be twittering, but a dancer is stretching deeply. Dance does not simply follow music, it derives from it. The choreography may move against a rhythm or phrase; it may echo it or argue with it; underline it or merely skim it. That is one reason dancers work to counts, rather than directly to music. A composer constantly iterates a phrase, but Balanchine chooses to illuminate that phrase from a different angle each time. In *Danses Concertantes* he uses similar steps in several sections with different music. A dancer works with the music, not to it.

Any work of art has a rhythm, an element of repetition that sustains it as the heartbeat sustains an animal. Balanchine never forgets it. His choreography may follow a melodic phrase, an orchestral swell or diminuendo, a theme-and-response or any other musical motif, but always, under it, is the pulse, even when fever speeds it or familiarity makes us forget it is there. From time to time, Balanchine will call it to mind, with a sharp lunge on the beat or a quick turn of a wrist, then submerge it again, as the body of the ballet becomes more interesting than the simple repetitious thrum of the basic life-thread.

The pulse, the momentum, the expansion and contraction of the music underlie the construction of the dance, even when disguised. Balanchine's ballets never ignore the music—they can't—although they sometimes hum a counterpoint to it, or answer it, or hint at what they would like to hear next. In effect, ballet makes music three-dimensional. To the elements of duration, tone and pitch, it adds that of space. Balanchine's ballets, especially, are not an illustration of the score but an extension of it, and spectators who look only for a physical echo often end up confused. Those who both look and listen, and keep their fingers on the beating pulse, soon understand, even when the dancers answer the music with stillness.

TUESDAY, MAY 29: Kay's finger is bandaged; she hopes to discard the wrapping in time for performance. Helgi is in class. He'll dance *Baiser de la Fée* tonight, "and see what happens." Nolan T'Sani is back, too. Around here, one day off is a rest cure.

On stage, Balanchine directs a dress rehearsal of *Liebeslieder Walzer*. Francis Sackett is doing it for the first time, in place of Tony Blum. It's a lovely, bright day, the first we've had in a week. A few dancers spent a free hour sunbathing on the roof: "We're not supposed to, but we do. It makes you forget what's going on inside the place." And there still are four weeks of repertory to go, plus a week of *A Midsummer Night's Dream*.

The performance goes well. Helgi dances as vibrantly as always, and comes off feeling "all right." Bonnie Borne's bone spurs have stopped pricking her—she doesn't need Jerry's ethyl chloride. *Liebeslieder* is lovely.

WEDNESDAY, MAY 30: Susie Hendl is on the mend. The doctor told her she can do a barre Friday and dance at the weekend, if the dancing isn't strenuous. In the afternoon, Mr. B. asks her if she can work in *Movements for Piano and Orchestra*. "You don't have to move. You just stand there." It's a lot more than standing, but she agrees. She feels she can't refuse Mr. B., he's more important to her life than the doctor.

Nolan dances in *Donizetti Variations* without damage to himself or the stage lights. Susie stands in the wings—she's only doing *Movements*—and whisper-sings "Margie, Margie," every time Marjorie Spohn reaches the down-right corner. "We always talk to one another during this," Susie explains. "I don't want her to feel lonely."

THURSDAY, MAY 31: Class, rehearsal, performance of *Jewels*. Nobody injured. Everybody exhausted.

FRIDAY, JUNE 1: The weariness doesn't show in performance,

but the dancers need a little prodding during rehearsals. Rosie herds an unenthusiastic corps through *La Valse*. Finally, she says: "Look, just because this part isn't all that interesting doesn't mean you don't have to do it well. You have to put as much into it as into the parts that really interest you. You think the audience can't tell, because there are so many costumes, but you see everything from the front—and the audience is paying to see a full performance." She wouldn't have used that scolding-teacher tone a month ago, but a month ago the corps kids would have been joking during breaks, not sprawling on the stage trying to get some rest.

Allegra's children have the mumps.

June is picking a path through the company like a sedan chair with a tired crew, but the weather is warmer and the injury list grows shorter. That exploding light bulb must have frightened away the hexing spirits—the accident rate began to diminish shortly after that performance.

There's still plenty to worry about. The Berlin trip may or may not be on. The producers want Balanchine to cede all his film rights to the ballets they will record; the dancers want residuals should the films be made into video cassettes and offered for sale here. The rumor that this may be the company's last summer in Saratoga becomes more persistent—"We're an expensive company . . . They could get American Ballet Theater for less . . . Lincoln will have to find another place for us to work in the summer . . . What about the people who have homes up there?" Nobody knows anything for certain, and reassurances from management do no good at all.

The Saratoga season is certain this summer, anyway. After that comes a session at the Greek Theater in Los Angeles, then the festival in Wolf Trap Park, then, possibly, Berlin. If nothing happens to change the schedule, the dancers will come home just in time to start rehearsing for the fall-winter season in New York—provided there is no musician's strike, and that there is a fall season. No wonder everybody is talking about the sun and the swimming pool at Saratoga.

Still, this season is almost finished, and the company seems to be gaining strength from the knowledge of that. "If we just stick it out; if we can only last another two weeks—ten days—a week— things will be easier." We're going to survive after all.

SATURDAY, JUNE 2: At the matinee, Bonnie Borne counts her way through the intricacies of *Concerto Barocco* after two short rehearsals. She had been an understudy for it, but she covered a different role than she danced, on the opposite side of the corps. The big injuries are healing; the little, everyday accidents, like the one that dropped Bonnie into *Barocco*, keep happening. During the evening performance, the kids talk about how relaxing it is up in Saratoga, where they'll be dancing as soon as this season is over.

SUNDAY, JUNE 3: Two performances, no damage, even more talk about Saratoga and still more about how nice it will be to rest tomorrow in between visits to the chiropractor, the masseur, the laundromat.

By now, the dancers are doing the same thing as the public school children, counting the days until the semester is over. Attendance in class diminishes; everyone needs more sleep than he required at the beginning of the season. The choreographers have to do a bit more urging during rehearsal. Faces are pale, skin is taut across foreheads and cheeks. Carol Sumner injures a foot and tries acupuncture. Bob Maiorano is taking pills prescribed by his own acupuncturist. Each one is about the size of a Ping-Pong ball and encased in wax inscribed with Chinese characters. Gelsey decides to take two weeks in the Carribean, her first real vacation in centuries, to catch up on her reading and resting. There's nothing she can do here, except be unhappy. Tony Blum shows up at the theater again, moving with his old sweep and power.

Psychiatrist Louis Shaw has been persuaded by Lincoln to visit the company and make some suggestions about lowering the level of stress in the theater. He sits backstage and watches, and listens, and talks, a small, graceful man with the dangerous eyes of a portrait painter and a mind as quick as Patty McBride's feet.

WEDNESDAY, JUNE 20: The evil spirits are back, and they have a nasty taste in humor. Allegra caught the mumps from her daughter.

11

The Powers That Be

The structure of The New York State Theater is a bit like that of a medieval castle. The orchestra pit serves as the moat, keeping the aliens beyond scaling-ladder distance. The fifty-one-foot-high proscenium is hung with the portcullis of the gold front curtain. Behind it is the great hall of the stage, the center of manorial life, where spectacles are presented, homage received and guests feted. Below, stark and functional, are the kitchen, dungeons, stables, armory, granary, well—the supports of the castle and workplaces of its dependents. Above is the battlement, where troops and sentinels drill and keep constant guard lest, through laxity, the castle fall. The level below the battlements, and high above the working smells and sounds, contains the rooms of the lords, furnished with carven chests, hung with tapestries against the cold, fitted with windows.

Balanchine's private office, on the fourth floor, is both an elegant seignoirie and a comfortable living room. The piano, the small stereo system and the neat stacks of scores and recordings testify to the occupant's profession and obsession. Cats, photographed and framed, play forever on the walls. The left-hand wall, as you enter, supports long shelves of books in French, Russian and English; modern dust-jacketed volumes share the space with leather-bound, folio-sized editions from the last century, including a magnificent, two-volume *Paradise Lost*. The shelves are crowded with books about dance, music, history, politics, psychology—"But I don't collect books," Balanchine insists. "I *read*. There is a difference. These are here because I have read them." It is a good room for reading; the furniture is upholstered and inviting. The office, like Mr. B.'s mind, is an organized but comfortable compendium; nothing is too neat for ease, but everything is there when you need it. A television set, independent as a cat, sits across from the piano.

On Thursday, May 17, ABC-TV's early evening news program includes a bit of film about the previous night's gala—a two-minute segment of *Cortège*—and an interview with Milly Hayden. Mr. B. has made his television set available for the occasion, and a small group of dancers gathers in his office. In the walk-in closet, along with suits, sports coats and denim shirts, hangs the beautifully sewn medieval gown, gray with black markings, of a Doctor of Humane Letters. Columbia University presented the degree to Balanchine yesterday morning, before he presented himself to Milly as a flower boy yesterday evening. Mr. B. turns down more honorary degrees than he accepts—"Usually, they only offer because they want something from you"—but he accepted the one from Columbia, and now his gown hangs in the closet like a hooded bathrobe.

Colleen Neary sits long-legged on the floor, watching the TV screen. She is in practice clothes, and the air is cool on her half-bare shoulders. She shivers very slightly; Balanchine notices. "Are you cold? Sit here," and he pats a place beside him on the sofa. Colleen sits and leans back, but Mr. B. is not satisfied. She still looks chilly, and no guest of his is going to be uncomfortable. He steps briskly to the closet, takes the doctor's gown and drapes it over her shoulders. Smiling at his joke, he arranges the gown as dextrously as if he were helping Colleen on with her cloak before escorting her to the opera. Most people have mannerisms; Balanchine has manners. Furthermore, whether or not he thinks of it that way, he has a keen sense of *noblesse oblige*.

By this time, followers of the arts know the basic biographical facts about Balanchine. Born in St. Petersburg to a Georgian family in 1904, named Georgi Melintonovitch Balanchivadze, son of a composer sometimes called "The Georgian Glinka," entered the Imperial Ballet School in 1914 almost by accident—his family had intended him for a military career—began studying piano at the age of five and, after graduating from the Imperial Ballet School in 1921, spent three years at the Conservatory of Music. Worked during the year the ballet school was shut by revolution as a bank messenger and sadler's apprentice. Made his dancing debut at the age of ten as a cupid in the Maryinsky Theater Ballet Company production of *Sleeping Beauty*. Also appeared, as a child, in dramatic theater productions, including *A Midsummer Night's Dream*—he played the role of a bug. Joined the corps at the Maryinsky at the age of seventeen, and staged one work, called *Enigmas*, for them. At the same time, he was studying his music and choreographing outside the company.

In 1923, he and some friends began to offer Evenings of the Young Ballet. A year later, he was one of four dancers who left the U.S.S.R. for a tour of Europe and ended up by joining Sergei Diaghilev's Ballets Russes in Paris. Diaghilev changed Balanchivadze to Balanchine, and hired him as ballet master, at the age of twenty. Balanchine made ten ballets for Diaghilev's company in four years. The official chronology of his works begins in 1925, with Stravinsky's *Le Chant du Rossignol*—"The Song of the Nightingale." (Not the version in the current NYCB repertory, of course; that one was made by John Taras.) The official chronology includes 135 ballets, including collaborations and a few rechoreographings, but it does not list his Russian works, his Broadway shows or his films.

Mr. B. has a sense of humor, and his stories generally have an edge, even when directed against himself. One of his favorites tells of the days when he was new to Paris, and Diaghilev took him to dinner at a celebrated restaurant. "The food was marvelous, but was not what I was used to, so I didn't like it. I said, 'Is no good.' I told the waiter, 'Bring me potatoes, and bread, and vegetables, a whole big mess.'—and I mixed it all up in a bowl." (He breaks imaginary bread into an imaginary dish and spoons it into his mouth.) "And I said, 'Now THAT is good.' I was young; I didn't know about food. That's how people are. They like what they know, and they think is good. Later on, maybe, they learn."

Some followers of the arts are more interested in the chronology of Balanchine's weddings than that of his work, a fact which irritates Mr. B. "I spent two hours talking with that man," he says of a reporter. "We talked about music, and ballet and a lot of things, and all he can find to write about is my five wives." Actually, four-and-one-half. Balanchine has not said for publication whether he and Alexandra Danilova ever went through a marriage ceremony—which just shows that Mr. B. has been ahead of his time in more ways than one. The official wives were Tamara Geva, Vera Zorina, Maria Tallchief and Tanaquil LeClerq—now we have that out of the way. Mr. B. is a couple of weddings short of Henry VIII, who also was an artist, strong-willed, devout and ahead of his time. He's also been more than politely affectionate with a number of other ballerinas, but his real darlings are the muses, and he is one of the most virile lovers they have had all century. There are no children by his wives, but his offspring by Terpsichore have peopled the dance floors of the world.

Balanchine can talk about women, as he can talk about almost anything else, and his ideas are personal and logical within his frame of reference. In a discussion of Women's Liberation he insists that women and men should be paid the same for their work—it's only logical—but work, he says, is not the purpose of a woman. Inspiration is. "Woman is the purpose of man's existence. I want a beauty to inspire me, that's what I want her to do. I don't want her to cook; I cook very well." (He stirs a non-existent pot and sniffs happily.) "I don't want her to wash dishes; I wash dishes every morning, very fast." (His hands wash, rinse and dry a rackful of plates and stack them neatly on shelves.) "I want woman to take flowers and give inspiration." (He presents a bouquet to the world's most beautiful inspiration, and bows.)

"But I don't hang on her. Women like you better when you don't hang on them. That is how they are." Then, with no gestures, holding your eyes with his, "But I am going to tell you this: I am free. I am old man. And nobody is going to get me any more."

Balanchine is touchy about his speech pattern; he prefers that reporters who quote him recast his remarks into "good English," but anyone who reinstates the omitted pronouns and articles is depriving his readers of the elegance of Balanchine's talk. Mr. B.'s English forms rhythmic patterns that suit the content of his sentences. Tampering with them is like removing the ornaments from baroque music. He has a greater command of the English language than most native speakers. He also is fluent in Russian and French, he has some German, is a student of the classical tongues, and demands that words in any language be used precisely. "You read in newspaper people are holding a 'symposium,' " he snorts. "Where is wine? You want to have symposium, you must have wine. That is what the word means. No wine, no symposium.

"People do not know what they say—they do not even know what they mean. If you do not know what words mean, how can we talk? You want to tell me something, you must use the right words. Otherwise, you are not saying what you want me to know."

Balanchine came into the world in a more orderly age, and his life has been devoted to the arrangement of patterns and rhythms. He values the proprieties, remaining a civilized being in a world that has discarded, for better and for worse, his ideas about civilization. He talks about the company's apprentices from The School of American Ballet, who learn, as he did in St. Petersburg, by being near the company. "They dance the same music; they get to know everyone; they respect you. When they dance here, you don't have to tell them, 'Be quiet.' They know. They are quiet. They don't dirty their costumes or spill things or drink and eat.

"In the high schools, it's terrible—they push, they smoke, they use knives, they make noise. And everybody *eats*. On the street, they eat. They can't wait until they get home. That's why streets are so dirty. Where are you going to throw things? There are not enough baskets. So everybody throws on the street, and it looks terrible."

In his art, Balanchine is a revolutionary, because he understood twentieth-century music and made dances to fit it. In much of his thought, he is a conservative, seeking the order of an age that no longer exists. Somehow, he manages to be a true revolutionary, turning things around as he examines them, showing the audience another aspect of a constant force, and to be a true conservative,

trying to maintain what is best of classical dance, music and manners. The revolutionary Balanchine sometimes disconcerts his audience; the conservative makes life difficult for the dancers. For himself, he has established a world and a way of life, and he lives
within them, ready to change when he senses the time, living each
moment without waiting for the one which is fair, learning, thinking and holding to his pattern.

He does not see his life as art. "Choreography is not inspiration—is necessity. When there are no dancers, I don't choreograph—I do other things." There are always other things to
do—one can cook, read, play music, play with cats, take a lady to
dinner—but during the season, he is at the theater early, and he
does not leave until the dancers do. He jokes with them, teaches
them, encourages them, and spends so much time being Mr. B.
that it comes as a shock when a visitor to the theater—Maria Tallchief, perhaps, or Mitch Miller—calls him "George." Everybody in
the company knows Mr. B.; there are a limited number of people
in the world who know George.

His talk is filled with animal imagery and food imagery: He
calls a ballet a "soup" or a "goulash," and has been known to say,
"Horses are beautiful; people are ugly." About teaching dancers,
he says, "The human body is lazy. You don't want to move." (A
pointing finger accuses you of lassitude.) "Nobody wants to move."
(The finger offers you forgiveness.) "Horse that wins race doesn't
want to run. Horse eats." (He bends from the waist to graze.) "But
you teach him and you spur him and you make him run, and he
wins race. You have to do with people, too."

You have to spur people; you have to make them run; and if
they don't want to, they had better withdraw from the race. Whatever you are doing, you must do it completely; then, you go on and
do something else. And you have to accept the fact that, whatever
you do, it is not going to be perfect; only God is perfect, we have
to get on as best we can. "Toumanova, you know, had wonderful
balances. She practiced all the time. She stood like this" (he
sketches in a pose on pointe); "her mother brought her lunch while
she stood. It was in France; she got paid in cash and she signed,
balancing." He mimes taking an envelope and signing the receipt

while on one foot. "So in *Le Baiser de la Fée*, I made a passage for her in which she stands on one foot, looking for him." He shades his eyes with his hand, looking into the distance. "In rehearsals, it was fine; she stood there forever. In dress rehearsal, she stood. Opening night, the curtain went up and—she fell. This is the way it happens."

However it happens, Balanchine maintains his principles, his beliefs, his word and his obligations. He has obligations to the music, to the public, to his company, his friends, himself, his dancers. NYCB is a fiefdom, not a democracy, and Balanchine's demands make it an unhealthy place for many people to live. Under the charm and the sophistication are a drive and a demanding force that must always be in control. He seems to accord respect to very few people—perhaps he has found very few who deserve it—and there often is something condescending in his attitude toward dancers. But Balanchine is an aristocrat, and treats people as his equals only if they have proven that they are. His dancers, much as they may love or hate him, admire or despise him, can never fully understand him. His manners and style are those of an age that is past; his ideas often are of a time that has not yet happened. He is a gentleman, a genius, a delighter in life and the steward of an art. And, as he tucks a dancer into his honors gown, he is the denim-shirted shepherd who protects his flock.

Lincoln Kirstein, falling into a metaphor of his army days, refers to the same obligation as "the responsibility of the command position." Balanchine's room is dominated by music and books, Kirstein's presence chamber by graphics. One wall presents a short exhibit of Oriental art—a subject on which Kirstein is expert—subtly detailed, clearly executed traditional subjects framed to entice the eye without distracting it. Other parts of the room display posters, cartoons, costume sketches, Lincoln's diploma from a posh Massachusetts private school, tributes public and private, and letters from the Governor of New York, signed "Nelson." The furnishings are more spare than Balanchine's, more stringent in style, less exuberant in character. You are in the presence of money, of social position and of the New England ethic, fortunately tempered by perception, inventive ingenuity and good taste raised to the level of genius.

The room has a neatness and clarity of focus you don't expect after seeing Lincoln, in his habitual dark, double-breasted suits, lumbering around the theater or nodding into sleep in his orchestra seat during dress rehearsals. The suits are remarkably reminiscent of those worn by Diaghilev, the great impresario and collator of Les Ballets Russes, and the similarity has been noted in the company. After all, Diaghilev brought together great dancers, choreographers, composers and scenic artists; he had superlative taste and a commensurate drive; he was a knowledgeable devotee of painting and sculpture. Lincoln himself wrote, in *Dance, A Short History of Theatrical Dancing:* "Since his work was correlation, discovery, presentation and propaganda, since he was neither painter, poet, musician nor dancer, his exact position during his lifetime was often obscure, and since his death it has tended to become mythical. Diaghilev was such a complex personality that it will need the accumulative testimony of all his collaborators before a final estimate is achieved. He affected through the medium of ballet, every field of art in his time, including painting, architecture, interior decoration, clothes and literature." Not a bad epitaph for a man to aim at—and a fluidly written one, too. However, the people who insist "Lincoln has a Diaghilev complex," sometimes do not follow the suggestion with a comparison of achievements, but with the remark that the great Russian innovator was autocratic, perverse, megalomaniacal and, possibly, nuts.

An interview with NYCB's director is a strenuous experience. Lincoln himself extends the invitation, with the absolute sincerity and warmth that charm the people close to him. Then the chase begins; "He's got to go to a meeting with the people from City Center . . . he's home working on his book . . . he's staging an opera in his house today." (That sort of casual remark makes you think about Lorenzo de Medici—or Ludwig of Bavaria.) The man never is engaged in only one project; he even writes his books two at a time. People in the executive branch of the company remark, "You don't really want to see him now anyway. He'll talk about Christ and Mohammed and Buddha. It would be very inter-

esting—he knows a lot about them—but you wouldn't learn much
about the company." A long-time associate warns, "Don't believe a
thing he tells you this week; he's going through one of those
periods."

He's also going through one of those periods during which making things up might be a welcome relief. The company is in debt;
the musicians may strike in the fall; the Berlin deal is as uncertain
as a Hollywood marriage; the company is suffering more injuries
than the Egyptians had plagues; morale is low; attendance is poor;
there is a rumor that after this summer, the company's contract
with the Saratoga Performing Arts Center, its summer home since
1966, may not be renewed. Lincoln sits Boston straight, looks
sharply through thick glasses, and begins to talk about stress.
"That's the real problem here; that's what you have to know about.
It's a question of stress."

He talks about the responsibilities of his office, the feeling that
he can't make any decision without thinking of the full result, the
sense of obligation toward the company, toward each member of
the company. He is totally honest, completely sincere, and incredibly condescending. "I am in the command position." He seems to
be saying that he knows more than the privates slogging it out on
the battleground; he is better educated, more experienced, has a
better perspective of the situation. He knows what's good for them.
The precision of speech, the impatience of gesture, make it very
clear that he is ole Massa looking out for his people, but it also is
clear that he cares about them.

Lincoln seems to be aware of the personal history of every
dancer in the company: This one's parents drink to excess; that one
is punishing himself because he can't face his homosexuality; X
lays everything but his morning eggs and can't keep his wife from
finding out; Y has this thing about his sister. His knowledge is astonishing; his interpretation even more so. Lincoln is hideously
perceptive; he not only sees a problem, he sees the attempted solution, and why the attempt won't work. If he has the same insight
into himself, you can understand why, from time to time, "he
makes things up." That sort of perception is one few men can bear.

He talks about his plans for the company. He wants to expand it to 125 dancers. He would like to hire a company psychiatrist. He is the one who persuaded Dr. Louis Shaw to observe the company for a few weeks this season. (Shaw agrees with Lincoln's diagnosis that the company's ailment is a surfeit of stress, but wonders whether Lincoln realizes how much he himself contributes to the problem.)

Supporting all the plans is Lincoln's admiration for Balanchine. He will protect him against anyone—uppity dancers, predatory females, carping critics. Lincoln's genius is correlative and analytical; Mr. B.'s is creative, and that is the sort of genius Lincoln wishes had been his. Obviously, he would have given anything to be a dancer, rather than director of a dance company; a painter, rather than a patron and historian of artists; an athlete, rather than a spectator. As a child he cherished such ambitions. He was defeated by his body. That hulking frame was not made to dance; those stiff arms would not be easy wielding a brush or sculptor's mallet. Perhaps some fear, either of success of failure, helped restrain childish muscles and shape the young body along unaesthetic lines.

Whatever the reason, Kirstein made his genius subservient to Balanchine's and in doing so created a link between them that seems almost a love-bond. What Balanchine wants, he will get, if it is in Lincoln's power to arrange. Any attack on the choreographer brings forth venom that is decidely un-Bostonian. It is not so much Balanchine that Lincoln defends as Balanchine's creative power. Anyone, or anything, that disturbs that is anathema.

Lincoln knows perfectly well why dancers become injured; he knows the stresses that weary and erode them, but a dancer who gets hurt is "an idiot"—because the resulting injury prevents him from performing Mr. B.'s ballets. Still, there is an undertone to the calling of names, "idiot . . . fool . . . bitch . . . cow . . . stupid," the sound of a mother badmouthing children she loves, wishing them stronger, safer, more secure and more obedient. Clearly, he would be happier if someone were to invent little plastic Build-A-Dancer kits, which once constructed, would never become depressed, injured, pregnant or rebellious. Unfortunately for Lincoln, those conditions, along with the driving creative force that generates them, are ingredients of art, and life, everywhere. A closed demesne like NYCB simply makes the tensions more obvious.

Kirstein does not have Mr. B.'s tolerant attitude about time. He does not say "maybe tomorrow, maybe next year, maybe never." He is too impatient for that. Balanchine is fatalistic; Robbins believes in the perfectability of dancers; and Lincoln Kirstein simply wants them to do what is right.

The indoctrination as to what is right begins in class. At The School of American Ballet—the official school of NYCB—girls in their early teens work at the barre the way sweat-shop girls once sat at their sewing machines. Their faces are so marked with concentration, their dedication so intense, that they seem far older than they are. It takes the sight of thin, immature hips and thighs to remind you that these are children—or that they would be children, out in the real world. They still can giggle, though, at least until class starts in earnest.

The pink leg warmers and toe shoes give their feet a blunt, heavy look, like some sort of medieval weapons. Grown-up hands, somehow more adult than those pubescent thighs, tremble with tension. Every step is considered, every plié is mentally analyzed while it is performed. An Irish-faced beauty-to-be, red hair beginning to unpile and tease the sides of her face, flirts with her tulle skirt as if she were Scarlett O'Hara, but does not miss a count.

If a few girls seem to be wandering, the teacher calls them back, gently, joking, but clearly. Her Russian-accented English reminds you that this discipline, this learning of craft rather than indulging in free expression, is a most un-American activity. "Not a difficult step," Madame assures them. "Just you have to be *here*, not somewhere else." And the wanderers return.

These are the girls discovered by Violette Verdy and other scouts in schools around the country, the ones who know they want to be dancers. They live with families with whom the school has placed them, study at the Professional Children's School, and take class. In a year or two, they will audition for ballet companies and begin work. One or two will make it into NYCB. They are slightly younger versions of Debra Austin, Wilhelmina Frankfurt and

Stephanie Saland, with the same motivations, the same dreams, the same ambitions. And to the few who graduate into the company, Mr. B. will beckon and say, "Come in front where I can see you. Now, you have to learn how to dance."

By the end of class, there is very little giggling and a good deal of panting. They have done barre, center work and combinations. They have polished their technique and been brought a bit deeper into the mystery, gone a step further on their quest for the impossible. They are learning to do what is right.

In the annual workshop performance offered by The School of American Ballet, they get a chance to do it. The students have more rehearsal time for their performances than the company gets, and they use it well. In *Stars and Stripes*, the lines are as straight as Rosemary Dunleavy could wish. Technically, the students are impressive. Many of them have great style, but few have anything else. So many of them seem to be made of plastic; perfectly formed, smooth, fresh, inanimate. They make the steps neatly and show themselves to the audience as performers, but they don't feel the music in their bodies. They have no idea of what the dance, as opposed to the steps, is about. There are a few egoists on stage who stand out because of their juvenile bravado, and there are many dancers who place themselves beautifully and execute the steps as neatly as a machine caps bottles, but only one or two show any signs of freedom or emotion.

These fifteen-and-sixteen-year-old dancers are professionals. They take the stage with panache. Their sweetly muscled bodies are beautiful and coltish, but most of them seem either terribly immature or too early jaded. Suddenly, one of the girls in the back row smiles with pleasure, and for a second, the stage comes alive. Then she goes back to smiling like a dancer again. These youngsters have had little time in which to be children; when will they find the time to become adults, and perhaps artists?

The too young-too old performers in the workshop exemplify the contradictions posed by classical ballet in a most unclassical time. Ballet is an artificial art, requiring an artificial environment. But even "popular" art—the movies, the record album, the contemporary concert—is as far removed from normal human endeavor as is professional football. Football depends on brontosaurian bodies, the popular arts on truckloads of mechanical equipment the use of which requires skill and training. The less highly trained the performer, the more complex the equipment through which he is presented to the public, and the more highly trained the technicians who present him. (Or perhaps, the more equipment available, the less we require of the artist—the more simplistic the statement, the more equipment required to convey it.) Ballet is artificial in a different sense—it demands modification of the body. It began by developing steps of social dances—opening the leg and stepping down on the side of the toe, to give the step a more gracious appearance—and continued until the steps were so demanding that only an altered body could perform them. Ballet is a convention developed in a time less rich than ours in machinery and, no matter what methods of lighting and stage design, and no matter what kinds of music are used with it, the art itself always remains based on humanity, not on technology.

Opera requires a performer to sing in a heightened, unnatural manner merely in order to be heard; a popular performer's voice is modified by electronic methods. The electronics allow the performer to be more human, but frequently they make his work less so because they stand between him and us. In contemporary art forms, a human being can be transformed into a superhuman being by mechanical means; in classical forms, he must transform himself. The self-transformation brings superior rewards, but it demands intense discipline and can be dangerous to the mental and physical well-being of the artist. Furthermore, a medium such as film, with its make-up, cameras and microphones, can make a performer appear to be behaving naturally, although he is truly in an unnatural situation. Therefore, a film can be more "realistic" than any stage play. In drama, and more so in ballet, the artist must admit to the audience that he is in an unnatural situation and then must, through his technique, make that situation seem right and proper for the moment. It is this that requires a dancer to become a mutated being; the artificiality of his performance depends on him, rather than on a mechanical intermediary.

This anachronistic quality is responsible, to a large extent, for the stress ballet exerts on those who perform it. Physical training and mental discipline require of those who would be dancers that they not only make themselves different from the rest of us, but that they live differently. Ballet is not a democratic art: It requires precision and absolute obedience to arbitrary rules. All art, which is an attempt to reflect experience, develops from the assumptions of the time in which it was conceived and grew, and ballet is a heritage of autocratic eras.

Classical ballet requires a restricted, ordered universe. One must be built to order, if need be, and Balanchine and Lincoln Kirstein have done just that. But can the universe, or the art, survive the changes in human society and thought patterns? Can we keep ballet—true, grand ballet—alive as costs rise, tastes change and a new, less pliant generation arises? Public school teachers tell you children are less disciplined than they were thirty years ago. That is bad for ballet, which cannot survive without discipline. They also tell you children are more creative, which is healthy. A generation of free-thinking, rebellious children can do quite a bit of damage to the greed, smugness and hypocrisy endemic to nations too comfortably established in their padded chairs, as the last decade proved. But a generation unwilling to learn history, or language, or anything that requires more than thirty minutes of apparently useless study is too restless to undergo the training required to become proficient in the craft of a major art. They damn their elders' achievements along with their failures, while the oldsters condemn fresh ideals along with the irritating noises they generate. There is hope in the Hegelian dialectic, but progress in one area often means a loss in another. If ballet is to survive, it must survive in a company that will combine classical discipline with contemporary individual values, and the founding of such a company will require a genius of Balanchine's scope, and half his years.

At NYCB, the dancer with too probing a mind or too highly developed sensibilities is in trouble. His growth either inside the company or outside of it will be stunted, or both may wilt. Violette Verdy, whose mind is very keen indeed, worries about the education of young dancers, not just in terms of ballet, or even of school, but also considering diet, exercise, personal growth and

"taking care of themselves." Violette, who could have been successful in many fields, knows what is wrong with her life and with the
company. "We're completely in Balanchine's hands; we sort of
marinate in here." But she chooses to stay in the brine, and to
dance. Allegra decided to augment her life at the expense of her
dancing. Both women are superior artists and human beings; neither is as happy as she deserves to be.

The problem, as Lincoln Kirstein knows, is stress. It injures
dancers; it gives them nervous breakdowns; it makes them seek any
possible release. A few seasons back, several dancers were fired for
using drugs. The use of marijuana, like the use of alcohol, is not
recommended before performing, a reality which deprives young
dancers of one of the pleasures of their peer groups. The use of ad-
dictive "hard" drugs is not recommended for anyone. A friend of
one of the fired dancers said, "She was using more than grass. That
place got to her, and by the end of it, she was a wreck." NYCB
plays havoc with the human system, but hard drugs do even more
damage—the combination could twist you like spaghetti. During
the spring, 1973, season, no addictives or stimulants other than
tobacco, coffee, tea and soft drinks were in use around the company. At least, they were not obviously in use, and several of the
performers who, if they were not dancers, might be expected to
use grass said, very distinctly, "We don't." The drug subculture
has made a minimal number of converts among the current roster
of NYCB.

Once it is established that you are writing a book about ballet,
the people who know dance ask you about technique, the company
fans ask you for gossip, and the yahoos ask you about sex. There
are two usual questions: About the women, "Do they fuck?" (Answer, "No, they reproduce by budding, like yeast.") About the
men, "Are they all queer?" (Answer, "No, some are merely peculiar.") Since the days when grand dukes ogled the pretty one in
the third row from the left, ballet dancers have been sex objects.
Well, dance is sexy; it's all part of the profession. On stage, that is.
Off stage, they behave pretty much like everyone else, and the
usual questions get to be a bore. Many of the older dancers who are
not married are living with someone; the others date when they get

the chance, just like actors, television crewmen and stenographers. Most, as has been said, form liaisons with people outside the company, generally outside the profession. Sometimes dancers live with stagehands, or musicians, or even other dancers, but mostly, they don't.

In addition to reasons noted earlier, the women in the company have a rather special problem. One of the corps girls decided, "This place is sick." It seems she was interested in one of the young men in the corps, and another young man challenged her: "Well, we'll see which of us can get him, you or me." He won. Not all male dancers are homosexual, but homosexuals do make up a sizable portion of the ballet population. (At this point, it is only fair to warn anyone reading this in the hope of finding a scorecard, that they are about to be disappointed: There is to be no detailed discussion of who does what, with which and to whom. As a general rule, sexual preferences concern only the practitioners.)

Homosexual dancers belong to two minority groups, instead of one. People in that situation tend to define themselves in terms of the least socially acceptable, and therefore most easily definable, group first. They consider themselves homosexuals first, NYCB members second, dancers third and human beings don't even place. The Gay Liberation Movement might relieve them of some of the need to exaggerate their manners, which would be nice, since it would bring the homosexuals in the company a bit closer to thinking of themselves simply as people. However, the first stage of every movement is ostentation, and the transition is going to take quite a time, which means that homosexual dancers will continue to regard themselves as doubly abnormal. Besides, the gay performers of NYCB are not active in any movement; they are too busy dancing.

The American Psychiatric Association has ordained that homosexuality is a matter of choice, not an aberration. Maybe so, but some psychiatrists continue to point out that homosexual practices do not afford the full, mutual discharge of tension afforded by heterosexual intercourse. However, the persecution of homosexuals is not likely to do anybody any good, either.

The contention that all male dancers are homosexual no longer is universal. A large number of male dancers are. Whether they become dancers because they are homosexual, or they become homosexuals because they are dancers, is a delicate point that deserves the attention of a talented social psychologist. Certainly the arts have a long tradition of homosexual participation, and of human tolerance. Dancers do not get fired or become socially ostracized because they are known to be gay and, in the theater at least, they do not have to disguise their preferences.

Secondly, people tend to "stay with their own." During the great waves of immigration to the United States, members of ethnic groups joined particular professions partially because it was expected of them and partially because their friends and relatives were already established practitioners. If you were an Italian and had a cousin who owned a barbershop, you got a job and learned his business. If your name was Ginsberg, and you had a brother-in-law who was a tailor, all of a sudden you were a tailor, too. Before the days of civil service examinations, every Irishman had a cousin on the police force. That's where all the jokes come from. And if you are a homosexual and, like the immigrants, feel safest among your own people, there's always show biz.

However, that argument does not work as well for dancers as for some other artists. Dancers begin class long before puberty and many are taken to the local academy by their parents. The character structure may be formed, the seeds of the future may be there just waiting for the spring of adolescence to make them grow, but it is unlikely that many mothers think: "It looks as if Billy is going to grow up to be queer—we'd better get him ballet lessons." It is more logical to assume that, if a tendency to homosexuality exists in an individual, it is developed by the congenial surroundings of a company in which homosexuality is encouraged and taken for granted.

Several astute observers of the company ask, "How can any man be a dancer and not have at least one homosexual experience? They're all in the dressing room together; they know one another and, one night, if they all get drunk . . ." Dancers, as has been noted, join the company in late adolescence; they want to be accepted by their peers; homosexuality seems part of the scheme of things; young men rely on the older ones to coach their dancing—in short, there is no lack of motivation. Even so, some dancers very obviously are straight. They may have had one experience; they may have had none. They are heterosexuals, and no amount of dressing room drollery is going to change that. One can only say that those young men who are likely to choose homosexuality are more likely to make the decision in the atmosphere of a ballet company.

The atmosphere thins considerably as one climbs higher in the company ranks. Of the eight male principal dancers with NYCB in spring, 1973, at least six are practicing (and, one assumes, believing) heterosexuals. The soloist group is more evenly divided, perhaps giving a slight advantage to the homosexual team. The corps seems to be overwhelmingly gay. There are a number of possible explanations for this sliding scale. The principals are a good deal older than the boys in the corps and less often in residence at the theater. As they matured, as dancers and as men, they very well may have put away youthful homosexual attachments—if they even had them—and gone on to make their peace with women and enjoy it. Dr. Kinsey shocked the American population when he reported on the number of adult males who admitted to having homosexual experiences in their young days, but were not homosexuals. More recent studies show his report was not exaggerated, and there is no reason dancers would not behave like a sociological sample. Life at NYCB seems to prolong adolescence in a number of ways, and it may well prolong a period of homosexual attachment along with everything else.

Another explanation for the smaller number of gay men in the higher echelons of the company is that a homosexual dancer, if effeminate, who allows his homosexuality to dominate his dancing is unlikely to become a superior performer. A homosexual dancer, effeminate or virile, who allows his homosexuality to dominate his life also is unlikely to become great. The effeminate dancers have the problem of needing to look very virile on stage. If a male dancer does not look masculine, in the nineteenth-century, masterful sense of the word, as he promenades his partner, if he cannot join in the seduction and triumph, enticing and enthralling, of the classical pas de deux, he won't make it. Ballet is about sex: *Swan Lake* is about sex; *Sleeping Beauty* is about sex; *Tchaikovsky Concerto No. 2* is about sex. They may be about love as well, but it is man-woman love and man-woman sex that is depicted, and no amount of rationalization or reinterpretation will change things. The love and sex are stylized, symbolized, civilized—remember, this is a classical art form—even repressed, but they are there.

Those homosexuals who rise to positions of power in ballet do so because of talent, not because of sex. A male dancer, like a female, may gain choicer roles by sleeping with the right man, but he is not likely to become a star if he cannot let the animal out, and unlikely to become a financially successful choreographer if he lacks the ability to become an artistically successful one. There is a charge, at least as tired as the one that all male dancers are gay, that the arts, and especially the dance, in America are controlled entirely by homosexuals. Homosexuals certainly are prominent contributors to the arts, and one reason is that so many middle-American heterosexuals take the attitude that "art is sissy stuff," and that no son of theirs is going to be a choreographer. A reasonable (or unreasonable) segment of the population remains convinced that the arts are a feminine consideration, opposed to the masculine pastimes of science, sports and making money. If these people decide that the dance is for sissies, the sissies might as well take it—it is all they are likely to get. In the end, of course, dance is controlled by businessmen and artists. There are homosexuals throughout NYCB, but it is not a "gay company." For one thing—one very important thing—Balanchine likes girls.

A dancer with another troupe once remarked, quite sincerely and without malice, that NYCB was controlled by Jews. A lot of people know it, she said, and she had had it on excellent authority—from a Russian, who certainly should know—that "Kirstein is Jewish, Robbins is Jewish, Balanchine is Jewish. . . ." Kirstein and Robbins, all right, but when Mr. B. takes a little time off each year to prepare his special delicacies for Russian Easter, he's not making gefüllte fish. Jews, blacks, homosexuals, all are said to "control things," things to which they have made contributions, sometimes because nobody else wanted to bother. The true con-

trol, the ultimate, if unseen clout, is held by people of talent, whoever they are, and people of power, who are far more likely to be
epitome canines than underdogs.

The homosexuals and the Jews can be accused, or credited,
with controlling NYCB, but nobody is likely to nominate the
blacks. Debra Austin is the only black swan in the pond. Arthur
Mitchell, the great, mercurial, energetic dancer who now directs
the Dance Theater of Harlem, was a principal with NYCB, and the
first black male principal with any great ballet company. Today,
there are a few black dancers in major classical troupes, but except-
ing Dance Theater of Harlem, no troupe has a great number. The
reason is simple: People who have never seen ballet do not want to
become classical dancers and, until recently, the majority of American blacks had not seen ballet. Now, as the black middle class gets
larger, more affluent, more interested in the things that traditionally attract the middle class, and as Mitchell's company and
school provide performance and a training ground within the poor
black community, we probably will be seeing more black dancers
in ballet.

Purists insist that the "true African silhouette" with high waist
and high, rounded buttocks and long, thin-calved legs does not
look right in the classical steps, forgetting that there is no one true
African silhouette, and that you never know how something will
look until you try it. Those on the other side accuse choreographers, and especially Balanchine, of racism. Balanchine has once or
twice used moderately offensive ethnic characterizations in his ballets, but he is not a racist. His characterizations, like his processions
and his pas de deux, are derived from a tradition he learned in St.
Petersburg, and one that is older than he. When he had a great
black dancer in the company, he made great roles on him. If Balanchine has racial prejudices they are of the kind most people have—
the kind that are so ingrained, so much a part of childhood learning—that they must be pointed out before we can even be aware
of them. When he and Arthur Mitchell pooled their companies and
talents to make *Concerto for Jazz Band and Orchestra* in 1970, Mr. B.
said he had wanted to do more work with black dancers "but
couldn't find enough," and he dreamed about a company like Dance

Theater of Harlem for nearly a decade before it began, and helped Mitchell in its formation.

It hardly is surprising that there has been little concern about the poor representation of blacks in classical dance companies. Human rights movements are concerned with dignity and economics. Since relatively few blacks want to be classical dancers— very few anybodies want to become classical dancers—only a small amount of dignity is to be gained. Since dancers are not highly paid, very few economic gains can be expected. There are more important fields to till first. As more blacks become interested in dance, more companies will become interested in blacks; Arthur Mitchell's graduates will provide the necessary quantity and quality, and more will follow.

What is interesting is that the women's movement has taken no interest in ballet. True, the ballerina is the light of the stage; she is an artist, a technician, a self-supporting human being—but she also is "a sex object." Her role is to be desirable, to be pursued, to be awakened with a kiss. Balanchine's plotless ballets don't have peasant girls dying of broken hearts, but they are made in the tradition of classical—which is to say romantic—ballet. And Mr. B. himself, with his daisy-full of "She loves me," wives, mistresses, delights, is certainly in that tradition himself.

NYCB does not discriminate economically or artistically against women, but their position in the world of ballet is not one of ultimate power. Modern dance has produced great female choreographers—it might easily be said that great female choreographers produced modern dance—but ballet has not. (Nijinska is the only example who comes to mind.) Women hold positions of prominence at NYCB; many have great responsibility and some have power. The ultimate power lives in Balanchine's office and nobody, male or female, is ready to dispute that. Female dancers are in subservient sociological place in the company, but so are male dancers. Mr. B. prefers to joke and talk with the women, but that is understandable.

The women-are-fragile-creatures mystique is in the air, although those fragile creatures have the strength of plow horses and the dexterity of watchmakers. It is part of the tradition. Dancers traditionally are called "men and girls," or sometimes, "boys and girls." Only Balanchine, at NYCB, sometimes refers to "men and women." He also makes roles that call for women, not girls. Many of the parts he has made on Karin von Aroldingen go beyond the traditional idea of the feminine, and Milly Hayden is no Giselle dying of a broken heart.

Ballet, which made a place for homosexual men, also has created one for strong women. Since they rose on pointe, the art has been devoted to ballerinas, and however fragile the roles they have danced, many of them have been a good deal more emphatic off stage. In white ballet, woman often is a prize to be won. In Balanchine ballet, she often has a stronger identity. Part of the reason, of course, is that Balanchine makes his work on specific dancers, and if he has an individualist woman, he makes a role to suit her. Still, the man wants a woman to inspire him, and the traditional role of the ballerina retains its hold on him, and on the audience. What is more interesting is that many of the young women in the company take, not so much a feminine, as a humanist position. A woman who has completed the training required of a dancer, and who has survived several seasons at NYCB, is not too likely to think of herself as a fragile blossom. Feminine, yes— femininity is part of her stock in trade—but dancers don't confuse femininity with weakness. The art of ballet is inclined to take a nineteenth-century view of women—they are either angels or predators—but the women themselves think along contemporary lines. At least, many of them do.

NYCB remains a castle, armored against change. In its financial policies, its artistic policies, its personnel policies, in the way it holds its members together as a cohesive society, the company is solid as a monument. But the vote against Berlin, even though it was reversed, was a sign of altered thinking. Production line workers, artisans, professional athletes, everyone who holds a job, is demanding more of life than the job can offer. Dancers are no different. Something happened to the United States during the 1960s, and although we may alter direction and even regress, we never will be quite the same again. Ballet, and NYCB, will have to adapt, perish, or change until it is quite unrecognizable. For the sake of the art, and of the artists, some accommodation must be reached.

It is true, as the young corps dancer said, that "the future of ballet is not with this company." NYCB will continue to produce great work, but it will not be a social model for the next great dance company. It was built by Balanchine and Kirstein, in the image of what they knew and what they believed would work and the environments that bred those men are passing. NYCB will change in particulars, but the job of designing a company in which a contemporary ballet dancer can survive and be happy belongs to someone else.

12

Midsummer Madness

NYCB owns three evening-long story ballets which punctuate the year with the regularity of the solstices. The winter repertory is bifurcated by five weeks of *The Nutcracker*, and includes, near the end, a week-long bout of *Don Quixote*. The spring season traditionally concludes with seven performances of *A Midsummer Night's Dream*—five evenings and two matinees. The dancers, accustomed to the varied diet of repertory, have little gusto for long runs. *Dream* troubles them least, because it has the shortest performance span, *Nutcracker* drives them nuts—"By the middle of *Nutcracker*, we're all going insane. The only thing that saves us is the New Year's Eve performance—we're all drunk and rechoreograph it as we go along. Every year it comes out a little different."

The company begins *Dream*-ing during the penultimate week of repertory, and rehearsals fill more of the squares on each day's schedule as the regular season dwindles. The fewer performances that remain, the fewer ballets from the repertory need practice time, and the more hours there are for *Dream*.

There also is time to train dancers into roles they may do in the future. Violette Verdy is teaching the *Emeralds* section of *Jewels* to Christine Redpath, who may get to dance it in Saratoga, or on tour, or not until the company is home again. For Violette, as for any gifted instructor, explaining the execution of a specific work is a vehicle for teaching the art. She leads Chris through each section, then watches as she does it alone, corrects, encourages and calls for a rest when her pupil has a sense of accomplishment rather than waiting until the session's achievements dissipate in exhaustion or frustration.

She tells Chris to work by herself on each section, "after you have the continuity in your head. Once you have that, you never lose it. Then you work section by section, as you do when you prepare an exercise in a good, proper class—maybe not one of our classes—but a proper drill class.

"You have to learn it, and to hear the music, so that on stage you don't keep thinking ahead. Too many people are so busy thinking, 'What do I do next?' they can't concentrate on the present and enjoy it. You want to feel the music and the joy of moving in the present. Otherwise, you aren't dancing, and you certainly aren't feeling good about it."

It's appropriate that the company should be rehearsing *Dream;* the theater is succumbing to midsummer madness. It's a new reaction to stress; the shock is wearing off and the only thing to do now is giggle. Gordon's piano selections for morning class include "I Whistle a Happy Tune" and "Who's Afraid of the Big Bad Wolf?" Most mornings, he has an audience of about twenty.

The wounded start to come around during the last week of repertory. Jacques d'Amboise comes to visit, but not to work for a while, natty in a red blazer and walking comfortably. Gelsey arrives without crutches, flaunting a touch of Carribean sun, looking brighter in the eyes and riper in the skin than she ever did before the accident. The dancers who are carrying a heavy end-of-the season performance load begin to topple under it. Jean-Pierre Bonnefous takes class and then rehearsal as usual on Wednesday, June 20 (seven performances to go until *Dream*) and is crippled by muscle spasms in his back. Bruce Wells, who started to regain his grin after that hellish *Dances*, stops smiling and starts rehearsing Jean-Pierre's role in *Waltzes* for the evening performance. A quick change in schedule is accomplished and inserts printed for the programs, so that *Illuminations*, scheduled to be danced on Thursday, also can be thrown into the Friday night and Saturday afternoon programs in place of *Scenes de Ballet*, which would require training a substitute for Jean-Pierre. Jean-Pierre Frohlich plays the lead in *Illuminations* because Bob Maiorano's knee still won't allow him out on stage. Jean-Pierre does very well with the role—it suits his intensity. Maiorano is eye-glowing angry with himself—he has tried everything but the waters of Lourdes to prepare for *Illuminations*—but subdues the beast with logic. "If you know you can't do it, you don't try. It would be worse if I danced this and put myself out for a year. At least I can do *Dream*."

Corps rehearsals for *Dream* are like corps rehearsals for everything else, only funnier. The company has not danced the ballet in two years; last spring, it was scratched for the Stravinsky Festival. Nobody can remember who goes where when, and the Main Hall echos with the bumps of colliding fairies. Every time it happens, we have a giggle-fest, and Rosie Dunleavy joins in. Surprisingly, even she can't remember all the steps. The only one who seems to be maintaining his sanity is David Richardson, performing his accustomed task of coaching the children who appear in *Dream*. His rehearsals go beautifully: The children take this seriously, even if nobody else does. Not having danced seven-and-a-half weeks of NYCB repertory, they aren't stir crazy.

Half-way through the last week of the regular season, John Clifford—who is rehearsing to do Puck in *Dream*—comes crashing into Betty Cage's office as if the character is taking too firm a hold on him. He's waving a long piece of paper as if it were an all-A report card and bubbling "Thank you, thank you." Then he kisses Betty and rushes out again. The long piece of paper is a principal dancer's contract. He's worked to earn it. Last Sunday he got another, lesser present—his very own costume for *Cortège*. It arrived just in time for the last showing of the season. Since taking over the role, he'd been wearing a *Diamonds* tunic which nearly fit.

During the last week of repertory, the principals rehearse their roles for *Dream*. There is less confusion than in the corps sessions; for one thing, these veterans have done the ballet more often than most of the corps dancers and have less trouble remembering the sequences. There also are fewer of them in one room at one time, and the giggles is a community illness. On stage, Melissa Hayden works with Peter Martins on the pas de deux of the divertissement. She calls the steps out by name like a teacher calling the roll. Her voice is so encouraging and authoritarian you half expect the steps to answer. Peter, his arm and shoulder hale again, is feeling each step as it makes friends with his muscles, to be certain they will remember one another at the next meeting.

At the last Saturday matinee of the repertory season, Peter and Kay perform Mr. B.'s *Tchaikovsky Pas de Deux*. It is a thriller and the audience loves it. Just now, the dancers don't. "It's too much—too demanding for this late in the season," Kay says, as soon as she can stop gasping. She's in pain again—a stiff neck this time; she woke up with it this morning. Peter sits off stage between variations, twisting his face in an effort to grab enough air. Dr. Louis Shaw, watching from a comfortably dark spot in the wings, says he probably lost a huge amount of potassium by perspiring so much. Shaw would like to see a good physician—an internist-endocrinologist-neurologist—backstage at all times. He thinks neatly timed injections of potassium and other minerals would help the dancers through the season.

The psychiatrist is one of those disconcerting physicians who is able to make a sound psycho-physical diagnosis on the basis of a quick visual survey, a light touch or two and a few minutes' conversation. He's usually accurate, "But you'd want clinical endocrinological and chemical tests to be sure." He trusts chemotherapy—the process of eliminating emotional malfunctions by correcting the individual's body chemistry—but adds, "After they had the treatments, they still would have to learn to live with themselves—and with this place. It's not just the stress of dancing that gets them; it's the stress of Lincoln, and Jerry and Balanchine pushing them and manipulating them—not to add what they do to themselves.

"This theater—any dance theater—is like a religious order. You have the same mortifications and the insistence to yourself that you are giving up the world for a greater good. That's all very well, but one generally is not absolutely certain that the higher ideal is worth it, and the conflict is devastating. The constant physical injuries are only one symptom. I doubt that anybody can stay in this place and be healthy."

Dream rehearsals continue to be confusing, so a showing of the company's movie of the ballet is scheduled. At last the football metaphor is complete—the team is going to watch films of the game. The corps dancers find it only moderately helpful. "The film doesn't show every step and besides we've changed a few things since it was made. But we were able to pick up some things and that helped a little."

The last performance of the regular season comes on the night of Sunday, June 24. Melissa Hayden does a beautifully articulated *Concerto Barocco*, dominating every measure of music, every foot of the stage and every seat in the house. It is her last appearance in repertory in this theater, and the galleries are filled. Humans are possessed by the desire for firsts and lasts; the period of gradual growth that separates them demands too much work and attention, and therefore lacks magic. Milly takes three solo calls before the curtain, walking along the apron of the stage and bowing like a queen on her balcony. Jenny Coleman, Milly's *Nutcracker*-aged daughter, stands in the first ring and claps her hands until "they tingle." She has a theater full of helpers. Afterwards, the whole company is backstage, telling Milly how fine it was—and they are right. Now, she will do *Dream*, Saratoga and the rest of the summer tour and finish at Wolf Trap Park, outside Washington, D.C. There are a lot of final performances required to end a career like Milly's—and she will get cheers and applause and bravos at every one of them. After dancing for more than twenty-five years, she has earned them.

Tuesday, June 26, brings *Dream* onto the stage. There will be a "Friends" rehearsal in the evening. The dancers warm up quietly, without giggles or games. They've just heard the news: John Cranko, choreographer and artistic director of the Stuttgart Ballet, died of a heart attack on the plane that was carrying his company home from its American tour. The talk is about the people in the troupe—one of the girls had danced with NYCB before joining Cranko, and dancers with international companies sooner or later get to know one another in any case. While the Stuttgart Ballet was appearing at the Met earlier in the season (they followed the National Ballet of Canada there), there was visiting back and forth between the theaters.

Sally Leland, Nicholas Magallanes and Kay speculate about the future of the Stuttgart company and its dancers. Who will succeed Cranko? Will he make changes in the company? What will the dancers do? What they carefully do not say is that Mr. B. is far older than John Cranko was, and what will happen to this company, and to them, if . . . ? (Mr. B. is healthy; he'll outlast us all, but . . .) America is too young, and too individualistic, to have the European traditions of continuity. Most of our dance companies are built by a choreographer, and grow with him. They are designed to dance in a specific style, and without that style, they have little reason to continue. The Royal Danish Ballet and the Bolshoi rely on a tradition of style; American Ballet Theater thrives on eclecticism; most American troupes, classical or modern, depend on a resident genius.

The manner of John Cranko's death affects the dancers, too. A heart attack is no longer necessarily fatal, but his one happened in an airplane; there was no help, no equipment, nothing to be done. An airplane in flight, like a theater, is a self-contained universe. There is no way out, no way in, nobody to hear if you scream. The big technical marvel is stuffed with little technical marvels—guidance and communications systems, comfortable seats, hot meals—but the necessary marvel, the wonder that could have saved John Cranko, was not included. With the choreographer gone, what will happen to his own technical marvels, the ones who leap like lightning and fouette on a dime? Mr. B. is healthy, Georgians live forever, but. . . .

Balanchine's appearance on stage makes the thought ridiculous. His denim shirt and bandanna, his tourquoise bracelet, his smile are too fresh and bright to allow even an imaginary heart attack. The corps is dancing a divided vote on the way a passage should be done. "That's the way it used to be . . . No, it used to be this way." Mr. B.'s voice shreds the ballots. "I don't care what it *used* to be. It's new. This way." (He steps the passage emphatically.) "Everything changes. Nobody can remember all that used to be, so the hell with it. You do it again, new, like this," and he dances.

Mr. B. sends the corps upstairs to continue working with Rosemary, and concentrates on the character roles. He rehearses the scene in which Titania, Queen of the Fairies, whose eyes have been rubbed with magic, becomes smitten with Bottom the Weaver, who has been transformed into an ass. Bart Cook snuffs out his genial face by pulling on the wooly ass's head; Kay Mazzo, enamored, takes his paw in her light-fingered hand and begins to lead him gently from the stage. Suddenly, Bottom has a terrible urge—he needs desperately to scratch; his fingers dig into his thigh. Balanchine interrupts. "It's not like that, not all-of-a-sudden," he says. "It's as if you're very aware of mosquitoes—I hate them, I know—and they come, and then, THERE they are." He winces in discomfort and scratches like a dog who has finally zeroed in on an experienced flea.

Titania gently dissuades her love from scratching and leads him off. As they go, Bart is distracted by a clump of grass and begins to nibble. Again, Balanchine interrupts, to teach Bart to graze. He looks down, sees the grass, wonders about it, nuzzles it, pulls against Kay's hand as if tugging at his leash. Within a few seconds, he has defined Bottom's complete thought process and the resultant action. One of Mr. B.'s most frequently quoted epigrams is: "There are no mothers-in-law in ballet." No relationship, no idea that cannot be expressed clearly and quickly in physical terms is allowed on his stage. Dance cannot provide complicated explanations, and the music allows only so many bars for each action. Pantomime must be explicit, refined, and broad enough to be seen and interpreted by the patrons in the top tier.

Balanchine is very aware of the audience. He insists that every gesture be, not exaggerated, but clear. "The public must be able to know that you see something. When you look over there, you must really look, you must really see. Don't just turn your head and then look back again."

Allegra is back from the mumps, as fairy-eyed as ever, but it hasn't been decided yet if she will dance. "We'll see how you feel," says Mr. B. She rehearses anyway, hoping. She and John Clifford are one of three couples practicing the divertissement pas de deux. The others are Milly and Peter Martins and Kay and Francis Sackett. (Francis is adding roles since he pinch-hit for Tony Blum in *Liebeslieder*.)

All the couples do the same steps at the same time, and each one does them differently. Looking at the women, you notice Allegra's supple bends and her long, yearning body line; Kay's fragility, masking her athlete's strength; Melissa's easy power and proud carriage. As they turn into arabesque, each draws the curving bow that leads from fingertips to pointed toe into a different shape. Allegra's raised leg is developed fully, arching high behind her back; Millie's is lower, but solid, piercing the air like an arrow; Kay's leg, still sore from injury, is lower still, but held so as to etch its roundness into the space around it.

Dream opens on the evening of Wednesday, June 27, and that day rehearsals begin after class and continue until five in the afternoon. Balanchine restages the sword fights between Demetrios and Lysander, working to make the action clear to the audience, rather than trying for any attempt at realism. Realism would be out of place anyway; the audience knows, or should know, that nobody in this ballet is going to get hurt.

Kay practices getting in and out of the couch on which she sleeps, a beautiful shell-shaped petal balanced uneasily on a pedestal. The petal has a tendency to tip when Titania curls inside it. As Mr. B. works on each scene, he explains the action in terms of the play—many of the dancers never have read it—often quoting Shakespeare, and quoting him with accuracy. He rehearses the end of the first act: Titania is released from the magic spell and Bottom from his ass's ears. The fairy queen leads her little changeling page, the object of all the contention, to her husband, Oberon, who sets him to work as a train-bearer. The fairy sovereigns, reconciled, exit at opposite sides of the stage. Balanchine clearly is not following the text of the play: Why should the couple not complete their peace and go off together? Because, says Mr. B., "They are like a married couple, but they are not lovers. They only quarrel about little boy. They cannot do it, because they have nothing to do it with—they are not human, you know. He is autumn, and she is spring."

He tells the story of the Germanic myth from which he derived his characterizations. Before beginning work on *Dream*, he read a great deal more than the play. Titania should be tall in his version, he says, "which is why, when I made it, I took Diana Adams," and Oberon is short, "which is why I used Eddie Villella." Oberon, according to the legend, was born of a nymph and a mortal. After his birth, there was a party, rather like the one in *The Sleeping Beauty*, to which various nymphs were invited. The slighted one left him with a curse, that he never was to grow, but the last speaker countered that with the gift of a face that would be beautiful forever. (Bullfinch recounts the legend in his retelling of "Huon of Bordeaux," in which version Oberon names as his parents Julius Caesar and "the fairy Glorinda.")

The sexlessness of Oberon and Titania—in fact, the purity of all the lovers in *Dream*—seems a bit strange after the passion, however formal, of Balanchine's pas de deux. Balanchine is, after all, a proper man. The greater the passion he wishes to show, the more formal his method of portraying it. The more realistic his convention, the more refined his delineation of emotion. It's an interesting sidelight on a man whose love-life has received nearly as much attention from the public as his artistic life, but then, Balanchine has never been the one to instigate the publicity. In his life, and on his stage, passion is to be enjoyed, not advertised; sex is too important a matter to be turned over to the public relations department.

What Balanchine's generation calls refinement a more recent one would call prudery. The formalization of physical love is a form of sublimation; so, of course, is the voyeurism of the sex show and the "dirty movie." Humans are the only animals to turn sex into a spectator sport and attendance seems to increase as a culture postures its way into decadence. Balanchine is something of a Victorian in his manners, his nearly automatic assumption of caste, his attitude toward women. He is of a generation which simply knew there were certain things a gentleman does not say, or do, in public. Freud developed his theses in a world peopled by such gentlemen.

Conventions of behavior in any era help shape conventions of art. A contemporary Aeschylus or Shakespeare might find it needful to write scenes of explicit violence or sex, but those two geniuses, working within their respective conventions, heightened their art by leaving some things to the imagination of the audience. We see Agamemnon dead; we do not see him murdered. We hear Romeo and Juliet meeting at night and parting at morning; we don't listen in on the panting. As a result, Agamemnon's death is more brutal, the youngsters' love much sweeter, because nothing we witness on stage can match what we see inside our heads. Balanchine's own inhibitions are expressed in stylization, which allows us to experience more than he shows us, and allows him to comment on human functions in a way he could not do if they were more explicitly staged.

The first performance of *Dream* goes very well; the fairies don't collide; Titania cuddles into her nook without tipping it over; the pantomime is clear, the dancing polished; and Karinska's costumes and David Hays' setting again prove themselves art works in their own right. John Clifford dances Puck, the role which was made on Arthur Mitchell, one role in which he can set free all his exuberance and Peter-Pan mischief. The audience loves him. Kay is pure delight as Titania; dancing with delicate finesse and winsomely falling in love with the ass. Eddie Villella recreates his commanding Oberon; although his dancing is somewhat restrained (his thigh still has not healed; he still is overworking), there is magic in his presence.

Balanchine's ballet—which is at least as much his tribute to Mendelssohn as to Shakespeare—surprises you again, no matter how often you have seen it, with the beauty and lyricism of its construction. The entire story—or as much of it as Mr. B. found it wise to use—is told in the first act. The second is given over to a divertissement at the court of Theseus and Hipollyta, reaching its climax in one of the choreographer's greatest pas de deux.

From curtain to curtain, Robert Irving and the orchestra fill the theater with the right romanticism of the music, and it is a pleasure to hear the "Wedding March" taken at proper tempo rather than being dragged along like a bride's too-heavy train, which is the way most marriage organists play it.

The rest of the week is devoted to performances of *Dream* with different casts, and with talk among the company about Saratoga.

"It's so different . . . it's so much more relaxed . . . we always dance better there than anywhere else." The wardrobe department is busy packing costumes; the halls are partially blocked by huge brightly colored crates.

Dancers already have arranged for their accommodations, either by reserving hotel rooms or by driving up to Saratoga Springs to rent houses or apartments. A few of the principals own property in the area, and others in the company are planning to buy. Robert Maiorano is purchasing a house in which he can live during the short Saratoga season, and in which his mother can live all year round. Anyone who has not yet subleased his city apartment is scrambling to find a tenant. Dancers, like other people, do not care to leave their apartments unguarded for long periods of time, nor can they afford to pay rent for several months of non-occupancy. Before the company goes on tour, the most popular sport is tenant-hunting. The need to sublease makes dancers susceptible to unscrupulous landlords and tenants. They come home from a tour to find their apartments rented out from under them, their furniture gone or their sub-lessee departed, owing several months rent.

Those who have found apartment sitters, and who are not scheduled to dance in the final performances of *Dream*, start for the country a few days early. The rest go up Sunday night, after the last performance, or Monday morning. Many drive their own cars, but a sizable contingent—mostly corps dancers—rides a bus chartered by the company. They check into motels, or check out their apartments, eat, shop, go to movies . . . Monday, after all, is the day off. Tuesday, everyone goes back to work.

Saratoga Springs, N.Y., can't be described as a one-horse town because its leading industry is the annual August race meeting, for which the hotel owners orbit their rates. It is, however, a two-bus town. (Like the "Looking-Glass" messengers, there is one to fetch and one to carry.) The buses only run during the summer months, when they ferry elderly Jews and Italians from New York City between their hotels and the town's other leading industry, the hot spring baths. Bath-takers pay to ride the buses. By courtesy of the local government, dancers don't. Anyone mistaken for a dancer and in the company of dancers also gets free rides on the old gray vehicles, but the trick only works during July. In August, there are no dancers, only horses. The first day the company was in town, bus drivers wanted to collect fares from dancers, but management straightened that out in a hurry. However, the owner of the swimming pool near the theater did reneg on his free-to-dancers policy of earlier years, and could not be persuaded.

Still, the town treats the company very well. The marquee of one motel reads "Welcome Back, New York City Ballet," and the innkeepers moderate their room rates for members of the company. (They also moderate them for friends of the company, but, again, you can only get away with that in July.) Resturant owners, bus drivers, waiters, shopkeepers—everybody in Saratoga tries to be nice to dancers, for a good reason. Dancers mean money. The generation that patronized the baths is dying or moving to retirement communities; the horses only work one month a year. Saratoga had the good sense to set itself down among a lot of colleges, but that population can't keep everyone in town fed. The Saratoga Performing Arts Center (SPAC) doesn't pull as many people as the races, but it certainly helps keep the summer active, and the town makes its living from the summer. Ask local residents what they do there during the winter; the answer is "shovel snow and shiver."

The Saratoga Performing Arts Center opened on July 8, 1966, with a performance of *Dream* by NYCB. By the time the company and the Philadelphia Orchestra had finished their seasons that summer, 140,000 people had paid their way into the huge amphitheater. The size of the theater has become almost a standing joke in the company. Balanchine will look out over the audience and say, "They hate us; the place is half empty." Virginia Donaldson, the press representative, who is as encouraging by nature as by profession, will remind him that SPAC holds twice as many people as the New York State Theater, so, even if the amphitheater is only half-full, "If we were at home, we'd be sold out."

The two-tiered theater, roofed over but open on the sides, is enormous, but the accoustics are excellent and the stage is good to dance on. The company, of course, brings along its own floor. The SPAC stage was built to the dimensions of the one at Lincoln Center, so the asphalt tile fits perfectly. The main rehearsal hall at

SPAC has filament lights instead of the fluorescent ones that burn the dancers' eyes at home and, even more wonderful, it has windows. On a July morning, they frame a soothing backdrop to class—green leaves and fir needles contrasting their textures against the sky. The first morning the company meets for class, July 3, most of the talk is about accommodations, the trip up, plans for relaxation. The dancers check the schedule carefully, and figure out at what times they will be free to go swimming. In Saratoga, you can tell what ballets are being rehearsed by noticing which dancers are not at the pool.

There's also a lot of talk about whether or not we're going to Berlin, and whether we will be back at SPAC a year from now. The prognosis, as usual, is pessimistic. Everybody is quite sure that SPAC has allowed its contract with the company to lapse, and that another, less expensive, dance group will be practicing on this floor next July.

At 11:30, dancers take their accustomed places at the barre; some hang on the paraphernalia that has been stored in this room during the winter. Peter Naumann clutches a tall flagstaff, complete with American flag. Karen O'Sullivan wraps her hand around the pedestal of an electric fan. Everyone is more relaxed, more ready for easy joking, than he was two days ago in New York. Dancers do their normal pre-Balanchine warm-ups; Dianne Chilgren plays the upright and Carol Sumner puts the company through its normal pre-Balanchine pliés.

Mr. B. comes in as usual, seven minutes after the scheduled start of class. In honor of summer, he is wearing sandals of shiny black leather. They have the unscuffed, stiffly elegant appearance that new shoes manage to keep for a few days before they begin molding themselves in the image of the wearer's foot. He tells Peter Naumann to put the flagpole back against the wall—Balanchine accords symbols their reverence—and helps him swing it into place. Peter joins the company at the barre. Karen maintains her friendship with the fan.

During the winter, vandals held a destruction party in Mr. B.'s dressing room: They ruined the couch, spurted catsup on the ceiling and dismembered furniture. Balanchine is merely sarcastic about the acts of the barbarians. The raised voice, the burning rage, the violent denunciation, are not his style: He almost never lets himself become truly angry. Perhaps it is because, during his long life, he has reached the conclusion that few things, and few people, are important enough to make him rage. He also is, as his tradition demands, a man of self-control. Even when moved, he speaks in an even voice, so sure of his ideas and opinions, that they seem to have become, for him, as factual as the multiplication table. His edged jokes, the irony in his twanging voice, are stylized anger, much as his great pas de deux are stylized passion. He, too, has been subjected to the discipline of dance, with its tradition of repression and control. He inherited the tradition, and he passes it on. But the Helots who invaded his dressing room are far less free than he—they, too, no doubt, were misdirecting anger, not allowing themselves to rage at true objects of their violence, but in their tradition there is nothing but destruction.

Balanchine is a crafter of things, a setter-in-order, an instructor to the world in rhythm and pattern. When he upsets a balletic structure, he does so because it has outlasted its time and needs rebuilding; he does not destroy for pleasure. He has built a house, not marred one. The house has been a prison to some, and a number of the tenants have been as thoroughly torn as Mr. B.'s dressing room couch, but any destruction that happens at NYCB is a by-product of creation. Balanchine's tradition allows no place to the stupidity of vandalism. "Idiots," he sneers, "They have nothing to do. They do not even know how to enjoy themselves, so they tear and spill and break things. Idiots." He is right. There is no sense in wasting words on them when one could be working. "Now," he says, "as normal. Battement tendu."

In the corridors, workrooms and dressing rooms, the keepers of the wardrobe, Mme. Pourmel and her ladies and Ducky and Arthur, are unpacking, pressing, sewing and hanging. Some of the square wooden crates that have arrived hold costumes, some hold backdrops, and some are gigantic compartmentalized sewing boxes, filled with snaps, bangles, ribbon, trim, hooks and eyes—the entire notions department needed to keep costumes in repair. The array is not as vast as the one in the workrooms at home—a fact which keeps Mme. Pourmel clucking in French as she scratches in the boxes for her gear—but the traveling cases are carefully organized and well-stocked.

On tour, as at home, the work of the wardrobe department is as unending as the rehearsals of the dancers. While the costume crew does not make the clothes—that is left to Karinska and to other shops—it is responsible for maintaining them. The costumes are durable but they are subjected to almost as much stress as the people who wear them. Every time the company does *Pulcinella*, the stage is peppered with little black balls which have fallen from the white costumes worn by Eddie and Violette. That means that after every performance of *Pulcinella*, Ducky, Mme. Pourmel and their associates are busy sewing more little black balls onto the costumes, so that they will be ready for the next presentation. Many of the costumes for other ballets are trimmed with spangles and sparkles and bits of bright glitter, and they always lose a few during performance and need to be refurbished. Torn cloth, opened seams and lost fastenings are regular occurrences. Ballet costumes take more punishment than any garments except combat fatigues and football and hockey uniforms and, unlike those outfits, they are designed to be decorative as well as utilitarian. The rapid turns, sudden lunges, lifts, stretches and body contact of ballet leave their scars on the costumes, and those scars must be made invisible by the next performance.

Even the simple white and black uniforms used in many Balanchine ballets, which have no black balls to float free, no bright spangles to break away, are subject to stress. Costumes removed from their crates must be examined for damage, repaired if need be, ironed and laid out for the dancers. After each performance the procedure is repeated and, after the final showing, the costumes are sent off to be cleaned, then packed away again.

While Mme. Pourmel, Ducky and Arthur are preparing the costumes for *Stars and Stripes*, *Duo Concertante*, and *Cortège Hongrois*, folding them and setting them out for performance, the stage managers supervise the setting of lights and hanging of drops on stage. The stage crew does not travel with the company, and although some of the Saratoga stagehands have worked with NYCB before, others are new. If Ronnie Bates, Roland and the rest of the company team did not have everything charted; if they did not know the choreography of their work as well as the dancers know theirs, this would be a terrible muddle. As it is, there is a bit of tripping over cable and misfocusing of lights, but things shape up quite well.

In the big orchestra pit, which catches sunlight coming in through the open sides of the theater, Robert Irving is rehearsing the orchestra. In the rehearsal rooms, and on stage when the technicians have left it, the dancers rehearse. Despite the fresh air and sunshine, the swimming pool and the soft lawns, the work is much the same as it is in New York.

After rehearsal, the dancers hurry back to town, either on the gray buses or in their cars, those who have wheels giving lifts to those who don't, for a short bask in the sun or a quick meal. There are a number of fast-food bars on the road between Saratoga and SPAC and the dancers, especially the corps dancers who are short of time, are regular patrons. There are some good restaurants in and around Saratoga, but the dancers don't always have time to eat sit-down meals. Besides, many do not eat before performance. The weight of the food in his belly slows a dancer and makes him sluggish and uncomfortable. In Saratoga, as in New York, many dancers wait until after the performance to do any serious eating.

Well before the half-hour call, everyone is back at the theater. It looks like rain, but the house is quite full. A comfortable, casually dressed audience has come to welcome the dancers back, and as the curtain goes up on *Stars and Stripes*, a happy burst of applause reverberates through the shell. The curtain itself is the drop from Anthony Tudor's ballet, *Dim Lustre*. The SPAC front curtain had been sent to New York for cleaning before the season, and somehow, it was lost. How anyone could lose a fifty-foot wide curtain is one of the more interesting questions of the summer, but it was done.

Stars goes very well; it is the perfect opener for a rural, summertime audience. The mechanical part of the performance is not as polished as the dancing. The curtain starts down smoothly, then drops the last five feet in a big hurry and hits the floor stage left a few seconds before the stage-right side clunks down. The batten around which the base of the curtain is furled records the landing with a resonant ker-CHUNK. There is no genial Hank here to adjust the rate-of-descent dial and push the button. There is no rate-of-descent dial and no button, just inexperienced stagehands and a rope.

Roland and Ned Waite—a young stage manager and a friend of Lincoln's, who joined the company in June—have difficulty with the chimes that announce the end of intermission. They place the chimes near a microphone and tap them with the handle of a screw-driver, with a hammer, with anything that happens to be handy. The chimes are unimpressed. Kevin Tyler takes a hand and hits the things at exactly the right place, summoning the audience. Later, he tapes the handle of the screw-driver so that it will bong more efficiently. Nobody thinks to borrow a mallet from one of Robert's musicians—perhaps union rules forbid it.

The second ballet is *Duo Concertante*. During the delicate by-play, the rain that threatened earlier begins to fall. The operator of the follow-spot, with insufficient experience and too little rehearsal, keeps the light surrounding Kay and Peter when he should be focusing only on their hands. Then, in an attempt to rectify his error, he diminishes the circle of light—and misses the hands altogether. The audience, which is much more attuned to *Stars and Stripes* than to the intricacies of *Duo*, applauds anyway, in all the wrong places. Kay comes back from her curtain calls in a fury.

During *Cortège*, the rain gives way to the mosquitoes. Saratoga mosquitoes, unlike Saratoga stagehands, are real pros. They can bite through Karinska's costumes; they can bite through heavy-weight denim; they can bite through just about anything. The people in the company are sure the little creatures post sentinels along the road, to watch for the NYCB bus. When it arrives, they hurry back to their swamp and hang a large sign which reads, "Tonight's Menu: Dancer under Lights."

They flit around the stage, arrogant in the knowledge that performers can't break a pose to swat at them. Some performers, though, have learned to execute quick arm-movements and wallop bugs at the same time. The stage managers' table is furnished with a can of OFF, which is as important up here as lamb's wool and El-mer's glue. Deni Lamont insists you don't feel the mosquitoes while you are moving, but Debbie Austin, who has to stand posed more often than Deni, says it's absolute hell to do a ballet such as *Swan Lake*, "because when you're standing still for long periods of time they can really get at you."

After the performance, the word comes around that Saratoga has claimed its first casualty. Danny Duell sprained an ankle during *Stars*. "It happened just before the tours," he says.

On July 4, some of the corps girls help celebrate the day by driving in a sulky race—they have experienced drivers with them, of course, and it's good publicity for the company. The local public relations man arranges horse races, TV interviews, fashion shows—anything to get people into the theater. Meanwhile, John Taras takes a rehearsal of *Concerto No. 2* on stage. What a superlative drillmaster he is. He takes the ballet apart and puts it together again, polishing every piece. "When you arabesque, let us see it— stretch, please . . . I want to see the leg . . . Look at one another . . . that's silly, why is the corps moving back there at the climactic moment for the principals? Let's change that, hold the move two beats."

By the time he has finished—and it's a long rehearsal, longer than scheduled—the corps lines are straight, the choreography is clear, the steps are precise. Some of the dancers are furious with Taras for holding such a taxing rehearsal up here, rather than in New York, and for elongating the day's schedule and making them spend time waiting to work at the theater when they could be at the pool. After all, this is their first chance in months to relax. Others admit they needed the drill, and that Taras did a brilliant job. "They ought to give him more time to do this during the regular season," they say. "They should let him do this with each ballet as it comes into the repertory."

Taras is the closest thing the company has to a classical ballet master, a man who devotes himself to perfecting the technical work of the company and the precision of performance. He has the patience and the knowledge for the job. Standing in front of the stage, tall, gray-haired, a slight paunch showing under his green shirt, he pushes the dancers relentlessly, never letting a passage go until he is satisfied with it, never allowing an "it's good enough" attitude to interfere with getting a perfectly straight line, a completely coordinated attack, a true sense of ensemble dancing. After the rehearsal, when complimented on his work, he says, "We'll see how much of it they remember. Doing this once in a while isn't enough. You have to take every ballet and work it through again and again if you want to polish it. It's not always the dancers' fault if the lines aren't straight, you know. If you want straight lines, you have to devote the time to get them."

In many ways, Taras is the forgotten choreographer at NYCB. His genius lacks the glamour of Mr. B.'s and Jerry's, because it is less a creative faculty and more a reproductive one. He has made some good ballets, but his finest talent is the ability to take a ballet—his or another choreographer's—and rub it until it shines. If he were given more rehearsal time during the regular season, if he, rather than Rosie, took some of the drill rehearsals, there would be fewer muddles for the critics to write about. Balanchine and Robbins are among the world's finest producers of ballet; Taras is among the world's greatest reproducers of ballet. It is a different talent, but no less difficult. If the company management is concerned about the lack of precision on stage, it has the remedy available—more rehearsals with Taras. There is no time during the season to hone every ballet, but if he were to give his full attention to a few each year, the repertory soon would be more crisply and precisely executed. When you first begin to observe the company, you wonder, "Why on earth do they need John Taras?" After watching him rehearse, you know exactly why the company needs him, and why it should use him far more than it does.

Barbara Horgan has been summoned from New York. Her arrival coincides with that of the German film producers, who want to finish negotiating the Berlin deal. There is a lot of meeting going on. Dancers spend as much time as they can at the swimming pool, making the other patrons look like clods. Dancers do not all have beautiful faces, nor do they all have beautiful figures in the Hollywood sense—but they invariably have beautiful bodies. The muscles are neatly defined, the shape of each limb is sculptured and

functional. Dancers in bathing suits are among the most ego-deflat-
ing beings in the world, not because they pose and show off, but
because they don't. They just sun themselves and swim like everybody else, and make you realize that your own chassis is not really
in running order, no matter how strong and trim it may be. Com-
pared to dancers, athletes look bulky and overdone; women with
voluptuous figures look somehow too rich, like overly sweet past-
ries; normal mortals just look dumpy. At the pool, even more than
on the stage, you realize how specialized an instrument is a dancer's body—and you don't even notice their poor, bruised feet.

The injuries are starting to happen again. Steve Caras, a gentle
young corps dancer, has an infected wisdom tooth that needs to be
pulled. Bonnie Borne hurts her foot doing *Jewels;* going onto pointe
she moves too far over her foot and strains it. She's out. During the
performance of *An Evening's Waltzes* Saturday afternoon, Chris
Redpath is so tired she doubles over as she comes off stage, as if
she'd taken a fist to the gut. She goes out for her curtain call
straight and smiling, comes off and curls again, goes out and stands
tall, comes off and bends again. Stephanie Saland, one of the first-
year corps girls, says, "I'm so tired that when I go to sleep I dream
about being tired. When that happens, you know it's getting to
you." Only a week ago, these people were talking about how
relaxing it is to dance at Saratoga.

Mr. Balanchine keeps his usual schedule—teaching, rehearsing,
watching performance. He's also occupied with the negotiations for
Berlin. On Sunday, July 7, the company gets the news: Berlin will
happen. The dancers will get their per diem allowance in marks;
Mr. B. will not cede all film rights; cassette residuals have not been
decided, but it doesn't look good for the dancers, because there is
no provision for such rights in the AGMA contract. Those who
always wanted to go are happy, the rest are disappointed. However, everyone is pleased when E. Craig Hankenson, general manager of SPAC, comes backstage to assure the dancers that they will
indeed be here again next year. Hankenson has heard the rumors
and come around personally to calm everyone. "Who else would we
get?" he asks. "You belong here. We have a rotating contract, and
if we don't inform you, or you us, long in advance that it is to be

cancelled, it is automatically renewed. You're our company. You'll be back."

The dancers know they will be back, but they wonder for whom they will dance. The Friday night audience numbered only 1,750, and although a near sell-out has been promised for Saturday night, most performances since opening have been poorly attended. Mary Porter, Lincoln's secretary, remarks that when the company first began to play SPAC, it sometimes drew only four or five hundred, so attendance is improving. And there are nights when the house is half-empty, if you listen to Mr. B., or half-full, if you listen to Virginia Donaldson. Sometimes, there is nearly a full auditorium. The audience is growing, and many of the regulars are as proprietary about NYCB as the fanatics back home. The theater is simply too big to fill very easily, and festivals which depend on a transient trade take a long time to develop a following. SPAC is much younger than Tanglewood (and not as perfectly sited for the summer trade) and a lot bigger than Marlboro or Jacob's Pillow.

Balanchine works as if he were at home and the theater was full. He worries about the box office, but he is more concerned with ballet. Milly Hayden says that he is "unsentimental," by which she means "he lives only in the moment. He doesn't worry about yesterday or tomorrow." He walks around the theater as comfortably as he does in New York, his gray-white hair smooth and neat, his bandannas as jaunty as ever, his step soft and springy. In class, he tells stories about famous dancers; he jokes; he bends to watch steps and says, "That's RIGHT." Milly insists, "Mr. Balanchine is superhuman. I know his faults—and he has them—and sometimes I feel he should be perfect. But even he can't be that."

Milly says that Mr. B. is not as patient as a teacher as he was when she joined the company twenty-four years ago, "He's nearly seventy now; he has less time. Once, long ago, he said he wanted me to learn to do entrechat six *his* way instead of the way I'd been taught. 'If you practice every day, in ten years you will do it,' he said. Of course, he was joking, and I did it in six months anyway, but I notice he doesn't talk about 'in ten years,' as often as he used to."

Milly isn't as indestructible as she once was, either. She rarely used to miss a performance. Now, performing *Cortège*, she hurts her foot, and Sally Leland has to go on for her in *Jewels*. There was an emergency rehearsal before the matinee—three corps dancers needed to be replaced. We might as well still be in New York, and there's a long tour ahead, especially now that Berlin is a certainty.

Balanchine takes the replacements, even Milly's, as part of the game; he always does. He stands at his place in the wings, watching, making comments, shooing the kids out for extra curtain calls when he thinks they can get them. For him, there are no certainties.

The biggest question in the company this season, the biggest one of every recent season, is that of a successor to Mr. B. Despite the contributions of Lincoln, Jerry, Taras and the dancers, Balanchine is this company, and he is sixty-nine years old. He looks good for another sixty-nine, but the question remains. Like Elizabeth I, he never has named a successor. Who can hold the company together? What will happen to his ballets, even with film records, like the ones that will be made in Berlin, and Jurg Lanzrein's choreology? It's a good topic for dance writers in need of column ideas, for dance buffs sitting around during intermission, and for dancers, who always are worrying about something.

Mr. B. doesn't worry about it at all. To him, the topic is of minimal interest. "I don't care," he says. "What will happen when I die? Who will take over? What will happen to the company, to the ballets? I don't care.

"Nothing is forever. There will be another kind of dancing, another way of dressing. Would you want Washington to be president today? Or Lincoln? Or Jackson? They were very great men, but they were in their times, not in ours. The Roman wars were very important at the time—today they are in the library. Caesar's reports are beautifully written but today, he'd probably be a failure in politics. Betty Grable just died. None of the children here know who she was.

"What is posterity? Fifty years? One hundred, two hundred? What about 1,000? Five thousand would be nice, too. And some day, in a short time—a few billion years—the sun will go and everything will end.

"But there is 'forever'—and is right now." The characteristic finger-point spears your attention. "Right now. Christ said it: 'Before Abraham was, I am.' Most people worry about time." (He writes an imaginary shopping list on his hand.) " 'Now I must be here, then I go there, then I rush there'—they're tied to the watch. But I only live now. That is the only forever, right now. But it takes a lot of" (the finger points at his forehead) "up here to live there."

People say Balanchine is selfish, that he should think about the future of his company, that he is too self-centered to concern himself with what will happen after him. To plan for the future would be the contemporary way, the logical, businesslike method. But Balanchine is not a contemporary man, nor a corporate one. He is an anachronistic individual, who lives for himself and his art because even his arrogance does not allow enough self-importance to plan the lives of future generations, and because his religion leaves such planning to God.

To even begin to understand Balanchine, you must accept him as a being beyond categorization. He is an individualist in a corporate age, a scholar in a time of slogans, a patient man in a culture devoted to immediate gratification. He has limitations and repressions, but can see through them and use his total being in order to work. He is a taskmaster and manipulator, but believes in human freedom. Like all of us, and more than some, he is restricted by his past, but unlike most of us, he can commit himself to the present.

Even when he talks about the future, he does so in reference to an immediate event. Rehearsing the corps in *Divertimento No. 15*, he tells them, "When I am gone; when I am not here but up there with Stravinsky" (and he points upward) "I don't want some ballet master to say, 'He never said he wanted the arm THERE.' So I say it. I will watch you from up there. Everyone worries, what will happen when I am not here any more? What will happen? I will tell you. SHE" (he indicates Rosie Dunleavy and smiles at her) "will take over, and she will remember where I said to put the arm. We put it HERE. That's RIGHT."

A few minutes later, he stops them again, with a familiar question. "Why are you stingy with yourselves? Why are you holding back? What are you saving for—for another time? There are no other times. There is only now. Right now."

Balanchine wears bright bandannas and Western shirts, beautifully tailored sports coats and old gray slacks, new country sandals and soft-soled rehearsal shoes. On certain occasions, he wears an old-fashioned tuxedo of perfect cut and style. Always, he wears his turquoise-and-silver bracelet, because an old Indian woman gave it to him—"When I was married to Tallchief, we were in Oklahoma"—saying it would bring him luck, and besides, its casual elegance suits him. He never wears a watch. A man whose time, always and forever, is now, doesn't need one.

Epilogue

* Before the season was over, Jerry Robbins left for Spoleto, where he choreographed an entrance and introduction to music from *Swan Lake*, and a finale for *Celebration—The Art of the Pas de Deux*, which was given its premiere at the Festival of Two Worlds on June 30, 1973, while the company was in New York dancing *Dream*. Pairs of dancers representing five countries took part in *Celebration:* Helgi Tomasson and Patricia McBride were the American entry; Jean-Pierre Bonnefous and Violette Verdy played for France. Violette and Jean-Pierre performed Jerry's Beethoven pas de deux, now named *Four Bagatelles*, as they had at the Spring Gala. Jerry sent the company a cheerful postcard.

* The company finished its tour and went to Berlin in September. Producers Reiner Moritz and Karl Shmitz put up $1.7-million to shoot six and one-half hours of color film of fifteen Balanchine ballets. The dancers put in six weeks of work on a bad floor, and nearly everyone came home with bruised feet. Eddie Villella was right when he told the company that a filming day lasts twelve hours, not five: work began at 10 A.M. and went on until ten at night, five days a week. (Of course, the dancers took their daily class with Mr. B. before facing the cameras.) Balanchine was in the studio throughout the filming. Every sequence had to be performed at least three times—for rehearsal, for setting angles, and for shoot-

ing—which allowed the dancers to learn some things they had not known about the ballets. For example, there are 202 hops on pointe in *Concerto Barocco*.

  * There was a strike. Although the musicians did not strike at the beginning of the fall, 1973, season, as had been expected, neither did they offer a guarantee they would not strike during the season. Everyone in the company suspected the musicians would play until it came time for *The Nutcracker*, NYCB's big moneymaker, and then walk out if their contract demands were not met. The expectation of such a move by the musicians prompted the dancers to ask management for a guarantee that they would either work or be paid for the fourteen weeks of the scheduled season. Management replied that it could not make such a promise without a no-strike guarantee from the musicians' union. On November 13, the day the season was to open, the dancers met in the main rehearsal hall, just as they had eight months earlier to vote on the trip to Berlin. This time, the vote went the other way: A strike was called by a vote of sixty-five to eleven with seven abstentions.

  Balanchine was quoted in the newspapers as saying, "I do not think they will strike." However, a number of dancers said that he had—well, hinted—that the only way they could get their guarantee was to walk out. It was not an angry strike. But, for the first time, the dancers dared to challenge the company. "It's history," said Eddie Villella. "Dancers for years have been subsidizing their art. Now, we want guarantees." Most of the anger was directed at the musicians' union. Its demands, which included a six-performance work week and a provision for sabbatical leave, were characterized by the dancers as "ridiculous." Some thought that the strike also would prove to management "that we have some rights, too. We need a little freedom and the right to make a living."

  Although the opening-night performance was postponed, the opening-night party went on as planned. It had been scheduled in advance, to celebrate the publication of Lincoln's history, *The New York City Ballet*. (Lincoln accepted the tributes patiently, then disappeared in the middle of the party. "He doesn't like crowds," one of the kids said, "and he's got better booze at home." The booze at the party happened to be an exquisite champagne.)

Before the party began, Gelsey Kirkland sat on the stone wall of the stage entrance stairwell, swinging her completely healed foot wistfully. "I wanted to dance," she sighed. "I haven't danced in five months. I hope it's over soon." Inside the main rehearsal hall, during the party, everyone also hoped the strike would be over soon and soaked up the champagne. Mr. B. suggested that if there were no early settlement, "We'll close the theater and everyone will go home. The girls will marry; the boys will go and drive taxicabs. Everywhere there's a strike. Everyone wants something." And he shrugged.

The men were looking for work as cab drivers before it was over, and the women for jobs as waitresses. They collected unemployment insurance, took class—with Mr. B.—and organized a benefit performance for themselves. The benefit went on just as the strike went off. Management reached a contract with the musicians—who got a good deal of what they wanted, but not everything—the dancers agreed to go back to work and the season began on December 12, four weeks late, with *The Nutcracker*.

* The Ford Foundation did not extend its grant to the company.

* In late summer, Patty McBride and Jean-Pierre Bonnefous were married in France. The bride's gown was sketched in *Women's Wear Daily*.

* Melissa Hayden retired, to begin her work at Skidmore.

* Conrad Ludlow retired, to head a company in Oklahoma. He returned briefly in February, to dance in *Don Quixote*.

* Nicholas Magallanes left semi-retirement for full retirement.

* Three corps members, Meg Gordon, who felt she would "never get anywhere with this company, I'm not tall and slim"; Karen O'Sullivan and Michael Steele, left the roster of dancers.

* Three corps members, Muriel Aasen, Richard Hoskinson and Elise Ingalls, were added to the roster of dancers.

* At the opening-night party without an opening night, Allegra was stunning in a floor-length gypsy-style skirt, which concealed the fact that she also was wearing white socks and sandals.

* On the night of the official premiere of *Four Bagatelles*, Allegra was stunning in *Swan Lake*, in which she was partnered by

Jacques d'Amboise, and set the audience buzzing. After intermission, Gelsey danced *Four Bagatelles*, and started more buzzing. She danced brilliantly, and kept it up throughout the season, gaining in charm, style and technical sizzle. Winter, 1974, was the season of the strike and of Gelsey.

* Violette Verdy needed a foot operation and did not dance during the winter season.

* Mr. B. choreographed *Variations Pour une Porte et un Soupir* on Karin von Aroldingen and John Clifford, to a musique-concrête score by Pierre Henry. The decor, a third partner in the pas, was designed by Rouben Ter-Arutunian.

* Jerry Robbins choreographed *Dybbuk*, to a score by Leonard Bernstein, on Patty McBride and Helgi Tomasson. He gave signs of mellowing, bringing apples in from the country for the dancers and giving them more leeway in rehearsal. "He's asking us to do things on our own now," the boys said. "In rehearsal, he's saying, 'Try something interesting . . . make up a step . . . show me what you can do.' "

Word also came around that when Patty was injured and Jerry needed a body to work on, he asked Gelsey to act as stand-in, proving that his quest for perfection had not diminished nor his tact increased. He used Deborah Koolish as the stand-in.

* Before the spring, 1974, season began, soloists Bruce Wells and Lynda Yourth and corps dancers Suzanne Erlon, Deborah Flomine and Polly Shelton left the company. Bruce said he'd simply "spent too many years in the dance factory—I simply have to live in a free atmosphere for a while where I can grow on my own." Lincoln Kirstein sent him a letter offering any help in his power. Suzanne Erlon made the even more unusual move of switching companies and went to dance with Eliot Feld.

* Gloria Govrin announced that she, too, had decided to leave NYCB. She would stay with the company until after the 1974 season in Saratoga, and then move to New Hope, Pa., and start a ballet school. "I've been here fore more than ten years—it's time for new people to take over. Besides, I've reached the point of hating New York; I just don't want to live here anymore. New Hope is beautiful—I'm really going to like it."

* Several apprentices and new corps dancers were taken into the company.
* Bobby Maiorano's knee healed.
* Merrill Ashley's foot mended; Jacques made a part on her in a ballet he was doing to Vivaldi.
* Bonnie Borne dispensed with her dentist in Los Angeles, lost weight and stopped being plagued by bone spurs.
* Christine Redpath somehow managed to become even prettier.
* Rosemary said, "Keep those lines straight."
* Mr. B. said, "Faster."

MARCH 6, 1974
NEW YORK CITY

Index

Balanchine, George (*continued*)
  dancers' views of, 11, 27, 48, 59, 61,
    101, 109, 128, 143, 156, 167, 172,
    177, 264, 293
  inventive role of, 19–20, 87
  and line, 35–36
  marriages and sex life of, 101–102, 253
  music and, 113–115, 244, 245, 246–247
  personal publicity and, 98, 139, 157,
    281
  personal style of, 19, 252–256,
    285–286, 296
  and Petipa, 123–124
  physical type preferred by, 22–23, 101
  private office of, 251–252
  racial attitudes of, 269–270
  at rehearsals, 48, 49, 53, 54, 55, 61, 67,
    70, 71–73, 117–124, 126, 127–133,
    135–137, 142, 146–147, 150–151,
    179, 183, 245–246, 278–281
  as revolutionary, 45, 254–255
  and Robbins, 52, 53, 177–178, 179,
    183, 185, 187–188, 200, 237
  rule of, in company, 22, 58–59, 96, 98,
    100–102, 107, 109, 110, 144, 157,
    163, 172, 256, 263, 264, 270–271,
    276
  speech pattern of, 13, 253–254, 255
  and speed, 26–28, 35, 38, 142, 301
  successor to, 294–295
"Balanchine dancers," 22–23, 26
"ballerina," title of, 9
ballet, as artificial art, 262–263
ballet, classical, *see* classical ballet
Ballet Comique de la Reine, Le, 24
ballet companies, 23
  European vs. American, 278
  Soviet vs. American, 96–97
ballet dancers, *see* dancers
Ballet Imperial, see Tchaikovsky Concerto No. 2
ballet masters, 13, 28, 291
balletomanes, 84–87, 157, 235–236
  dances popular with, 216
ballets, naming of, 126–127

ballet shoes, *see* shoes
Ballet Society, 24, 213
Ballets Russes, 252, 257
Ballet Theater, *see* American Ballet Theater
Barnes, Clive, 80, 178
barres, barre exercises, 27, 28, 30, 32, 34, 78
Bates, Ronald, 15, 68–69, 74, 79, 81, 148,
  149, 150, 184, 190, 200, 207, 288
battement tendu, 30–31, 36
Bayadère, La, 124
Beethoven, Ludwig van, 145
Beethoven Pas de Deux, A (Four Bagatelles),
  145, 149, 151–152, 153, 182, 297, 299
benefit audiences, 88, 94, 138
Bennett, Tracy, 123, 144, 189
Berlin, NYCB film-making in, 57–59,
  101, 236, 248, 258, 285, 291, 292,
  294, 297–298
Bernstein, Leonard, 300
Bigelow, Edward, 58, 59, 131, 133–134,
  145, 146, 196, 197, 199, 201–202,
  213, 236
bitch boxes, 69
Bizet, Georges, 234
Black, Maggie, 38
black dancers, 269–270
Blasis, Carlo, 119, 120
Bloom, Claire, 21
Blossom Music Festival, 56
Blum, Anthony, 145, 146, 232, 237, 238,
  241, 249, 280
Boelzner, Gordon, 30, 31, 33, 66, 68, 71,
  72, 118, 122, 127, 129, 130, 131,
  132–133, 238, 274
Bogan, James, 239
Bolshoi Ballet, 23, 96, 117, 278
Bonds of Work, The, 103
Bonnefous, Jean-Pierre, 22, 34, 53, 56,
  114, 117, 118–119, 120, 129, 134,
  135, 143, 145, 151, 152, 153,
  170–171, 175, 191, 193, 197, 201,
  234, 235, 236, 237, 238, 240, 241,
  274, 297, 299